PUBLIC NEGOTIATIONS

GLOBAL LATIN/O AMERICAS
Frederick Luis Aldama and Lourdes Torres, Series Editors

# PUBLIC NEGOTIATIONS

GENDER AND JOURNALISM
IN CONTEMPORARY
US LATINA/O LITERATURE

ARIANA E. VIGIL

THE OHIO STATE UNIVERSITY PRESS
COLUMBUS

Copyright © 2019 by The Ohio State University.
All rights reserved.

Library of Congress Cataloging-in-Publication Data is available online at catalog.loc.gov.

Cover design by Christian Fuenfhausen
Text design by Juliet Williams
Type set in Adobe Minion Pro

# CONTENTS

*Acknowledgments* vii

## PART 1 • DOMESTIC NEGOTIATIONS

INTRODUCTION  Latina/o Literature, Journalism, and the Public Sphere  3

CHAPTER 1  Rubén Salazar, Historical Memory, and the Gendered Contours of the Chicana/o Public Sphere  25

CHAPTER 2  The End(s) of Representation: Media and Activism in Cherríe Moraga's *Heroes and Saints*  67

## PART 2 • TRANSNATIONAL NEGOTIATIONS

CHAPTER 3  Femininity, Journalism, and the Necessity of a Transnational Public in *The Long Night of White Chickens*  97

CHAPTER 4  Photojournalism, Militarized Conflict, and the Boundaries of Latinidad in Graciela Limón and Ana Menéndez  117

CONCLUSION  Publics Unbound: Undocuqueer Activism  155

*Works Cited*  169
*Index*  179

# ACKNOWLEDGMENTS

I WANT to thank the people and institutions who supported my work and made completing this book possible. Thank you to Kristen Elias Rowley and the staff of The Ohio State University Press. Thanks to the Global Latin/o Americas editors, Lourdes Torres and Frederick Luis Aldama; I'm honored to have my work included in this new series.

This project reflected a new area of research for me as I sought to place media and communication studies in dialogue with my area of expertise in literary and cultural studies. Thank you to Maggie Franz for many conversations, recommendations, and feedback regarding public sphere theory. Thank you to the Department of Women's and Gender Studies at the University of North Carolina at Chapel Hill and especially our chair, Professor Silvia Tomášková, for providing a stimulating and supportive environment in which to work and grow as a scholar and teacher.

The University of North Carolina at Chapel Hill supported research and travel necessary for this project. Thank you to the staff of the Chicano and Latino Collections at the University of California, Santa Barbara, where I was able to access the Oscar Zeta Acosta papers. Eve Kelemen generously put me up at her house in Santa Barbara so I was able to conduct that research.

I was fortunate to receive a fellowship with the Latino Research Initiative of the University of Texas at Austin, which allowed me to work on a significant portion of the book manuscript. Thank you to the staff and faculty of the LRI, the Department of Mexican American and Latina/o Studies, and the Center for Mexican American Studies, especially Deborah Parra-Medina, John Morán González, Karma Chávez, and Nicole Guidotti-Hernández. Thank you to Rebecca Hey-Colón, whose friendship and camaraderie greatly benefited my time in Austin. And thank you to my community in Texas—Cristina, Whicael, Rockie, Tane, Trinity, Ron, and Debra—for always welcoming me home.

The final drafting and revision of this book was completed while I was a Faculty Fellow of the Institute for the Arts and Humanities at UNC. Thank you to the Faculty Fellows Director, Michele T. Berger, and to my colleagues who worked alongside me.

As I worked on the manuscript, I received great feedback from students and colleagues at Virginia Tech and the University of Texas at Austin—I thank organizers and audience members for those opportunities.

Anonymous peer reviewers offered important insights and critique and encouraged me to think through and refine aspects of this manuscript—I thank them for their time and attention.

As I've written and revised this manuscript I've negotiated a few major life transitions and have reflected on my own relationship to writing and communication. My dedication to writing and intellectual pursuits is in no small part indebted to my mother, Vicki Blum Vigil, who imparted a love for writing and thinking to me and who always encouraged my scholarly pursuits. I dedicate this book to her and to my own daughter, Eliana Amaya.

# PART 1

# DOMESTIC NEGOTIATIONS

INTRODUCTION

# Latina/o Literature, Journalism, and the Public Sphere

IN THE satirical 2004 film *A Day Without a Mexican* (dir. Sergio Arau), California grapples with the disappearance of all of the state's Latina/o population.[1] While agricultural fields lay untended and individuals worry about the loss of their families, friends, and co-workers, even anti-immigrant politicians are forced to ask that the Latina/os "come back." Only one person seems to have escaped this mysterious plague, Mexican American reporter Lila Rodríguez (Yareli Arizmendi). Lila becomes a signal of hope and a specimen to be studied; a doctor seeks to discover her "L Factor," or what makes Lila Latina, and the US government plans to create a vaccine with her blood to keep the remaining Americans safe. Throughout Lila's ordeal, a close family friend—Aunt Gigi—exhibits a suspicious unease. When Lila is on the verge of participating in a dangerous experience to find "her people," Aunt Gigi (Caroline Aaron) confesses the truth: Lila is her biological niece and they are Armenian. The parents that Lila has known, Teresita and José, are her adoptive parents. Lila grapples with this newfound information; in tears she declares, "You belong to the people who taught you the world;

---

1. Despite the title, the film does a good job of pointing out that not all Latina/os are "Mexican."

my heart is Mexican." Lila then promptly disappears. As mysteriously as it arrived, the dense fog that signaled the mass disappearances leaves and California's Latina/o population returns to a newly appreciative state.

While the film clearly pokes fun at US racism and hypocrisy, it also raises intriguing and pertinent questions regarding identity, community, and representation. After Lila disappears, the producer of her show is dumbfounded, declaring "she's not Mexican!" and therefore cannot have disappeared. The film, however, articulates Lila's own sentiment, that one's membership in a particular racial or ethnic community is not necessarily delineated by biological ties. Lila's stance as a reporter also broaches questions of voice and representation. She is initially hired when the station is looking for a "Latina reporter," although at other points in the film she refutes this label, asserting instead that she is "a reporter." The film and characters seem to recognize that Latina/o reporters should not be tasked with being (only) a representative voice for Latina/o communities while also illustrating the responsibility that Lila feels toward "her people." While Lila is revealed to have a more complex relationship to Latinidad than originally assumed, the film further questions the essentialist links between individuals and racial/ethnic populations. At the same time, Lila becomes a necessary and effective means of shedding light on the catastrophe, affirming the value of members of the media who can speak to and from specific constituencies. In its choice to focus on a reporter, then, *A Day Without a Mexican* affirms the relationship between Latina/o media and Latina/o communities, without making reductive or essentialist claims.

*A Day Without a Mexican* touches on the central concerns of this book: the relationship between Latina/o media and Latina/o publics; the ways in which the boundaries of the Latina/o public sphere are negotiated through and by mass media; and circulation of these inquiries and ideas within Latina/o cultural production. This book examines a range of late twentieth- and early twenty-first-century Latina/o literature that takes up these issues. Works that feature Latina/o media workers—specifically journalists and photojournalists—reflect how this literature demonstrates a sustained interest in the relationship between

Latina/o media and Latina/o publics.[2] These works utilize the figure of the journalist, and tropes of journalism more largely, to reflect conversations and contestations about the shape and constituency of the Latina/o public sphere. Within these conversations, gender plays a decisive role. The book's title, *Public Negotiations,* captures the idea that the role that gender plays is not static or consistent—in some texts gendered concerns (for example, the relationship between masculinity and militancy) prove divisive, while in others they become a way to move toward cohesion. The plurality of the word *negotiations* is meant to capture the multiplicity of these movements and conversations as well as the carry-over between literature and culture; the texts both reflect and participate in discussions about the Latina/o public sphere. Following a brief history of Latina/o mass media, this introduction reviews the important theoretical terms and scholarly terrain upon which the project relies and then offers an overview of individual chapters.

## LATINA/O MASS MEDIA IN HISTORICAL CONTEXT

Latina/o journalism has as long-standing a history in the US as Latina/o peoples themselves. Because such media tended to be produced and distributed in areas populated by Latina/os, the south and southwestern parts of the country played an important role in the development of Latina/o mass media. Early publications often served as a means of connecting Spanish-speaking peoples within the US to those in Latin America; thus, US Latina/o media has been and remains transnational. The first Spanish-language newspaper published in the US, *El Misisipí,* stems from New Orleans; published in 1808, the periodical was produced by and for merchants who traded in the Spanish (and formerly Spanish) colonies of the Caribbean (Rodríguez, *Making Latino News* 25). Later, Spanish-language newspapers played an impor-

---

2. This study focuses on Latina/o texts that center on Latina/o media workers; it is not an exhaustive analysis of the role of media writ large in Latina/o literature. Thus, a text such as Luis Valdez's *Zoot Suit,* in which both mainstream and alternative media play an important role, but are represented by non-Latina/o characters, is excluded.

tant role during periods of national conflict, such as during and after the Mexican–American War (1845–48) and the Mexican Revolution (1910–20). Of newspapers published in the earlier period, some were subsidized by the state of California and were part of the larger process of colonization that Mexicans and Mexican Americans suffered (15). At the same time, some privately owned newspapers employed Mexican journalists to work as translators of Spanish sections in their English-language newspapers (15). Félix Gutiérrez describes newspapers such as *The Californian* as "linked with the Anglo power structure" and their function as a means of social control over the people in these newly acquired territories (38). Such connections, however, did not preclude the publication of pieces advocating Mexican American unity and resistance to Anglo cultural imperialism; newspapers in Texas and California also called for Spanish-language instruction in public schools and tax resistance on the part of residents who did not receive adequate public services (Gutiérrez 41). These histories underscore the role that mass media plays in times of conquest as well as the varying roles—from oppositional to accommodationist—that individual journalists and newspapers may embody.

In the early twentieth century, as immigration from Mexico increased because of the Mexican Revolution, areas with large Spanish-speaking populations were served by local newspapers. Papers in Los Angeles such as *El Heraldo de México* and *Regeneración* spoke out against abuses by Anglo-Americans against Mexicans and underscored the importance of the revolution for those living in *México de afuera* (Rodríguez, *Making Latino News* 16–17). Just as the native-born and immigrant Mexican population was diverse, so were the perspectives of different papers. For example, San Antonio's *La Prensa* was directed toward an elite of Mexican exiles who were educated and middle-class (17). Some of these papers adjusted their stances over time and, particularly in the years following World War II, began to influence local elections and encourage voter registration and voting on the part of their readers (19–21). The heterogeneity of these newspapers and their readership is an issue that Latina/o and non-Latina/o media continue to grapple with. Despite the diversity—linguistic, racial, and economic—that has existed and continues to exist within Latina/o communities, this diversity is seldom fully recognized or reflected in mass media.

The early twentieth century also saw the establishment, and growth, of Spanish-language radio and television in the US. Again, these broadcasts were first established in the south and Southwest. Dolores Inés Casillas explains that between the 1920s and 1940s, the US airwaves hosted a series of "Latin-themed" shows that treated Latin Americans as exotic guests and served to "charm and culturally enlighten" English-speaking Americans (25, 22). Shows such as *Pan American Nights* and *Mexican Music* featured artists from Latin America (25, 22). This apparent celebration of ethnic, cultural, and linguistic difference, however, existed in tandem with political disenfranchisement and social exclusion of Spanish-speaking peoples and their descendants in the US. Of this period, América Rodríguez explains that Anglos in power displayed contradictory attitudes toward Mexicans and Mexican media. On the one hand, US stations sold blocks of time to Spanish-language programming; on the other hand, state and federal authorities illustrated hostility and intolerance by massively deporting thousands of Mexicans and Mexican Americans and campaigning to ban Spanish from the airwaves (30).

One important difference between Spanish-language newspapers and Spanish-language radio at this time was that the former were owned by members of the Mexican community but the latter were not (Casillas 37; Rodríguez 28). Initially, Mexicans were not considered a market, and so local radio entrepreneurs would purchase airtime on Anglo-owned stations during undesirable hours (for example, during the early morning) for Spanish-language programs. These entrepreneurs operated somewhat autonomously and paid themselves back by selling ads (Rodríguez 28). Much of the Spanish-language programming came from Mexico; media mogul Emilio Azcárraga Vidaurreta transmitted music from his Mexico City station to a station in Los Angeles, which then relayed it to other stations (Rodríguez 31). This arrangement allowed Azcárraga to use his considerable capital as well as to avoid anti-Mexican attitudes on the part of Anglo media. As time went on, however, Spanish-language media not only connected Mexicans in the US with Mexican culture and politics but also contributed to a distinctly Mexican American identity by highlighting issues pertinent to their US-based audiences, such as labor disputes within the Latina-dominated garment sector (Casillas 41). Latina/os in the US continued to seek more control over programming as well as over the perception of them as an audience. The first Chicano to own a Spanish-language radio station was Raúl Cortez, who owned KCOR in San Antonio (Casillas 43–44). But Cortez still had to fight to have his listeners recognized as a viable audience by his advertisers, at one point asking listeners to mail in box tops to prove they existed (and consumed!) (Rodríguez 33).

Spanish-language radio shared with Spanish-language television an early reliance on programming from Latin America and, along with Spanish-language newspapers, an evolving role concerning advocacy for Latina/o peoples in the US. Radio continues to play an important role in Latina/o organizing. The immigration reform marches that took place in 2006, when millions of Latina/os and their supporters walked out of school and work to protest HR 4437, were significantly impacted by Spanish-language disc jockeys who encouraged Latina/o communities to participate. At the same time, we can see in debates about audiences issues relevant to immigration. That is, are the consumers of Spanish-language radio to be considered foreigners living abroad, or domestic ethnic minorities? English-language radio had the former approach and Spanish-language radio the latter: "The distinction highlighted how Mexicans located afar on the other side of the border were depicted or even envied as 'cultured' while Mexicans in the US were racialized as unruly and yet-to-be-assimilated citizens" (Casillas 15). This issue remains pertinent in other forms of mass media; for example, while high-profile Latin Americans in the film industry such as Mexican directors Alejandro González Iñárritu and Guillermo del Toro have recently earned acclaim (in Iñárritu's case, two Oscars for Best Director two years in a row), recognition (and funding) for efforts spearheaded by US Latina/os lags behind. Finally, radio remains an important medium for working-class Latina/os in particular. Currently, Latina/os make up 10 percent of radio listeners, and broadcasts in Spanish make up 5.5 percent of total broadcasts in the US. Moreover, over 50 percent of Spanish-language listeners make less than $25,000 (Casillas 11). Radio is and remains an important component of Latina/o and Spanish-language media in the US.

Despite the remaining significance of radio, this form of broadcasting was unambiguously overshadowed by the growth of television in the early twentieth century, a form of mass media that remains dominant across the globe. In terms of Spanish-language broadcasting,

Latina/o television was hugely influenced by the aforementioned Mexican media mogul Emilio Azcárraga. In 1961 Azcárraga, who at that point owned a Mexican television network called Televisa, expanded into the US market through a new subsidiary, the Spanish International Network (SIN) (Rodríguez 35–36). Throughout the 1960s and 1970s, SIN functioned as a branch of Televisa; via stations in Los Angeles, San Antonio, and other parts of the Southwest, the network broadcast Mexican-produced programming to the US (37). Unlike early local Spanish-language newspapers that understood themselves as related to different Spanish-speaking constituents, SIN approached Latina/os as a homogenous group united by their tie to the Spanish language. As Rodríguez explains, the network ignored issues such as race and class, instead "[assuming] that its Spanish language programming would appeal to all U.S. Latinos" (38). This attitude on behalf of a Mexican-affiliated station illustrates that the heterogeneity of US Latina/os may be ignored not only by Anglo entrepreneurs and advertisers but by Latin Americans as well. According to the FCC (Federal Communications Commission), networks functioning in the US may not be owned by a foreign entity (Rodríguez 61). This rule was ignored in the case of SIN for the first twenty-five years of its existence, but in 1986 Azcárraga was forced to sell the network, doing so to Hallmark Cards, who renamed it *Univisión*. At the time, seeing the value of having Spanish-language media in the control of US Latina/os, several Latina/os organizations attempted (unsuccessfully) to block the sale to Hallmark, pointing out the corporation's lack of ties to the Latina/o community (63).

While Azcárraga was building his television empire, Latina/o and Chicana/o newspapers and journals affiliated with the Chicana/o civil rights movement were being established across the country. Magazines such *Caracol, Con Safos, El Grito, De Colores, El Pocho-Che,* and *Revista Chicano-Riqueña* published poetry, editorials, and political analyses from a politically engaged perspective. One of the most significant publications of this period was the newspaper *La Raza,* which for ten years (1967–77) chronicled and furthered the Chicana/o movement. The newspaper had a high enough profile that two of its editors, Eliezer Risco and Joe Razo, were part of the "East LA Thirteen," who were arrested after the LA Blowouts of May 1968 and charged with disturbing the peace, trespassing, and conspiracy to commit those crimes

(Haney-López 25–27).³ While male leaders and editors were often the most visible, Chicana feminist organizations and publications made significant contributions to the movement as well as to Chicana/o print culture more broadly. As Maylei Blackwell demonstrates, the Chicana feminist newspaper *Las Hijas de Cuauhtémoc* transformed Chicana consciousness and inaugurated an imagined political community that linked university campuses to national readers ("Contested Histories" 61). Importantly, such media offered a space where feminist activists could articulate demands as well as one where ideas, theories, and strategies and negotiations over gender and sexuality could be discussed (61). Chicana print communities constituted a Chicana counterpublic; within the movement they reworked "the discursive frames of social struggle" to create space for women and established the historical base for Chicana feminist scholarship (80). Newspapers and journals of the Chicana/o movement illustrate how print media provided an important space for the dissemination, deliberation, and contestation of diverse ideas and contributed to the formation of a Chicana/o counterpublic.

In the case of all three mediums—print, radio, and television—Spanish-language and Latina/o media in the US are marked by their overwhelmingly transnational character. These media have both sought to connect Latina/os in the US with their counterparts in Latin America and worked toward establishing and strengthening Latina/o communities and political and social power in the US. In the case of SIN/ *Univisión* and television, of particular interest is that for many decades, the network broadcast Mexican-produced content to the US. This flow of culture would seem to reverse what we commonly assume regarding the dominance and exportation of US media to audiences abroad. While US advertisers and owners were slow to recognize Spanish-speakers in the US as a viable audience, their counterparts in Latin America were not. Rodríguez explains that for Latin America media, US Latina/os are often considered simply part of the northern Latin American market (48). Moreover, these transnational ties are increasingly bidirectional. While about half the Spanish-language television programming that is aired in the US is produced in Latin America,

---

3. In addition to Risco and Razo, members of the Brown Berets, UMAS (United Mexican American Students), and high school teacher Sal Castro were arrested. Oscar Zeta Acosta represented the defendants.

nearly all the Spanish-language television produced in the US (much of it produced today in Miami) is distributed to Latin America (48–49). This means that television circulates in a more consistently transnational circuit between the US and Latin America than perhaps almost any other kind of cultural exchange.

Many of the issues discussed above, in particular the independence of Latina/o media from Anglo owners, the attempt by Latina/o leaders to have Latina/o audiences taken seriously by networks and advertisers, and the role of Latina/o media in establishing a distinct US Latina/o community identity, can be found in the literary works that provide the basis for this book. As individual chapters illustrate, these issues continue to be negotiated within a specifically Latina/o context as Latina/o authors turn to Latina/o media workers to explore and establish the relationship between Latina/o journalists and the Latina/o public sphere.

## LATINA/O MEDIA STUDIES

As Latina/o media has grown in terms of diversity (newspapers, television, radio) and reach, so too have the fields of Latina/o media studies, feminist media studies, and Latina/o feminist media studies. These fields look closely at the production, dissemination, and reception of Latina/o-oriented mass media. Scholars such as María Elena Cepeda, Otto Santa Ana, Angharad Valdivia, Dolores Inés Casillas, Mari Castañeda, and others have looked at the representation of Latina/os in network news shows and popular culture and the history, growth, and dissemination of Latina/o-oriented film, radio, and television. Arlene Dávila argues that while Latina/o media have often been understood as "media that are supposedly marketed and packaged" to Latina/os, a more expansive scope that considers a media landscape that includes mainstream TV, network news, video games, and the internet is necessary for understanding and theorizing Latina/o media (Dávila and Rivero 3). At the same time, Dávila and Rivero acknowledge that Latina/o media may be defined as media that is marketed, packaged, and circulated as such—in other words, Latina/o media is media that self-consciously understands itself to be in relation to Latina/os (3). This definition encompasses the creation (production), distribution, and consumption of media. Regarding questions of production and distribution, scholars have noted the unavoidably transnational origins and present state of Latina/o media. Much of the media that is targeted at US Latina/os is produced in Latin America and largely influenced by Latin American–born elites (Cepeda 349). The Latin American production of Latina/o-oriented media is a reflection of the high costs of media production within the US but also exhibits a reliance on overly narrow ideas of gender, race, and class (349). Of course, just as much of Latina/o media must be understood as a transnational phenomenon, we must also understand its close relationship to capitalism and market forces. The "Latin media boom" of the late twentieth and early twenty-first centuries was as much tied to changing demographics as it was to a process of marketing and commodification. As María Elena Cepeda explains, Latina/os gained media attention insofar as they were acknowledged as potential consumers; in other words, "'Latina/os can spend, therefore Latina/os exist'" (348). Like the influence of Latin American elites on the content of Latina/o media, marketing both enabled and constrained particular images and representations, and "gendered articulations of Latinidad" in particular are constricted by market forces (349).

Building on existing scholarship, this book engages with Latina/o media studies and Latina/o feminist media studies by taking into consideration how issues of production and dissemination are reflected and reflected upon in literary works. For example, the discussion of Rubén Salazar in chapter 1 contextualizes the journalist's literary representation within the social and political milieu of the mid-twentieth century and Salazar's historical position as the first Chicano reporter for a mainstream television station. Salazar's own movement from Spanish-language to English-language media reflects the Latin American (and specifically Mexican) origins of much Latina/o media, while his relationship to fictional Chicana/o movement activists broaches important conversations about gender and sexuality that were taking and continue to take place. Chapter 2 also considers Latina/o media production and dissemination by examining how a Latina/o public health crisis, pesticide poisoning among migrant farmworker communities in California's Central Valley, is covered by Latina/o and non-Latina/o media. That chapter, which focuses on the fictional female reporter Ana Pérez, also looks at how gender not only is something that is imposed by media and market forces but may be harnessed for self-representations which may include "subversive self-tropicalization" (Cepeda 350). The transnational focus of chapters 3 and 4, which examine fictional journalists and photojournalists who work in Guatemala, Mexico, Turkey, and the US, captures the importance of Latin America while introducing different geographical, national, and political contexts. The Guatemalan and Guatemalan American characters in *The Long Night of White Chickens* call on us to consider the place of non-Mexican and non-Chicana/o subjects within the Latina/o media landscape while also examining how Central American–American communities are gendered in relation to other US Latina/o communities. The final chapter considers how a non–Latin American transnational context may impact how we think about Latina/o media and Latina/o publics. As a whole, then, the works in this study reflect the transnational origins and importance of Latina/o media and the way in which gender works within and between Latina/o and non-Latina/o audiences and communities. The attention to production, dissemination, and reception throughout the book is in dialogue with how these facets of Latina/o media are taken up in Latina/o media scholarship, while the privileging of literary analysis also allows us to consider how the realm of the creative and imaginative offer new possibilities for reflecting and shaping the Latina/o media landscape.

## LITERATURE, JOURNALISM, AND THE PUBLIC SPHERE

This project relies equally on considerations of questions of production, representation, and distribution of Latina/o media and theoretical considerations that draw on the relationship between mass media and publics. Contemporary discussions of the public sphere draw heavily on Jürgen Habermas's *The Structural Transformation of the Public Sphere: An Inquiry into a Category of Bourgeois Society*. According to Habermas, the bourgeois public sphere arose in Europe following developments in the sixteenth and seventeenth centuries, specifically the circulation of goods and news. This "public" was occupied by people who did not hold public office and indeed defined themselves in opposition to those who did and began to understand the sphere of civic society as one that was "properly theirs" (18, 23). Such a public, however, was made up not of all people who did not hold public office but rather of a more privileged and educated group. The reading of fiction as well as the consumption of newspapers played a formative role in terms of how this public sphere was formed and shaped. Private individuals came together—in salons, reading houses, or coffee/tea houses—to "reflect critically and in public on what they had read" (51). The exclusion of particular people from these spaces and conversations went hand in hand with the public being established as a space inhabited by citizens (107).

While Habermas delineates the public sphere (composed of private citizens) from the political sphere (occupied by political actors), feminist theorists have been careful to point out that these demarcations do not always hold up and, moreover, rely on heterosexist ideas. In "Sex in Public," Lauren Berlant and Michael Warner rethink commonly held assumptions regarding the relationship between sexuality, intimacy, and the public sphere. The critics point out that "intimacy is itself publicly mediated," and that ignoring the ways in which heterosexual institutions mediate intimacy allows myths concerning the ability to separate "personal life" from the public sphere to remain (553). In a similar vein, Warner explains that one of the terms central to public deliberations—"rational-critical debate"—is sexed and gendered (*Publics* 51). For Warner, publics organized around sex—and that of gay men, or lesbians—and which exist in "tension with a larger public" constitute counterpublics (56). Similarly, Nancy Fraser argues that counterpublics contest bourgeois norms and are explicitly linked to social movements (61). These counterpublics have an awareness of their subordinate status and are not, or cannot be, formed through a "bracketing" of embodiment and status (Warner, *Publics* 56–67).

The Latina/o public sphere shares with the bourgeois public sphere a long-standing relationship to print culture and media circulation while also abiding by Warner's and Fraser's definitions of a counterpublic. Raúl Coronado's history of Latina/o print culture, *A World Not to Come: A History of Latino Writing and Print Culture*, explains that the public sphere energized by print culture in the early nineteenth century was both capacious, because of transatlantic circulation, and constrained, because of the limited number of printing presses (18). His study of a transatlantic Hispanophone public sphere offers important historical grounding for work that looks at contemporary issues of

Latina/os and publics. Taking up Habermas's definition in the contemporary moment, Lázaro Lima homes in on the relationship between subaltern groups and the bourgeois public sphere.[4] Lima asserts that Habermas's assumption regarding "equal access to public articulation of group concerns" creates a "quandary" for subaltern groups who are asked to uncritically accept "bourgeois inclusionary norms" (7). He argues that in moments of crisis, "the organizing principle of Latino public sphere identities offered context specific strategies," and details specifically patriotic, assimilationist, and gendered Latino engagement strategies (8). Here we see the links between gendered and racialized subaltern publics.

Latina/o studies scholars have also looked at how social and literary movements coalesce to form counterpublics and the relationship between counterpublics and print culture. According to John Alba Cutler, a Chicana/o literary counterpublic emerged between 1953 and 1990 (148). Building on Warner's discussion of a "reflective circulation of discourse," Cutler explains that Chicana/o literary works function as "performative acts" and participate in a counterpublic (140). Other scholars have built on the work of Warner and Fraser to characterize Latina/o publics; Urayoán Noel suggests that New York Puerto Ricans may be a subaltern group, but that the Nuyorican poetry movement functioned as a counterpublic (54). Concerned with the relationship between counterpublics and mass publics, Noel argues that in moving from performances in the Nuyorican Poets Café to ones on Broadway, for example, Mayda del Valle moves from the former to the latter. He states that the tensions he identifies reflect the ways that Nuyorican poetry "has self-reflexively addressed the terms and mechanisms of its circulation," including its "publicness" (59). Indeed, as Cutler points out, this "publicness" is what allows one to enter, and presumably leave, counterpublics and discursive spaces (149). The Chicana/o movement of the 1960s and 1970s, within which Latina/o-oriented publications flourished, further affirmed the relationship between counterpublics and social movements. Maylei Blackwell's study of Chicana feminist organizations highlights the importance of newspapers such as *Las Hijas de Cuauhtémoc* and *Encuentro Femenil*. According to Blackwell,

---

4. Warner points out that counterpublics are often called "subaltern publics" (*Publics* 57).

"Chicana public spheres were forged and expanded by linking community and political organizations and Chicana print," adding that these journals created a "counterpublic" (¡*Chicana Power!* 147, 146).

Counterpublics of course, exist alongside and excluded from dominant publics, a point that Marta Caminero-Santangelo drives home when she considers works by and about undocumented Latina/os in relation to Fraser's "subaltern counterpublics" to argue that such texts "[challenge] their exclusion from the public sphere" (11). In addition, both Blackwell and Marissa López are attuned to the importance of gender in terms of who and what circulates within Chicana/o or Latina/o publics. In her discussions of Mexican and Chicana/o emo culture, López points out that the role of femininity in emo expression contributes to its denigration, explaining that "Mexican emo's intimate publics deploy a strikingly feminine, or androgynous, personal aesthetic whose putative deviation from the norm has clearly hit a Mexican nerve" (904). López builds off Lauren Berlant's concept of "intimate publics" to understand Mexican and Chicana/o emos and strives to place them somewhere between the "mass marketing of emotionality and sentiment" without ties to any political intervention and a context that considers emo performance within a context of "Latin@ belonging and ostracization from broad national and global communities" (897, 899). These scholars touch on the long-standing history of Hispanophone print culture in the Americas; the ways in which artists and activists use(d) newspapers, journals, poetry, music, and performance to articulate counterpublics; the ways in which Latina/o peoples and cultures challenge commonly held understandings of the bourgeois public sphere and the importance of gender and sexuality when considering Latina/o counterpublics. The approach to a Latina/o public sphere in this book consciously builds off the work of these thinkers. Like Coronado's and Blackwell's histories, this manuscript affirms the importance of the circulation of texts across the Americas and elsewhere. Like Blackwell and Cutler, this study connects counterpublics to their articulation through literature and journalism and social movements. Underlying this project is the assertion, also made by Lima, Caminero-Santangelo, and Noel, that Latina/o literature is able to question the terms of access and articulation—namely questions of citizenship and belonging—upon which ideas of the public sphere are formed. The project further considers, as do Blackwell and López, the way in which gender functions in terms of both the construction and the reception of a Latina/o public in a transnational space. Finally, following Noel, *Public Negotiations* contends that Latina/o authors have self-consciously engaged with questions of publics and counterpublics.

## METHODOLOGY AND LITERARY STUDY

This analysis draws from several scholarly traditions and fields and employs multiple methodologies in its execution. As stated earlier, the book is situated within and between the fields of Latina/o media studies, Latina/o literary studies, and feminist and Latina/o feminist variants of these areas. The project likewise uses methodologies from each of these fields, including contextualization within social, historical, and political moments and applying theoretical inquiry to primary literary sources. While working within a variety of disciplines, *Public Negotiations* privileges literary sources as well as the act of close reading, and it is in its focus on literary works that the project seeks to make methodological, theoretical, and cultural interventions. First, by asserting that literary works—namely novels—may be examined with attention to issues of rhetoric and content analysis, tools often used in mass media analysis, the project suggests the relevance of media studies approaches to literature. This assertion has theoretical implications as well, urging us to understand literary works not only as exemplars of public rhetoric but as a component of it as well. Thus, literary and cultural works don't only apply or illustrate ideas about publics but actively contribute to these ideas themselves. For example, the film *A Day Without a Mexican* does more than reflect an extended kinship network. As an independent film that has high visibility within Latina/o communities, it contributes to larger conversations about how individuals and families may define themselves and the ramifications of such definitions within ethnic and mainstream public spheres. Combining media studies and Latina/o studies theories and methodologies implicitly argues for the potential connections between these fields, while the use of literature specifically argues that creative writing as an object of study can help forge these connections. Attending to the interdisciplinarity and intersectionality of Latina feminisms, the manuscript demonstrates how feminist analysis specifically facilitates the productive conversation between media and literary studies. Finally, from a cultural studies standpoint, this project breaks new ground in affirming the deep relationships between literature and journalism while suggesting that literature itself is an opportune place to investigate these relationships.

This book contends that Latina/o texts have used the figure of the Latina/o journalist to invoke, contest, and problematize the Latina/o public sphere. The project also implicitly engages with the significance of Latina/o journalists and their relationship with social justice movements. Juan González, the former minister of Education of the Young Lords and current co-host of the radio and television program *Democracy Now!*, often quotes the columnist Jimmy Breslin, who quipped: "The Young Lords produced more good journalists than Columbia J [journalism] school" (González). Similarly, Caminero-Santangelo has recently discussed, and problematized, the work of Latina/o literary journalism in relation to accounts of undocumented immigration. Certainly, much work remains to be done, and the chapters on politically engaged journalists, whether fictional ones such as Graciela Limón's Adriana Mora and Cherríe Moraga's Ana Pérez or historical ones such as Rubén Salazar, aim to invoke this particular history. More so than reflecting particular histories or events, these literary works allow us to imagine new iterations of Latina/o publics. While the particular focus on journalists and journalism in Latina/o literature suggests a specific mechanism to take up these questions, the breadth of the project—covering several decades of literature from a diversity of ethnonational, geographic, and political perspectives—points to a cohesive and established interest in the relationship between Latina/o journalists and Latina/o publics. In addition, focusing on how gender plays a formative and dynamic role in how texts and characters negotiate the boundaries and possibilities of a Latina/o public sphere allows us to consider the race, sex, gender, and ethnic iterations of publics and counterpublics.

Finally, the focus on literary works in conversation with the production, dissemination, and reception of mass media broaches new ways of thinking about literature and journalism. This book excavates and highlights the robust and long-standing relationship between literary and journalistic concerns and between writers of fiction and journalism. As a result, we can see that literary and mass media studies can and do engage in productive conversations around representation, ethnicity, gender, and Latina/o peoples in the US. At the same time, while the manuscript draws equally from literary and mass media studies theory and scholarship, it privileges literary texts and creative portrayals of journalists and journalism. This approach argues that literary works and authors have a particular role to play in contributing to a conversation about the relationship between mass media and Latina/o publics. These texts don't only reflect the important role that Latina/o journalists have and do play in the creation and articulation of a Latina/o public; they also present literature as a realm where ideas and articulations of Latina/o peoples and publics, approaches to gender and community-building, can be imagined, contested, and negotiated.

## CHAPTER INTRODUCTIONS

The manuscript is divided into two parts. The first part looks at Chicana/o texts that take place within the US (specifically California) and that touch on historical events from the early 1970s to the early 1990s. Chapter 1, "Rubén Salazar, Historical Memory, and the Gendered Contours of the Chicana/o Public Sphere," examines Oscar Zeta Acosta's *The Revolt of the Cockroach People* and Lucha Corpi's *Eulogy for a Brown Angel,* two novels set during and in the aftermath of the Chicana/o Movement. Both texts deal with the 1970 Chicano Moratorium during which *Los Angeles Times* and KMEX reporter Rubén Salazar was murdered. Focusing on discussion of Salazar and specifically how he is depicted in relation to the texts' protagonists and other characters, we can see that each of the texts' narrators, Acosta's Brown Buffalo and Corpi's Gloria Damasco, use Salazar's life and death to put forth a vision of a Chicana/o public. That is, both narrators suggest that Salazar was commensurate with the larger Chicana/o public. However, they differ in what kind of public this is/was. For Buffalo, Salazar reflects a militant masculinism that mirrors and supports his own perspectives and tactics. For Damasco, Salazar reflects an egalitarian public in which women and Chicana feminists could play a role. This chapter illustrates how these two Chicana/o texts use the figure of a prominent Chicano journalist to make claims about a Chicano public as well as the way that gender impacts the differing ideas of this public.

Chapter 2, "The End(s) of Representation: Media and Activism in Cherríe Moraga's *Heroes and Saints*," examines a fictionalized portrayal of another significant facet of Chicana/o history—the struggle against pesticide poisoning in California's Central Valley. This play treats a historical subject through a fantastical lens which includes a prominent character who consists of a headless body (representing the ravages of pesticide poisoning on children), her family and community members, and a Latina reporter. Looking at mainstream network news coverage of the events to contrast them with the reporting produced by the play's journalist, Ana Pérez, this chapter illustrates that Pérez employs a different tactic in her broadcasts, foregrounding the voices and perspectives of those impacted without granting "equal" voice to the perspectives of agribusiness or government agencies. Considering Pérez's status as a translator, a role that invokes La Malinche, highlights the gendered and sexed stakes in questions of voice, visibility, and representation for Chicanas. Via a close reading of the final scene of the play, when Pérez abandons her role as a journalist to join the townspeople in burning the fields, this chapter argues that Pérez's actions reflect an acknowledgment that media representation of Latina/o issues does not (or will not) translate into increased Latina/o political power, what Hector Amaya terms the Latina/o "public sphere paradox." This chapter, then, acknowledges a relationship between Latina/o social justice issues, Latina/o media, and the power of a Latina/o public while suggesting that the relationship may be vexed and complicated.

Reflecting the transnational orientation of Latina feminist media studies asserted by María Elena Cepeda, the second half of the manuscript looks at Latina/o texts that move outside the confines of the US. Chapter 3, "Femininity, Journalism, and the Necessity of a Transnational Public in *The Long Night of White Chickens*," examines Francisco Goldman's debut novel to understand how the Guatemalan American text engages with questions of a Latina/o public in a transnational space. Like the other texts examined in this manuscript, *Chickens* responds to recent historical events, in this case the Guatemalan Civil War and US intervention in the region. Looking closely at the journalist in the text, Luis Martínez Moya, and the portrait of journalism more broadly, the chapter demonstrates how media is feminized and portrayed as disempowered. Furthermore, this chapter seeks to understand how the history and legacy of US intervention in Central

America can alter ideas of a Latina/o public, pointing to the ways in which transnational connections necessitate a rethinking of the boundaries of the Latina/o public sphere to incorporate non-Chicana/o and Central American–American identities and experiences. While Moya and Graetz are two principal actors in the novel, it is the character of Flor de Mayo Puac who best illustrates this point. Thus, Moya and Graetz's investigations amount to a search for the role of Central American–American subjects within the Latina/o public sphere. As a young female character who is chiefly developed and portrayed in relation to mass media, Flor urges us to consider how gender impacts the position of Central American–Americans within the Latina/o public sphere as well as how Latina/o and non-Latina/o media respond to the so-called Central American migrant crisis going on today.

The last chapter also takes place largely outside the US and in militarized spaces, examining the novels *Erased Faces,* by Chicana author Graciela Limón, and *The Last War,* by Cuban American author and journalist Ana Menéndez. These works offer the opportunity to examine how texts set outside the US present different visions of a US Latina/o public via their characters' lives and professions. This chapter also affords us the opportunity to look at a different kind of mass media worker—the photojournalist. Reading these novels in relation to work that takes up the role of photography in representing militarized conflict, specifically questioning how photojournalism may render static or transformative particular peoples and viewpoints, we can see how the two protagonists engage in disparate journeys. While one delves into her own past and subconscious to connect further with the subjects she is photographing, the other eschews engagement and interacts only at the surface level. This analysis relates the work of the characters to the ways in which US Latina/os have (and have not) expanded their sense of a US Latina/o public sphere to incorporate the Zapatista struggles and the occupation of Middle Eastern nations by the US. In this reading, each of the texts reflects, on the one hand, US Latina/o (and specifically Chicana/o) expansion of the US Latina/o public sphere to include the Zapatistas and, on the other, the lack of incorporation of Middle Eastern, Arab, and Muslim concerns into the US Latina/o public sphere.

The conclusion briefly considers how media is being harnessed not only to articulate a Latina/o public sphere but also to challenge the relationship between citizens and publics. This section examines specifically how undocumented artists and activists and their allies are using internet-based mass media to intervene in commonly held assumptions about how citizenship functions within the public sphere. As Marta Caminero-Santangelo argues, undocumented narrators "understand themselves in some sense part of what critics would call a 'public'" (154). Analyzing the work of Julio Salgado and Yosimar Reyes, this section shows how undocumented artivists reshape the idea of a Latina/o public sphere, placing necessary pressure on the concept of citizenship while deploying an intersectional feminist framework.

Our current political climate, unfortunately, points to the relevance of this project and its necessity and importance. While President Trump's attacks on mass media—in the form of banning BBC, CNN, the *New York Times*, and the *Guardian* from an off-camera briefing and declaring media "the enemy of the American people"—have deservedly made headlines, his disrespect for media workers has a much longer and more racialized history (Siddiqui). Notably, in August 2015 he ejected popular *Univisión* anchor Jorge Ramos from a press conference in Iowa, telling the journalist to "go back to *Univisión*" (Schleifer). The dismissal of course echoed the popular xenophobic attack on immigrants that tells them to "go back to" whatever territory they supposedly belong in / come from. By ejecting Ramos and dismissing *Univisión* and its viewers, Trump voiced his explicit perspective that Spanish-speaking media consumers and immigrants are not, or should not form, part of the US public sphere.

While members of the press within the US have faced new hostility in recent months, journalists around the world have been enduring grave threats to their work and life. According to the Committee to Protect Journalists, in the last twenty-five years, eight hundred journalists from around the world have been murdered. While Iraq is ranked the deadliest country for journalists, three nations in the "top ten" are from the Americas—Colombia, Brazil, and Mexico. News of cartel violence against journalists in Mexico in particular has made headlines in the US. In addition to the high-profile murders of Anabel Flores, María del Rosario Fuentes, and Rubén Espinosa, many others have been kidnapped, killed, or forced to flee. The *Washington Post* notes that the danger to journalists in Mexico is something that the country has in common with Middle Eastern nations, such as Iraq and Syria (Garza

Ramos). These dangers to journalists threaten the ability of the press to educate and inform the public, and threaten democracy itself. While this manuscript does not focus on threats to journalists per se, it does engage with this issue via the analysis of Francisco Goldman's *The Long Night of White Chickens,* set during the Guatemalan Civil War, which included severe repression of mass media. In addition, the book as a whole takes place within this larger context, cognizant of the relationship between attacks on journalists inside and outside the US and the importance of media workers and media outlets.

Public mobilization in defense of journalists, whether those threatened physically or verbally, is necessary but also offers important opportunities to examine the relationship between journalists and publics. The Ramos incident, for example, was of course widely covered by mainstream and Latina/o-oriented press; *Univisión* ran an article quoting prominent Latina/o and Latin American figures (from Ricky Martin to María Elena Salinas) decrying what occurred and affirming their Latina/o pride. These Latina/o responses simultaneously sought to affirm that Latina/o media (and Latina/os) belong in the US and to acknowledge their continued marginalization from mainstream political spaces. No doubt buoyed by this incident, Ramos has become a valuable and vocal critic of the current administration and a voice that seeks to represent immigrants, Latina/os, Mexicans, and Mexican Americans. Without underestimating his political commitments, however, the conflation of Ramos with all Latina/o immigrants bears scrutiny and raises important questions—just what kind of Latina/o community does Ramos (or *Univisión*) represent? What kinds of gender, race, class, language, and citizenship differences are experienced by US Latina/os? Who is this "Latina/o," "immigrant," or "Mexican" community that Ramos and *Univisión* speak to and perhaps for? In what languages do they speak? Affirming the importance of exploring these questions, this book turns to the field of Latina/o literature to seek answers. Looking at contemporary Latina/o literature allows us to appreciate the extent to which Latina/o cultural workers have been in active dialogue with Latina/o media around questions of access, production, distribution, and representation. Privileging the realm of the creative and literary does not deny the existence and importance of the relationship between Latina/o media workers and the Latina/o public sphere. Rather, I argue that this relationship has been and remains in a state of flux and is one that literature and authors have sought to negotiate, reflect, problematize, and create. Literature, then, can invaluably reflect current and historical issues surrounding media and the public sphere and help us imagine new, hopefully better, possibilities.

CHAPTER 1

# Rubén Salazar, Historical Memory, and the Gendered Contours of the Chicana/o Public Sphere

IN HIS iconic article covering the death of Rubén Salazar, the late journalist and author Hunter S. Thompson situates Salazar's death and the controversy surrounding it squarely within the context of Los Angeles race relations and, more specifically, the city's marginalized Chicana/o population. Published in *Rolling Stone* in August 1971, one year after Salazar's death, the article, "Strange Rumblings in Aztlán," bears Thompson's trademark perspectives on some of the seedier sides of US culture and society while also revealing his own ties to Chicana/o peoples and the Chicano movement. A sort of abstract appears at the beginning of the article, offering phrases and bits of information: "The . . . murder . . . and resurrection of Ruben Salazar by the Los Angeles County Sherriff's Department . . . Bad news for the Mexican-American . . . Worse news for the pig" (Thompson, *Fear and Loathing* 44). As the article continues, readers are told that Thompson went to LA at the invitation of Chicana/o civil rights lawyer and activist Oscar Zeta Acosta. Readers familiar with either figure, Thompson or Acosta, likely know that the two had a long-standing friendship, with Acosta occasionally functioning as Thompson's lawyer. In Thompson's most well-known book, *Fear and Loathing in Las Vegas*, Acosta is referred to as Thompson's "Samoan" lawyer, although in the movie version of the book, released in 1997, this historical figure is played by Puerto Rican actor Benicio Del Toro. Exemplifying Thompson's relationship with Acosta, Thompson's article offers near-insider information about the Chicana/o movement to provide readers with the necessary context for Salazar's death. Thompson's choice to use the word *Aztlán* in the title—a term that describes the mythical homeland of the Aztecs and one that Chicana/os commonly invoke to mark their state of belonging in the US Southwest—evidences the writer's familiarity with important Chicana/o terms and concepts. As Thompson's article continues, the author attempts to present readers with a thorough portrait of the social and political landscape of Los Angeles in 1970 as he offers information and conjecture about the death of Salazar.

Salazar's death occurred in the midst of one of the most significant events of the Chicana/o movement. On August 29, 1970, Chicana/os in the Los Angeles area mounted what was likely the largest Chicana/o civil rights mobilization of the time; called the Chicano Moratorium, the march was meant to draw attention to, and to protest, the large numbers of Chicanos drafted into the US war in Vietnam, the disproportionate deaths of these soldiers, and the overall state of US imperialism. Thousands of people—estimates range from 20,000 to 30,000—marched through the streets of East Los Angeles, the historically Mexican American *barrio* of that city. Police who were sent in to monitor the event at some point began to attack protestors. Accounts of how clashes between protestors and police began vary: some claim there were intoxicated protestors in the crowd and that a liquor store had been robbed; others accuse the police of provoking violence and state that there were very likely undercover agents among the protestors. Regardless of the provocation, what followed were brutal attacks by police on unarmed protestors. Police chased protestors into nearby Laguna Park, firing tear-gas canisters at close range and beating unarmed civilians. More than 150 people were arrested, and four were killed: Gustav Montag, Lyn Ward, José Diaz, and Rubén Salazar. Among these, Salazar's death had the greatest ramifications within the Chicana/o community and outside it.

Salazar, a journalist, was covering the Chicano Moratorium for the local Spanish-language station, KMEX. Unlike other protestors, he had not been forced by police into the park. Rather, he and a friend had stopped into a bar, the Silver Dollar Café, on Whittier Boulevard. In a 2014 PBS documentary about Salazar's life and death, *Rubén Salazar: Man in the Middle*, the friend who accompanied Salazar that day, Guillermo Restrepo, explains that he and Salazar had entered the bar in an attempt to throw off a person who was following them. A short time later, LAPD sheriff's deputies began to gather outside the bar, claiming that they were called in to respond to a report of someone in the bar carrying a gun. What happened next is again disputed: the deputies claimed that they shouted warnings and asked those inside the bar to leave. Survivors claim that no such warnings were given. What is not disputed is that sheriff's deputies fired a tear-gas canister into the bar. The canister struck and killed Salazar.

As a journalist, credited with inventing a style he called gonzo journalism,[1] Thompson was keenly aware of what the death of Salazar meant for Chicana/o peoples. He explains in his essay that Salazar meant so much to the Chicana/o communities that he reported on, partly because those communities were keenly aware of the power of media. Thompson writes that after becoming the news director for KMEX, Salazar "quickly transformed [the station] into an energetic, aggressively political voice for the whole Chicano community" (*Fear and Loathing* 50). As Thompson's article aptly captures, Salazar's death was a watershed moment in Chicano history and continues to reverberate in legal, political, and cultural spheres. Several inquests have been held regarding what happened that afternoon in 1970 but no charges have been filed, and only recently has the LAPD released files regarding the case.

Since his death, Salazar has become an icon of the Chicana/o movement, a symbol both of Chicana/o activism and of police brutality and a racist criminal justice system. His image has been reproduced and disseminated frequently, most notably by the artist and print-maker Rupert García and by the US Postal Service, which released a Salazar

---

1. In a short profile of Thompson published by *Playboy* in November 1973, the magazine writes: "His method, known as Gonzo Journalism (his term), involves participating in the story, filling his notebooks with whatever comes up and printing all of it with few if any changes. It produces a very cranked-up style and he stays well cranked in order to maintain the pace: Guacamole, Dos Equis and MDA are the staples of his diet" (quoted in Calderón 88). Acosta's letter in response, in which he "[takes] issue" with the credit given to Thompson, is discussed later in this chapter. Oscar Zeta Acosta Papers, Chicano and Latino Collections, Special Research Collections, University of California, Santa Barbara Libraries.

FIGURE 1. Rubén Salazar commemorative postage stamp

stamp in 2008 (see figure 1). In addition to these visual representations, Salazar has appeared as a character and historical reference in several works of Chicana/o literature published since his death. These works offer us an opportunity to explore and understand how Salazar's death impacted Chicana/o authors and literature. Furthermore, to the extent that such works consider Salazar not only as a Chicano activist or participant in the Chicano movement but specifically as a Chicano journalist, they provide ample fodder for considering how Salazar's life and death shaped how Chicana/o authors and activists understand the relationship between journalism, Chicana/o political and social aspirations, and a burgeoning Chicana/o public.

This chapter focuses on two literary texts, Oscar Zeta Acosta's *The Revolt of the Cockroach People* (originally published in 1973) and Lucha Corpi's *Eulogy for a Brown Angel* (1992). Both texts deal centrally with the Chicana/o movement of the late 1960s and early 1970s, and both include Salazar as a character or reference. The two texts are also well known; Acosta and Corpi are important Chicana/o authors, and their works are widely read and taught by Chicana/o and non-Chicana/o students and scholars. Despite their critical and popular importance, no one has yet undertaken a comparative analysis of their portrayals of Salazar. Indeed, there exists no significant analysis of artistic representations of Salazar in any medium. As this chapter argues, the two novels use Salazar to invoke a specifically Chicana/o public and to posit that

Salazar speaks to and from such a public. While this may seem like a somewhat noncontroversial claim, it is distinct from other, more mainstream representations of Salazar as a man whose relationships with, or allegiance to, Chicana/o communities was indeterminate. Moreover, considering the period during which these works were set and published, they predate by at least a decade more widely accepted historical markers of the existence and importance of Chicana/o or Latina/o "markets." At the same time, the texts are not uniform regarding who or what makes up the Chicana/o public. Corpi's and Acosta's characters claim that Salazar represents a "we" or an "us," but the constituents of these groups are distinct in the different texts. In Acosta's novel, the plurality is subsumed under an individual, his narrator, while for Corpi this plurality is a heterogeneous Chicana/o community. Within both texts, gender plays a decisive role, as differences regarding sexual and gender equality within the movement divide characters. Salazar, in his life and in his death, is drawn into these discussions so that we can see in these literary portrayals a reckoning with questions of voice, representation, and agency. Overall, this chapter argues that representations of Salazar's work and life provoke a rethinking of Chicana/o movement peoples and politics that affirms the relationship between Chicana/o journalism and a Chicana/o public while nevertheless failing to put forth an uncontested portrait of this public.

This analysis relies on a close reading of the cultural products alongside Chicana/o and Chicana feminist literary, media, and cultural studies scholarship. The texts are analyzed within their historical context to examine how the works position Salazar's life and murder in relationship to biographical information and Chicana/o movement politics. Considerations of Salazar's life and work are made alongside attention to the authors' own positionality. That is, Acosta himself was a prolific writer and journalist, whereas Corpi, who continues to publish, has made a name for herself not only as a significant Chicana feminist voice but also as a pioneer in the genre of Chicana/o detective fiction. This chapter employs an intersectional framework, paying attention to matters of race, class, gender, and sexuality as sites of simultaneous and interlocking oppression. However, questions of gender and sexuality are highlighted in terms of how these factors shape characters' interactions with Salazar, his legacy, and Chicana/o publics. Seeking to foreground the texts themselves, a close reading of Salazar's portrayal in these works makes up the bulk of the analysis. The last section builds on the literary and cultural analysis to consider how these works intervene in discussions about the public sphere.

In both novels Salazar is affirmed as a member of the Chicana/o community and as supportive of principal actors in the texts. This portrayal, stemming from the characters themselves, suggests the importance of these texts and characters claiming a Latina/o journalist as part of their larger movement and is at odds with other representations of Salazar that emphasized his liminality in relation to Chicana/o politics. Characters recognize the relationship between Chicana/o journalists and Chicana/o social movements and underscore the dual nature of this relationship and the affirmation that each receives from the other. At the same time, the texts themselves focus on a small, nameable group of Chicana/o activists, and Salazar is scripted in relation to particular people. These people reflect different values, attitudes, and tactics with regard to political praxis and sex and gender politics. The salience of gender to these differences points to the diversity within Chicana/o movement viewpoints and of the gendered concerns that were largely ignored during the movement itself, but which continue to play an important role in our understanding of the movement's focus and operation. Both Acosta's and Corpi's texts evidence a sustained interest in portraying and exploring the connections between journalism and the Chicana/o public sphere while demonstrating the decisive role that gendered representations and politics play in negotiating this relationship.

## SALAZAR

According to Mario T. García, Salazar is best understood as a "border correspondent" because in his life and work he straddled, and crossed, multiple borders. He was born on the US–Mexico border in Ciudad Juárez, Chihuahua, Mexico. Months after his birth in 1928, his parents moved to Juárez's sister city on the US side, El Paso, Texas. Salazar joined the US Army after graduating from high school and then returned to Texas to attend Texas Western College (now the University of Texas at El Paso), where he studied journalism and wrote for the school paper, *El Burro*. After graduation, he became the first Mexican American reporter to write for the *El Paso Herald-Post*. It must be noted that El Paso is an overwhelmingly Mexican / Mexican American city; that the local newspaper did not hire its first Mexican American reporter until the mid-twentieth century underscores the segregation and discrimination that has marked and continues to mark English-language media in the US. After several years at the *Herald-Post*, Salazar relocated to Northern California to write for the *Santa Rosa Press Democrat*; soon after, he moved again, to the *San Francisco News* and later to the *Los Angeles Herald-Express*. In 1959 Salazar obtained the job that would define his career as he began working for the *Los Angeles Times*.

In Los Angeles, Salazar himself was not initially thrilled at being assigned to report on Mexican American issues, worrying that he was being pigeonholed as a writer. However, he was a good reporter and "in time became quite committed to the Mexican American community" (García 12). In his columns, Salazar reported on the dissatisfaction of the Mexican American peoples in Los Angeles, who complained about the bracero program, the discrimination and poor education that Mexican American students received in public schools, and their lack of political clout. Between February and March of 1963, Salazar published a five-part series on Mexican Americans in Los Angeles. The series touched on language, the history of Mexicans in the US Southwest, and views on assimilation/acculturation, education, and political power. Many of the issues resonate in today's social and political climate; Salazar quotes Professor George I. Sánchez, a founding figure in US ethnic and Mexican American studies, who asks, "Why is it all right to continue to call many of our cities and streets by Spanish names, encourage Mexican-Spanish architecture, praise and eat Mexican food and still expect Mexican-Americans to become wholly Anglicized?" (92). Interestingly, although the first article in the series is titled "Spanish-Speaking Angelenos: A Culture in Search of a Name," Salazar never uses the term *Chicano*, which suggests that the descriptor was not yet circulating in mainstream circles at that time.[2] The series received mixed responses from *Times* readers; some lauded Salazar for writing "truth," others accused the journalist of unfairly and negatively

---

2. Many of Salazar's headlines refer to "Latins," although the articles themselves use the terms *Spanish-speaking* and *Mexican-American*. Throughout this chapter I use the terms used by individual authors and scholars.

stereotyping Mexican Americans and Mexican American barrios, and at least one reader found in the series evidence to support the idea that the "blame" for the state of Mexican Americans "lies wholly on us individually and as a community" (García 107–9). Although he took the concerns of Mexican Americans seriously, Salazar took a decidedly liberal viewpoint that took US institutions to task for not fulfilling their responsibilities to Mexican Americans without fully grappling with the depth and intensity of US structural racism. His political philosophy, García explains, was "linked to accomplishing reforms through established channels," and his perspective did not waver, even when he reported on the decidedly radical Chicana/o movement (18). In a January 1962 article on Juárez and El Paso, Salazar notes that although until recently Mexican Americans faced segregation (not being allowed to swim in Anglo pools), the city is now "a model of democratic living" (García 66). His fundamental beliefs in US institutions and ideals can be found in some of his early writings as a foreign correspondent. Sent by the *Times* to cover the 1965 US invasion of the Dominican Republic, Salazar echoed US State Department rhetoric that the military had no choice but to intervene in the name of "democracy" (21). Salazar then spent almost a year in Vietnam, covering the escalating US intervention in the region. He eventually came to oppose the war, although apparently on pacifist, as opposed to political, grounds (23). In 1966 Salazar was assigned to a third foreign post, this time as the bureau chief in Mexico City. He had married Sally Robare in 1960, and the couple brought their three children with them. From that post he reported on not only Mexico but also Caribbean and Central American nations. His reporting at this time continued to favor official government perspectives. For example, he portrayed members of the Salvadoran oligarchy as liberal reformers, when in fact they were at the forefront of the increasing political, racial, and economic repression that would soon lead to that nation's civil war. Covering the Tlatelolco Massacre of October 1968, when the Mexican government murdered hundreds and disappeared an unknown number of students and other activists, Salazar parroted the Mexican government's lower number of casualties (24). The president and general manager of KMEX, Danny Villanueva, speculates that Salazar's poor reporting on the massacre, in which as a non-Mexican he was not able to fully access or understand the story, led to his being recalled by the *Times* to Los Angeles in

1969. Salazar's response to his reassignment affirms that the move was a demotion; he called this career change "professionally defeating and distressing personally" (*Rubén Salazar: Man in the Middle*).

While Salazar was covering events in Mexico and Latin America, the US was being transformed by social movements spearheaded by people of color. By early 1968 Chicana/os in Los Angeles had received significant media attention for a series of high school blowouts (walkouts) on the part of middle school, high school, and college students. The actions were facilitated by a network of organizations, including the Brown Berets and the United Mexican American Students (UMAS), and supported by sympathetic teachers in the community such as Sal Castro. These protests were the culmination of decades of grievances against racist educational institutions, but they reflected a new, more militant way of voicing Chicana/o dissatisfaction and claims to equality. The Chicana/o movement in LA was also closely linked to other political and social developments that Salazar had covered, including the war in Vietnam and the growing student movement around the world. Despite his reservations about returning and concerns over being stereotyped as a "Chicano reporter," Salazar was sympathetic to movement demands. Of concerns regarding bilingual instruction in schools, he explained that Spanish was a language indigenous to the Southwest, and he described David Martínez, the leader of the Brown Berets, as a "clean-cut Mexican American boy" (28–29). Such descriptions of young men of color were hardly commonplace in mainstream, Anglo-owned and Anglo-oriented newspapers of the time (or today).

Perhaps the firmest illustration of Salazar's commitment to Chicana/o people was his decision to leave the *Times* for the Spanish-language station KMEX. Salazar explained his decision as stemming from a desire to communicate *with* the people he had been reporting *on*. "I really wanted to communicate in their language with the people I had written about so much," he told another correspondent, also mentioning that Spanish-speaking peoples relied on television and radio more so than newspapers (García 30). The move to Spanish-language media suggests the Salazar was himself, and sought to connect with, what former *Univisión* CEO Joaquín Blaya terms "born again Hispanics," that is, "bilingual people who have been using more English language than Spanish language media, but for a variety of reasons (affirmative action, racism, family concerns) have recently renewed their feelings of ethno-racial solidarity" (Rodríguez, *Making Latino News* 67). Salazar's move underscores both the linguistic fluidity of Latina/o media producers and consumers and the significance of the Spanish language as a symbol of Latina/o ethnic identity and cohesion.

Although he moved to KMEX, Salazar continued to write a weekly column on Chicana/o issues for the *Times*. For García, this meant that Salazar functioned as a "translator," explaining Chicana/o concerns to an Anglo readership and connecting him to the earlier tradition of Latina/o journalists who had Spanish-language columns in English-language newspapers (30). Salazar's articles for the *Times* throughout 1969 and 1970 focused on various aspects of the Chicana/o movement—including high school protests, Alicia Escalante's East LA Welfare Rights Organization, and college students' demands for more representation and important conferences. An April 1, 1969, article covered the Chicano Youth Liberation Conference held in Denver, Colorado, and led by Rodolfo "Corky" Gonzales, while an article a few days later touched on the demands made by students at UCLA. The students from UMAS demanded an increase in Chicana/o enrollment on campus and fought against the university's tendency to count Latin American students as Chicana/o, an issue that students and faculty of color frequently contend with to this day (García 208). Salazar's columns give lots of space to Chicana/o activists and often cite Anglo experts who support their claims. As such, he does not exhibit an overreliance on "official sources" (who are overwhelmingly white and male) and rather views community leaders as a "legitimate source" (Nishikawa et al. 244, 252). However, Salazar's columns also use standard, stigmatizing language when he denotes figures such as Reies López Tijerina as "extremist" (García 195).

At KMEX Salazar took on state racism more directly. According to a friend, at the time of his death he was writing a book on police abuse (García 31). Salazar's reporting had certainly caught the eye of the LAPD; Chief Ed Davis wrote a letter to the editor to the *Times* demanding that a misquote by the reporter be retracted. Salazar's friend Guillermo Restrepo reports that Davis called Salazar and told him to stay quiet, while another friend, Earl Morris, says that Salazar was told to "stop stirring up Mexicans" and affirms that "Rubén didn't like cops" (*Rubén Salazar: Man in the Middle*). Pressure seems to have come from all sides, as Bill Thomas, an editor at the *Times*, explains that Davis called him and told him to fire Salazar (García 32). Despite Anglo hostility to him that would suggest otherwise, Salazar was never a militant. He continued to reject the adjective *Chicano* when placed before *reporter* and relished returning to his suburban home in the majority-white Orange County at the end of a long day of work (34). His daughter, Rachel Salazar Cook, also saw her father as enacting a strict separation between his home life and his work life. "I don't know how much he [identified] with being a Mexican," she told interviewers. "My father led a completely Anglo life. He was a professional. He was part of the establishment" (*Rubén Salazar: Man in the Middle*). Of course, the differing perspectives on Salazar may say as much about these individuals as they say about Salazar himself. Notably, Chicana/o reporters and activists such as Villanueva and Restrepo seem to have taken Salazar's sympathies with the Chicana/o movement and the threats against him more seriously. Those with less contact with Chicana/o communities, including Thomas and Salazar Cook, view him as more aligned with Anglo institutions. There is no doubt, however, that Salazar's relationship to the Chicana/o movement and to the Anglo-controlled criminal justice system evolved in the last years of his life.

## ACOSTA

At the end of his first book, *Autobiography of a Brown Buffalo*, Acosta's narrator returns to Los Angeles, a move that echoes Salazar's own return to LA from Mexico City. Acosta's subsequent book, *The Revolt of the Cockroach People*, illustrates the narrator's growing involvement with the Chicano movement, again paralleling the trajectory of Salazar's life. In this latter text the character that refers to Salazar, named Roland Zanzibar, is portrayed as similar to and sympathetic with the narrator, Buffalo "Zeta" Brown. The portrayal of Zanzibar and Brown as alike is no doubt based on some of their demographic similarities— both are Chicano heterosexual men who were born in nearly the same city (Juárez / El Paso), and both are in their late thirties / early forties and completing the most significant periods of their careers in Los Angeles when the book takes place. The close relationship between Zanzibar and Brown may also allude to Acosta's own interest in journalism. While best known as the friend/lawyer and co-conspirator of Hunter S. Thompson, Acosta himself in fact claimed equal credit for the development of the "gonzo" style of journalism with which Thompson is most heavily associated. Thompson was no doubt inspired by Acosta; the term *gonzo* refers to the fictionalized version of Acosta who appears in the former's iconic *Fear and Loathing in Las Vegas* as "Dr. Gonzo." In response to a *Playboy* story about Thompson in which "gonzo journalism" is described as "his [Thompson's] method," Acosta wrote the magazine a letter:

> I beg to take issue with you. And with anyone else who says that. In point of fact, Doctor Duke and I—the world-famous Doctor Gonzo—together we both, hand in hand, sought out the teachings and curative powers of the world-famous Savage Henry, the Scag Baron of Las Vegas and in point of fact the term <u>and</u> methodology of reporting crucial events under fire and drugs which are of course essential to any good writing in this age of confusion—[3]

He signs the letter "Oscar Zeta Acosta, Chicano Lawyer" and then adds "P.S. The guacamole and XX he got from me." Acosta's portrayal of Salazar can thus be understood within the context of his own portrayal by Thompson and an indication of Acosta's investment in, and identification with, journalists.

Outside of his relationship with Thompson, Acosta was a considerable figure within the Chicana/o movement with which he worked as a lawyer, writer, and activist. Born in El Paso, Texas, in 1935, he moved with his family at the age of five to the rural farming town of Riverbank, California. After high school he enlisted in the US Air Force and spent several years as a missionary in Panama. He was discharged from the Air Force, married his first wife, Betty Daves, and the two had a son, Marco Federico Acosta. According to Ilan Stavans, this period of Acosta's life is marked by mental breakdowns, psychiatric treatment, and at least one suicide attempt.[4] In the mid-1960s Acosta enrolled in

---

3. Letter to the Editor of *Playboy*. 15 October 1973. Oscar Zeta Acosta Papers, 1936–1990. Chicano and Latino Collections, Special Research Collections, University of California, Santa Barbara Libraries, Santa Barbara, CA.

4. See Mendoza's critique of Stavans's work on Acosta in which the former claims that the latter exploits and pathologizes Acosta while appropriating his identity for his own purposes.

San Francisco State University Law School, earning his degree by taking night classes. While at SFSU he also studied creative writing, and both his personal papers and his published works exhibit a strong identity as a writer. For example, his papers include a 1972 letter to a friend in which he says "I'm not just a writer . . . I would like to write so-called journalism, too," as well as a sketch of his next book, to be titled *The Rise and Fall of General Zeta*.[5] In 1968 Acosta moved to East LA and became well known for his work on several high-profile cases. By this time the United Farm Workers had been founded, and several other significant events, including the Chicano Youth Liberation Conference in Denver in March 1969 and the National Chicano Moratorium in LA in August 1970, were just around the corner. Acosta worked as a lawyer with the movement; he represented "the Chicano 13," a group of students who were charged after orchestrating a series of "blowouts," or walkouts, at East LA high schools, demanding culturally relevant education and school reforms. He also defended a group of Brown Berets, known as the Biltmore 6, accused of disrupting a speech by then California governor Ronald Reagan.[6] Acosta also defended Rodolfo "Corky" Gonzales against weapons charges after he was arrested the day of the Chicano Moratorium. During this time, Acosta's work inside and outside of the courtroom earned him the attention of the FBI, who

---

5. Letter to the Editor of *Playboy*, 15 October 1973; Letter to Alan, 12 November 1972; Letter to Helen, undated. Oscar Zeta Acosta Papers, 1936–1990. Chicano and Latino Collections, Special Research Collections, University of California, Santa Barbara Libraries, Santa Barbara, CA.

6. The Acosta papers contain numerous newspaper articles about the Biltmore case and Acosta's role. One article not attributed to a specific paper titled "Jailed Attorney Complains" explains that "the 36-year old attorney was sentenced to five days in jail Thursday after making a cryptic remark in connection with a ruling by Judge Alarcon on a question by the prosecution." A headline in an unnamed Spanish-language newspaper declares, "zeta expone el racismo en las cortes." In notes that are part of his personal papers, Acosta wrote: "I was defending the 'Biltmore Six,' six young Chicanos who were busted for allegedly trying to burn down the Biltmore Hotel one night in 1970 when Reagan was delivering a speech there. They were indicted by a Grand Jury and I contended that all Grand Juries are racist since all grand jurors have to be recommended by Superior Court Judges and that the whole thing reeks of 'sub-conscious, institutional racism.' I was trying to get the indictments squashed on that basis. To prove my contention I subpoenaed all 109 Superior Court judges in Los Angeles and examined them all under oath about their racism. After almost a year of work on this the judge on that case, Arthur Alarcon, who is Mexican American, rejected the motion."

began to keep a file on him as part of the COINTELPRO program.[7] In 1974 Acosta departed for Mexico; he was last heard from in June of that year when he called his son and told him he would be returning to California via a friend's private boat. After none of Acosta's friends or family members heard from him for five years, Marco began the process of having his father declared dead and having the rights of his father's books reverted to himself. By the late 1980s Marco had succeeded in obtaining the rights to *Autobiography* and *Revolt*, and, with the help of Chicana/o academics who vouched for the literary and social significance of Acosta's writings and Jann Wenner, editor of *Rolling Stone*, whose subsidiary, Riverhead Books, had originally published both works, he was able to republish both works through Viking Press. Acosta's old friend Thompson lent a hand as well, writing a memorable forward to the second book in which he declares the author "too weird to live and too rare to die" (Acosta 7). In his afterword to the 1989 edition of *The Revolt of the Cockroach People*, Marco Acosta writes that "no one, to my knowledge, knows for sure what happened" to his father and describes him as "a fearless and committed fighter" in the "struggle against racism and oppression in America" (259, 261). Marco Acosta was instrumental in the reissue of his father's books, which had been out of print since the 1970s, as well as in the establishment of the Oscar Zeta Acosta papers as part of the Chicano and Latino Studies collection at the University of California, Santa Barbara. In the 1989 afterword, he also alludes to a film portrayal of his father's life, which has just come to fruition.[8]

Acosta's works have received sustained attention from Chicana/o studies scholars. Given that his books correspond closely to important moments in Chicana/o movement history, it is no surprise that issues of politics and ethnic identity are foremost in scholarship on the author. The vast majority of scholarship focuses on his first book, *The Autobiography of a Brown Buffalo* (originally published in 1972), and

---

7. These FBI files are part of the Acosta collection at the University of California, Santa Barbara. In his review of Ilan Stavans's *Bandido*, Louis Mendoza criticizes Stavans for failing to mention the files, explaining that they "illustrate how the FBI, the Secret Service, and the L.A.P.D. conducted an intense campaign of surveillance on Acosta" while also struggling to impose a racial identity on him—as the author is variously described as Mexican American, Spanish American, and white (82).

8. *The Rise and Fall of the Brown Buffalo*, directed by Phillip Rodríguez, was released in 2017.

on the process of ethnic self-realization that the narrator undergoes.[9] Michael Hames-García, however, asserts that Acosta's take on issues of identity and authenticity are premised on satire and suggests that we read Acosta's style as premised on the grotesque and the gonzo journalism style he invented. This style, with roots in both satire and *testimonio*, "reveals that what seems like a search for an essential identity . . . is in fact a satirical critique of the standards of authenticity often implied in such a search" (470). Juan Bruce-Novoa also examines Acosta's writings in light of his and Thompson's journalism, explaining that Acosta uses the Gonzo style "to push aloof events or people to the edge of chaos; when the subject is already there, traditional forms create an appropriate juxtaposition of order and chaos" ("Fear and Loathing" 44). This explains why in situations that are so "abnormal"—such as the murder of Salazar—the Gonzo style is not necessary and not used. Frederick Luis Aldama and Raymund Paredes highlight magico-realist elements in Acosta's work and the author's tendency to present historical facts in a manner that is "impressionistic without any significant concern for objectivity" (Aldama 65; Paredes 243). Such elements of Acosta's writing of course are also that of Gonzo journalism. Referencing William Faulkner's assertion that fiction is more "more true" than journalism, Thompson asserts that both fiction and journalism "are artificial categories" (*Great Shark Hunt* 106). He goes on to explain that his idea of Gonzo journalism was based on the idea of writing events as they happened, so that the "eye and mind of the journalist would be functioning as a camera," although he later acknowledges that "this is a hard thing to do" (106). The presence of these elements in Acosta's work highlights the significance of journalism and specifically gonzo journalism for the author.

In addition to its historico-political context and invocation of gonzo journalism, Acosta's work is marked by blatant misogyny and homophobia. Sara Bishop confronts the homophobia of Acosta's writing, in which the epithet "fag" is used widely and almost indiscriminately, but suggests that the fictionalized portrayal of Acosta and Thompson's relationship (in the guise of the characters of Oscar and

---

9. For example, Marta E. Sánchez reads Acosta's first book in light of questions of ethnic identity pertinent to the Chicana/o movement, arguing that Acosta's protagonist exists in a liminal space in which he moves "from a not-anymore quasi-assimilated Mexican American into a yet-to-be Chicano" (103–4).

Karl King) "transgresses the boundary between homosocial male friendship and queer love" (211). The meaning and significance of the misogyny and homophobia in Acosta's text and their relationship to Chicano male subjectivity and the Chicano movement continues to provoke various responses. Was Acosta offering a satirical takedown of "the idea of the Chicano warrior-hero," as Hames-García suggests, or was he reflecting an extreme version of what today we might call toxic masculinity and which was undoubtedly part of the movement? (474). While scenes such as the homosocial exchange of gifts between Oscar and Karl King in *Autobiography* and Brown's use of the "Chicano handshake" with Liberace (whom the narrator refers to as a "world famous fag") suggest some nuance to his treatment of gay men, there remains little doubt as to the role of *heterosexuality* in the works. That is, regardless of his portrait of gay men or lesbians, Acosta's narrators engage in "continual self-glorification" as "heterosexual superstud[s]" and align themselves with exploitative masculinist heterosexuality (Bruce-Novoa, "Homosexuality" 73–74).

This chapter seeks to forge new ground and place existing scholarship in conversation by combining a focus on Acosta's political engagement, his relationship to journalism, his interest in questions of ethnicity and ethnic cohesion and questions of gender (specifically masculinity) and sexuality. As the next section demonstrates, these issues are broached specifically through the figure of Roland Zanzibar (a clear reference to Salazar) in *The Revolt of the Cockroach People*. Focusing on these questions through Zanzibar belies Acosta's sustained engagement with and interest in journalism while also presenting a different perspective on the relationship between media workers, Chicana/o peoples, and social movements. Specifically, by portraying Zanzibar/Salazar in a way that emphasizes his alignment with Buffalo Brown, Acosta suggests his own investment in the idea of a specifically Chicano media. Given that this portrayal is less ambivalent about questions of ethnic allegiance than Salazar himself was, and given the relationship between Brown's Chicanismo and exploitative masculinity, the portrait of Salazar rendered in *Revolt* emphasizes the important, but not uncontested, role of Chicana/o journalists in relation to larger questions concerning Chicana/o peoples and the public sphere. The gendered nature of so much of Brown's personality means that questions of gender and sexuality remain at the forefront of these negotiations.

## *REVOLT*: SALAZAR AND THE MASCULINIST CHICANO PUBLIC SPHERE

*Revolt* is part memoir and part fictionalized rendering of Acosta's own participation in the Chicano movement. Acosta's protagonist and narrator is, like the author, a Chicano lawyer who has a varied and at times contradictory relationship to Chicana/o peoples and movements. When the book opens, the protagonist, named Brown, has recently returned to Los Angeles in January of 1968 to pursue his dreams of being a writer. He proclaims: "I had no intention of practicing law or of pitting myself against anything. I was only anxious to find 'THE STORY' and write 'THE BOOK' so that I could split to the lands of peace and quiet where people played volleyball, sucked smoke and chased after cool blondes" (22). But Brown has arrived in LA in the midst of significant social agitation on the part of people of color, and he is drawn to the movement. His sister asks him if he's heard of the Chicano Militants, whom she describes as "sort of like the black Panthers" of East Los Angeles and he finds himself reflecting on his own status as a marginalized US citizen (25). He decides that the Chicano movement will be his big story:

> My brain goes off like explosions and by dawn I have made innumerable resolutions. I will change my name. I will learn Spanish. I will write the greatest books ever written. I will become the best criminal lawyer in the history of the world. I will save the world. I will show the world what is what and who the fuck is who. Me in particular. (31)

Brown becomes involved in the Chicana/o movement and goes on to represent various Chicana/o activists facing charges related to demonstrations and to lead actions himself. These include defending the Chicano 13, leading a group of Chicana/os protesting the corruption of the Catholic Church by gathering at St. Basil's Catholic Church on Christmas Eve in 1969, and even running for sheriff of LA in 1970.

These events reflect Acosta's own life and work; like Brown, he ran for sheriff, receiving over 100,000 votes with just one campaign promise: to dissolve the office of sheriff if elected.

Acosta's book details these high-profile and historically grounded actions undertaken by his narrator, Brown. And as indicated by his resolve to "save the world—me in particular," Acosta's narrator is self-aggrandizing and hyperbolic. Alurista's early take on the novel attributes the portrayal of Brown to the genre of the novel, explaining that the novel is a bourgeois form "that tends to glorify the individual" (94). Contributing to the focus on the individual is the fact that Acosta's novel is written in the first person; this allows Brown to act "as the protagonist who triggers the plot and ends up as its antihero" (95). Not only does Brown make himself the focus of the novel; he also continuously portrays himself as both the most militant and most level-headed of his activist *compañeros,* while nevertheless leading others in activities such as dropping acid to plan a political demonstration and launching Molotov cocktails into a grocery store being picketed by the United Farm Workers. Along with the consistent allusion to Brown's own ego and heavy alcohol and drug use, the book is marked by its misogyny and homophobia. Men whom Brown confronts are often referred to as "faggots," and almost no woman is mentioned without a description of her breasts, buttocks, or legs. The homophobic and misogynistic aspects of the text have been extensively discussed by other scholars, but Brown's heterosexism and misogyny bear mentioning because to the extent to which Brown portrays himself as commensurate with Chicano political leadership, he by extension portrays this leadership as male-dominated and sexist. It is within this misogynist and Chicano context that Roland Zanzibar is introduced.

Zanzibar is scripted into an explicitly Chicano context in Acosta's book. The narrator tells us that Zanzibar is the "news director at the Pulitzer Prize winning Chicano station, KMEX" (134). While KMEX is and was a Spanish-language station (it was an early acquisition of Azcárraga's SIN), the extent to which it is or was "Chicano" is less clear. That is, "Chicano" is both an ethnoracial and a political designation that is meant to describe not only someone's heritage as having roots in the US Southwest or Mexico but also a political commitment to *la causa* of Chicana/o civil rights. Within the book, characters argue among themselves about their ethnic and political loyalties, and occasionally a character will assert "I'm a Chicana/o" in order to foreground their political commitments and their resolve in the face of opposition. For example, Brown is most definitely a "Chicano," whereas the judge before whom he tries several cases or the police who infiltrate the Chicana/o movement—despite their Mexican American heritage and Spanish surnames—are definitely not. Thus it's notable that Brown names Zanzibar and his station as Chicana/o. He is saying that both—the individual and the news station—are on the side of the people. In fact, as América Rodríguez explains, as the oldest and most institutionalized station in the US's largest Latina/o market, KMEX has played and continues to play a particularly significant role in US Latina/o culture and society. Much of the station's most significant endeavors, however, occurred in later decades. For example, in 1980 the station urged Latina/os to participate in the 1980 census; the station also emphasized that its viewers were part of the US when it began live broadcasts from the Tournament of Roses New Year's Day Parade and later raised money for the 1985 Mexico City earthquake (118). Later, when Californians were debating the anti-immigrant Proposition 187, KMEX broke with industry protocols that emphasized objectivity and spoke out against the ballot initiative (119).[10] Rodríguez credits stations such as KMEX and KVEA with disseminating political information that impacted the Latina/o community and, by extension, with encouraging Latina/os to register and vote. Indeed, in the years that saw the passage of Proposition 187 and other anti-immigrant legislation, Latina/o voter turnout increased 30 percent (119). During the events of the novel and Salazar's life, however, KMEX had been broadcasting for less than a decade. Given the diverse history of Spanish-language broadcasting in the US, KMEX's ties to Mexican elites, and the fact that Latina/os were not considered an important "market" until at least the 1980s, the station's establishment of itself as an important part of a largely working-class community was not necessarily a given.[11] Indeed, when KMEX began broadcasting in 1962, the term *Chicano*

---

10. The initiative, which passed in 1994, prohibited undocumented immigrants from using state services such as emergency rooms and public education. The law was ruled unconstitutional and by 1999 had been repealed.

11. Rodríguez explains that in terms of media consumption by Latina/os, the English language may be a "proxy for class." Middle-class Latina/os are more likely to be bilingual or English-dominant, while working-class Latina/os are more likely to be monolingual or Spanish-dominant (131–32).

was not in wide circulation and would not have been applied to the station. Rather, we can understand this programming to be a response to the demographics of LA's Spanish-speaking population as well as to the mobilization of this population in the 1960s and 1970s. From this perspective, KMEX became "Chicano" through actions like hiring high-profile, community-oriented journalists such as Salazar; for his part, Salazar's employment by the local station solidified his own commitment to Chicana/os and, according to Acosta's protagonist, to *la causa*. Finally, Brown's assertion that KMEX is a "Chicano" station that has hired the "Chicano" journalist Zanzibar is not uncontested. The recent PBS documentary on Salazar is titled *Rubén Salazar: Man in the Middle*—suggesting that Salazar occupied a liminal position—neither Mexican nor American, neither a wholly mainstream journalist nor a community voice. When Brown unequivocally scripts Zanzibar and his employer into a Chicana/o context, he underscores the importance of being able to align a station and a journalist with the movement while gesturing to the bidirectional process through which media outlets and workers come to be affiliated with social movements.

In the novel, Zanzibar invites Brown to the KMEX studio for an interview, and during their interview the latter announces his bid for sheriff and spells out his plan for the sheriff's office: to dissolve it. At the conclusion of their interview, Zanzibar laughs and shakes Brown's hand and the two go next door for a beer. Zanzibar then tells Brown about his job, describing himself as "the only articulate Chicano in the business at the time," and declaring his intention to bring the "barrios to the public's attention" (137). At their parting, Zanzibar somewhat ironically warns Brown to be careful. In this scene, Zanzibar and Brown offer a mutual validation of one another and their status as members of the movement. Echoing the importance of terminology circulating in subaltern publics through mass media, Brown takes the opportunity of being on-air with KMEX to use and define his term *cockroach*. Speaking of the case of Robert Fernandez, he surmises that Fernandez's murderer could have been "another prisoner . . . a Chicano or some other Cockroach" (135). After prompting by Zanzibar, he offers his definition: "you know, the little beasts that everyone steps on" (135). Given that the title of Acosta's book is *The Revolt of the Cockroach People*, this scene is significant, as it marks the first time that Brown is able to disseminate his terminology to a larger public. He's able to do so through a sympathetic Chicano journalist, echoing the way that Salazar and others disseminated the term *Chicana/o*. Brown's invitation to the KMEX studio suggests a recognition of his importance as a Chicana/o leader. At the same time, Brown's decision to officially announce his campaign while on-air establishes KMEX as the appropriate medium through which to reach his potential constituents. Brown's presence at KMEX and his interactions with Zanzibar also affirm the latter's status as a Chicano. Zanzibar is portrayed not as marginal or ambivalent about Chicana/os and Chicana/o issues but as firmly supportive of the popular uprisings. His sympathy toward the erratic character of Brown underlines just how firmly he is on the side of the movement.

Interestingly, the idea that Zanzibar has come to work for KMEX to increase, as he calls it, "the public's" knowledge of Chicana/o issues is a bit more complicated. Recall that KMEX is and was a Spanish-language station. Non-Spanish-speakers (i.e., non-Spanish-speaking Chicana/os and Anglos) do not watch/listen to Spanish-language programming—thus, this cannot be the "public" whose attention Zanzibar is hoping to catch. "The public" Zanzibar is directed toward, then, are Spanish-speaking viewers only, presumably primarily Latina/os and Chicana/os. This suggests that he is not trying to translate "barrio" issues for mainstream/Anglo audiences but rather trying to speak to Chicana/o audiences in particular—in effect mobilizing and helping to fortify this public itself. Here Zanzibar affirms Salazar's own movement from an Anglo- to a Chicana/o-controlled news outlet. In a television interview with Bob Navarro, Salazar explains: "The most important thing about my move to me was that I was frustrated. I wanted to really communicate with the people about whom I had been writing for so long" (*Rubén Salazar: Man in the Middle*). Zanzibar's move also suggests a movement away from mainstream journalism that has a heavy reliance on "authoritative sources," primarily government leaders, and a move toward incorporating more "dissident voices," such as those of working-class people, racial minorities, and activists (Nishikawa et al. 244). These early scenes, then, portray Zanzibar as transforming himself as a Chicano journalist to more firmly reflect his investment in a Chicana/o public whom he wants to serve; they also establish Zanzibar and Brown as personal and political allies.

The relationship between Brown and Zanzibar is solidified later in the novel when, following Zanzibar's murder, Brown positions himself as the only one capable of understanding the motives behind the reporter's murder and of taking his place as a chronicler of the movement. The last third of the novel largely centers on Brown's defense of Corky Gonzales, who was arrested during the Moratorium. At this point, the work blends fact and fiction, as Acosta has his narrator not present for the actual march but rather finding out about the events and returning to LA soon after. In the narrative, Brown has escaped to Acapulco; there, news of Gonzales's arrest and Zanzibar's murder reaches him via a newspaper and phone call. At the end of chapter 14, Brown declares: "It is Sunday afternoon, August 30, 1970, in the year of The Cockroach. Our first martyr, Roland Zanzibar is dead" (197). Brown returns to Los Angeles to defend Gonzales and others who are facing charges. Historically, Acosta defended Gonzales against charges of inciting a riot, but in the novel Brown suggests that Gonzales is being accused of Zanzibar's death. This point is somewhat confused, as Brown repeatedly claims that Zanzibar's death is being blamed on Gonzales, while other characters correct him (206). Ostensibly, Gonzales's trial has nothing to do with Zanzibar or his death, although the defendants face charges of public disorder that took place on the same day as his murder, the day of the Chicano Moratorium. This alteration, however, allows Acosta to center Zanzibar's/Salazar's death in the narrative and to, through Brown's courtroom antics, do something that has never been done—put Salazar's murderers on trial.

As Carlos Gallego points out, Acosta intertwines Zanzibar's murder with this case to depict both as part of a political strategy and to portray the event as a "political assassination and not an accidental misfire" (169). For Brown, the charges against Gonzales amount to an intelligent conspiracy against the Chicano movement: "If anybody set out to destroy the Chicano movement, he couldn't do better than murdering Zanzibar and hanging it on Corky. Corky makes things happen and Zanzibar makes what's happened important" (246). Here Brown portrays himself as the only one who is truly able to understand the political implications of what has happened and to place Gonzales's arrest rightfully within the larger schema against Chicana/o people. He simultaneously affirms the importance of Zanzibar as a reporter and of himself as a strategist and activist.

Brown claims that the motive for the murder of Zanzibar was evidence of police misconduct and brutality that the reporter had. Later, while cross-examining a police chief, Brown suggests: "And that's exactly why they first ordered the death of Zanzibar . . . He talked too much . . . the motive for the death of Zanzibar was that he'd expose the true facts of the day . . . He could show who started the riot and document the specific acts of brutality" (246). These claims are not without merit within the context of Salazar's own life, as the recollections made by Salazar's friends and co-workers quoted earlier demonstrate. Moreover, this was likely an enduring interest on the part of Acosta because he himself was the subject of FBI surveillance. Undated notes as part of his collected papers include a paper by Acosta asking "How powerful is the media? Why was R. S. killed?"[12] In the context of the novel, Brown attempts to answer the questions that continued to plague Acosta.

In this section, Brown laments the death of Zanzibar but also manipulates the events to serve his own political purposes. "Now that Zanzibar is dead," he thinks, "there is nobody to tell our story to the world" (207). In fact, however, as Brown repeatedly reminds readers and other characters, he is a writer, and thus Zanzibar's death may open up the space that he has been seeking to become the voice and chronicler of the movement. Thus, unsurprisingly, the lament about nobody being left to tell "their story" is followed several lines later by Brown's resolve to finish the trial, "destroy the courthouse," and "write my book" (208). In spite of his role as a lawyer, Brown never loses sight of his goal of becoming a writer, and his involvement in the movement promises to provide necessary material for his writing career.

Despite Zanzibar's murder not being the focus of the trial, Brown continues to make it relevant. He explains his strategy: "I have no desire to make a martyr out of Zanzibar. I know he has been murdered . . . But now there is no Zanzibar to tell our story, no way for us to use the media to get us back our land. I shouted it to the rooftops: we *need* writers, just like we need lawyers. Why not me? I *want* to write" (230). Distancing himself from the earlier assertion that after Zanzibar's death, the movement had its first martyr, Brown now suggests that he has a more complex and meaningful solution for moving forward from the impasse posed by this tragedy. He proposes the importance of media workers, affirming Zanzibar's particular relation-

---

12. Undated Paper, Box 7, Folder 29. Oscar Zeta Acosta Papers, 1936–1990. Chicano and Latino Collections, Special Research Collections, University of California, Santa Barbara Libraries, Santa Barbara, CA.

ship with the Chicana/o counterpublic—invoked through the multiple use of plural pronouns *us, our,* and *we*—but then proposes that he has a solution that involves both writing and him.

Throughout the trial, the presiding judge continually tries to rein in Brown's reach into Zanzibar's murder, at one point threatening: "Mr. Brown, I am not going to allow another public airing of the causes of the riots or the causes of the death of Zanzibar" (247). Brown is persistent, however, invoking Zanzibar's murder and asking witnesses about it at every chance. These last chapters also illustrate how both Brown and Acosta attempted to put the racism of the Anglo-controlled court system on trial by subpoenaing every judge in the LA circuit and inquiring about their race, religion, and feelings toward Chicana/os. A year after the events of August 1970, the defendants are found innocent, although Gonzales is found guilty of the misdemeanor charge of possessing a weapon (253). In the final chapter, a bomb is set off in the courthouse, killing a young man, and Brown leaves Los Angeles for San Francisco.

While the murder of Salazar is and was relevant in the context of Chicana/o movement politics and culture, within the space of the novel, Brown is forced to make this argument/connection against the protestations of other characters. That is, Brown insists on making Zanzibar's death an important aspect of the case when, as he is told by the judge, Zanzibar's death is irrelevant. In a sense, Brown is trying to put the murderers of Roland Zanzibar on trial when what he's supposed to be doing is defending his own clients. In so doing, Brown/Acosta makes Zanzibar/Salazar central to questions of Chicana/o politics. If we are to believe the accusations made by Brown, the murder of Zanzibar is the key to understanding events during the Chicano Moratorium, and prosecuting Zanzibar's murderers is the means through which to both defend Chicana/os accused of misconduct and to mount or continue a Chicana/o civil rights crusade against the LAPD. Thus, Zanzibar is not merely a casualty of a war between Chicana/os and the LAPD; he is a direct target in that war. In his death, and according to Brown, Zanzibar has shifted from a reporter who reports—however sympathetically—on Chicana/o causes to a Chicana/o political leader whose power is such that he must be killed by the LAPD.

This particular rendering of Zanzibar is worth considering in light of earlier sections regarding his relationship with Brown and with

Brown's persona in general. Recall that at the start of the novel Brown is solely focused on his own ambitions—his stated objective is to write a book, and he claims that "me in particular" will save the world. Brown is also an unrepentant misogynist and homophobe. When Brown, via his court arguments regarding the defendants and Zanzibar, is portrayed as the only person who is fully and accurately able to understand and expose the political machinations that lay beneath Zanzibar's murder, his character suggests that his mode of politics is the most effective. Only a man as brutally and crudely honest as Brown, who unabashedly spouts racial and sexual epithets, has the political clarity and bravery to understand and expose the forces working against Chicana/os in LA. While Zanzibar had hoped to reach a Chicana/o public, Brown portrays himself as commensurate with this public, thereby equating the Chicana/o public with masculinism and hyperindividuality. Brown appropriates Zanzibar's death to become the one legitimate, militant voice of Chicana/o politics.

## LUCHA CORPI

Just as aspects of Salazar's murder continue to provoke disagreement and questions, portrayals of Salazar in Chicana/o literature are not monolithic. In Acosta's novel, Salazar's death is used as a means to legitimate the continuation of the masculinist political praxis of the narrator. A novel published several decades later, Lucha Corpi's *Eulogy for a Brown Angel* (1992), presents a very different portrait. In this text, which focuses on a Chicana feminist detective, Gloria Damasco, Salazar is contrasted with a misogynist Chicano activist, and his death provokes mourning for the loss of political possibilities. Unlike in *Revolt*, Salazar is never alive in *Eulogy*; the book opens on the day of Salazar's murder, and his death is conveyed via one character to another. His death is mentioned as an example of Anglo state violence against Chicana/os, but as time passes (and the murder mystery unfolds), the legacy of Salazar and his life takes on new meaning, particularly for Damasco. As in Acosta's text, the continued invocation of Salazar and his death illustrates the enduring importance of the reporter. However, the incorporation of his murder into a specifically Chicana feminist novel urges us to understand the gendered dimensions of his life and work in relation to the Chicana/o movement and the movement's own legacy. In *Eulogy for a Brown Angel,* Salazar's figure exposes the salience of gender within the Chicana/o counterpublic and contributes to the text's larger calls for a full accounting of gendered inequities and hopes for a more egalitarian future.

Corpi's book is a murder mystery and the first of four novels featuring the Chicana private investigator Gloria Damasco. The text opens on the day of the Chicano Moratorium in East Los Angeles, where Gloria and her friend have left the crowd to seek shelter from the police and tear gas. While walking on Whittier Boulevard, the two women stumble across a horrible sight—a dead four-year-old boy. The text inserts a fictional murder, that of young Michael David Cisneros, into the historical events that took place the same day that Salazar and three others were killed. Damasco works somewhat reluctantly with an Anglo cop, Michael Kenyon, to solve Cisneros's murder. The two are aided by a young gang member, Mando, who was present when Cisneros was murdered and has clues regarding the culprit(s). Their investigation is somewhat hindered by Joel Galeano, a Chicano journalist who refuses to do anything with the police. Damasco's attempts to solve Cisneros's death are at first unsuccessful, and, pressured by her husband, she puts the case away. However, eighteen years later, and following the death of her husband, she returns to the investigation into the death that has haunted her for decades. This time she joins forces with Justin Escobar, who continues on as her partner in subsequent novels. To solve the mystery, the two must revisit—geographically, politically, and mentally—the date and time of the murder, the Chicano Moratorium of 1970. The text thus comments on the enduring significance of the events of that day, including Salazar's murder, which is mentioned frequently throughout the narrative. Before the novel concludes, Damasco and Escobar solve the mystery of Cisneros's death, although his murderer is killed in a shootout that also takes the life of Damasco's best friend.

Existing criticism on *Eulogy* and other works by Corpi have placed her (rightfully) within the context of female-led and "ethnic/minority" detective fiction. When *Eulogy* was published in the early 1990s, Corpi joined other Chicano detective novelists, including Rolando Hinojosa, Gregory Nava, Michael Nava, and Manuel Ramos; however, she was the first Chicana writer to portray a Chicana detective.[13] Critics of Corpi's work emphasize how she writes against both the Anglocentrism of the detective novel and the male- and individual-centrism of male writers of color. The commonly held assumption that detective fiction is white, however, is not uncontested. M. Michelle Robinson argues that "the genesis of detection, its very design and development, is interracial," and that early detective fiction from the eighteenth and early nineteenth centuries illustrates a "continued investment in interrogating the limits of and possibilities for interracial sociability and economic interdependence" (203). Robinson's perspective throws into question the significance of a growing corpus of ethnic detective fiction, as she writes that attributing such work "to a liberal project and pursuit of the public sphere ignores that detective fictions' devices are literary products of an interracial modernity grounded in the nineteenth century" (204). From this perspective, Corpi is continuing, not subverting, an interracial tradition within detective fiction. However, Corpi does undoubtedly buck male-centrism and other aspects of the genre. Specifically, she shifts culpability from an individual toward society in general, which is complicit in the maintenance of a social structure that discriminates against women and people of color.[14] Similarly, Donna Bickford points out that in Corpi's works, it is not individuals who are guilty so much as structures—including racism, misogyny, and police violence. While Corpi undoubtedly focuses on structural inequalities, this chapter will shed light on the issue of media representation, which is broached through the death of Rubén Salazar. In addition, gender is at the forefront of Corpi's and Damasco's interventions, and the importance of gender underlies all aspects of the novel, including the crime itself and how it is reported. Damasco is "overtly a feminist" who brings "a new Chicana feminist aesthetic and cultural perspective to the genre of detective fiction" (Méndez-García 74; Maloof). Her feminism is intersectionally bound with her ethnicity; Damasco struggles with monolithic ideas of Chicana/o cultural identity associated with the Chicana/o movement but also credits her "gift"—a sense of vision

---

13. The first Chicana detective was Elena Oliverez, a character created by Anglo writer Marcia Muller, who first appeared in Muller's 1983 *The Tree of Death*, as well as several subsequent novels.

14. Steblyk, qtd. in Rosell.

and intuition that helps her solve crimes—to her Mexican heritage (Rodríguez, *Brown Gumshoes* 55). *Eulogy*, with its explicit grounding in Chicana feminism and racial, gender, sexual, and economic justice, sets the stage for future Damasco mysteries in which commitments to Chicana/o peoples and gender equity are similarly displayed.

## *EULOGY* AND CONTRASTING MODES OF GENDERED ENGAGEMENT

In *Eulogy*, discussion of Salazar engenders two developments. First, the journalist serves as a focal point around which characters voice shared knowledge and experience. His murder and the lack of accountability that followed establish a point of commonality for characters who find in Salazar's death a reflection of their own experiences with and attitudes toward the police and Anglo institutions. Second, his death, both the immediate aftermath and its longer-term implications, becomes an opportunity to explore gendered differences as well as the legacy of the events of that day for Chicana/o peoples. This exploration occurs through contrasting Salazar with another Chicano reporter, Joel Galeano, and through the thoughts and comments of the Chicana feminist protagonist, Gloria Damasco.

Salazar's death is mentioned at the outset of the novel and occurs the same day as the murder that animates the rest of the plot. By writing the fictional murder of Michael David Cisneros into the historical events of the Chicano Moratorium, Corpi foregrounds the significance of that date for her characters and for Chicana/os more generally. Readers are first told of Salazar when Damasco goes to the Galeanos' house to phone the police to report the body that she has just found. There she finds Reyna Galeano and her husband, Joel, a Chicano who at first thinks Damasco is making a phone call about Salazar and asks her "is it about Rubén Salazar?" Damasco tells him it is not, but Galeano is still uncomfortable with her calling the police. He tells her: "I really don't think you should be calling the pigs. We're almost sure one of them shot Rubén," and then: "Rubén Salazar is hurt. He may even be dead. We don't know for sure" (20). The text offers no explanations about Salazar, his death, or this larger context of racial marginalization of

Chicana/os in Los Angeles; readers unfamiliar with the historical figure might think he is another fictional character. This lack of initial context allows the novel to signal that it is a novel *for* Chicana/os and one in which non-Chicana/o, and in particular Anglo readers, will have to either pursue additional knowledge or remain ignorant of some of the historical and cultural details behind the narrative. At the same time, the fact that Corpi's characters do not require much explanation of who Salazar is establishes him as a public figure. Similarly to Acosta's novel, this portrayal suggests a process of legitimation that goes both ways—the relevance of Salazar to Corpi's characters affirms him as a member of a politicized Chicana/o community, while their knowledge of him portrays them as individuals who pay attention and have a stake in the Chicana/o politics of LA.

The pronoun *we* is used frequently to refer to the larger community of which the characters, and Salazar, are a part. Recall Galeano's information: "Rubén Salazar is hurt. He may even be dead. We don't know for sure." His use of the pronoun *we* is unclear but could refer to journalists, Chicano journalists, or Chicanos—all groups to which he belongs. However, Galeano and Damasco are soon shown to share similar attitudes toward the police, suggesting that the "we" of his sentence includes her and other Chicana/os. Although Damasco interacts with the LAPD, the novel makes clear her own mistrust of police, aligning Damasco with Galeano's perspective and characterizing both of them as members of a Chicana/o population that has firsthand experience with racial profiling and judicial marginalization. When she first calls the cops to report the boy's death, for example, she pauses when the dispatcher asks for her full name, explaining: "a Spanish surname always meant a delay of at least an hour in emergencies" (21). This commentary is representative of attitudes toward the police in all of Corpi's mystery novels, in which, significantly, the police never end up solving the crime. As Donna Bickford points out, resolution comes only through the community-embedded work of Damasco and her partner Escobar (94). The documenting of police racism against Chicana/os and the suspicion of Chicana/o characters toward the police is also part of the larger context surrounding Salazar's murder. What Corpi's character can't possibly know—but the author surely did—is that in fact the police let Salazar lie prone on the floor of the Silver Dollar Café for hours before checking on the body. The tear-gas canister was shot into the bar at 2:00 p.m. but no one entered it—and police kept passersby from entering—until 6:00 p.m. Thus, individual characters in Corpi's novel reference collective experiences of marginalization that include circumstances surrounding Salazar's death. The parallel deaths in the novel, Cisneros's and Salazar's, show the overlap between historical and fictional events and drive home the point that while the boy's murder was invented, the deaths of Chicana/os during the Moratorium and at the hands of state forces were not.

Salazar's death continues to function as a way to gesture toward a larger Chicana/o experience and to provide the impetus for conversation and deliberation relevant to the Chicana/o counterpublic. Mentions of his murder are pervasive in the text. When LA police officer Matthew Kenyon arrives, he and Damasco each repeat the names of the other victims of that day: Rubén Salazar, Angel Gilberto Díaz, and Lyn Ward. Kenyon reads their names from his notebook, and later Damasco names them to herself, noting that unlike her, they will not be returning home that evening (27). This repetition—and the memorization of the names of the victims on the part of Damasco—suggests that these deaths have become a part of Chicana/o collective memory. The text makes clear that the deaths have reverberated beyond the Los Angeles area; when Damasco calls her husband in the San Francisco Bay Area, she is relieved not to have to tell him about the day's events because he's already heard about them on the news (30). Knowledge about the deaths is something that Chicana/o characters share, but Salazar's murder in particular provokes group discussion. At the start of chapter 5, Damasco tells us that she left the Galeanos' house, where "the conversation centered around the death of Rubén Salazar" and characters speculated on how justice can possibly be achieved within an Anglo-controlled court system (41). Damasco comments: "After all, Salazar wasn't just any Chicano; he was a reporter and a TV news personality. The *Los Angeles Times* would definitely put pressure on the Internal Affairs Division of the L.A.P.D. to conduct a thorough and fair investigation" (41). The conversation among a group of characters speaks to the reverberations that Salazar's death had within a larger sphere; although some, like Joel Galeano, knew him personally, most of the other characters did not. Rather, they knew Salazar as a public Chicana/o figure and as someone who was able to contribute to and mediate within that Chicana/o public.[15] His death, then, has implications for the physical and political safety of the Chicana/o public, indicating the vulnerability of Chicano peoples. If even a "TV news personality" can be killed in broad daylight, what hope might there be for other racial minorities? Once again, the characters (either wittingly or not) reference aspects of the case; the *Times* did indeed pressure the LAPD for an inquest into Salazar's death, but as editor Bill Thomas recalls, the inquest didn't come up with anything that was not already known, only determining that "he [Salazar] was killed by another person" (*Rubén Salazar: Man in the Middle*). Within the novel, Salazar's life and notably his death provoke group deliberation on their role in relation to state institutions. They reflect on his significance to Chicana/o people as well as his relative insignificance to Anglo forms of power and justice. In this way the text affirms the significance of Chicana/o journalists and specifically the role they play in the formation of a counterpublic.

In addition to serving as a figure through/around which other characters negotiate their relationship to Chicana/o politics, Salazar is also used as a referent in key events in the story. In chapter 13, characters discuss the whereabouts of Mando in relation to the whereabouts of Salazar. In fact, they place Mando at the scene of Salazar's murder, with the former "watching the riot from a liquor store across from the Silver Dollar Café" (94). Joel Galeano was also there, having walked out of the Café before the sheriff's deputy arrived. The characters cite differing stories, Mando claiming he heard gunshots, and a neighbor of Luisa's, Tobias, saying there were no shots fired while Salazar was inside (96). Here Salazar functions in a fashion somewhat similar to how he functions in Acosta's text, but rather than the two characters affirming each other's status as important Chicano leaders (as Brown and Zanzibar did), Salazar and Mando affirm each other's relevance in terms of historical events and their importance to the characters. Sala-

---

15. At this point, Oscar Zeta Acosta is also briefly mentioned, described as "a Chicano writer and attorney . . . defending those arrested at the Moratorium"; he appears at the Galeano house looking for another reporter (41). Luisa suggests that as a lawyer, Acosta may be able to help with their investigation into Cisneros's death, but Damasco never calls on him.

zar's death is important because it occurred adjacent to the kidnapping at the heart of Damasco's mystery, and the kidnapping is elevated in importance because it happened on such a politically significant day. In this case, the mention of Salazar serves to suggest that the kidnapping of Cisneros is as significant to Chicana/o peoples as the murder of the journalist.

In addition to serving as a significant public figure whose death echoes the racist treatment of Chicana/os by Anglos in power and provokes conversations around group identity and experiences, Salazar is contrasted with a fictional journalist in the novel. By juxtaposing Salazar with Joel Galeano, the text comments on gender politics within the Chicana/o community as well as on how these politics have impacted / will impact the legacy of the 1960s and 1970s. While Galeano might at first appear to have much in common with Salazar because of his status as a Chicano reporter, the text distinguishes between the two characters, with the latter serving as an absent foil to the former. Akin to the fictional Brown, Galeano is a militant, masculinist activist who espouses hard-line political stances while treating those around him with disrespect.

From this perspective, Galeano's "we" is narrower than we might at first understand. His understanding of a Chicana/o community is one that is masculinist and heteropatriarchal, led by domineering Chicano men such as himself. Damasco critiques the masculinist posturing of Galeano and other male characters in the book. After she calls the police, Damasco and Galeano return to where she found Cisneros's body; there they are approached by a young gang member, Mando, who witnessed a man (presumably the murderer) leave the boy's body. Although he is being helpful, Galeano is mistrustful of Mando, and the two men soon engage in threats against one another. Galeano accuses Mando of the murder, Mando spits on the ground between them, and Galeano invites him to fight by saying "cuando quieras" (any time) (25). Following this exchange, Kenyon arrives, and when the wheels on his police car screech to a stop, Damasco wonders: "why is it that cops and tough men, young and old, have to brake or start up a car with a screech. . . . do they think they are establishing turf . . . ?" (25). Here, the narrator lumps all three men—the reporter Galeano, the young gang member Mando, and the Anglo cop Kenyon—together and pinpoints their commonality: their exaggerated, performative masculinity. She quickly establishes gender as a definitive component of social and political engagement and makes clear that questions of race and class are not the only issues that divide characters. Taking place in 1970, but written several decades later, *Eulogy* offers a critique of both Chicana/o and Anglo heteronationalism prevalent during the *movimiento* (and today).

While the above scene implicates all three men in masculinist performance, the text soon makes clear that Galeano's masculinity is the most violent. Soon after, Mando is murdered, and Kenyon suspects the reporter, telling Damasco that Galeano harbors a deep-seated hatred for gang members as well as the capacity to kill, based on his status as a former Marine. Speaking of Galeano, including his work as a journalist and approach to politics, the cop invokes Chicana/o politics and Salazar. He tells Damasco that Galeano is "almost [obsessed with] that *la causa* of yours" and adds, "he thinks that . . . people like Rubén Salazar are the ones who will redeem your community" (75–76). Kenyon offers an explanation of Galeano's investment in Salazar's life and career but considers only the ethnic dimensions of this relationship, overlooking Galeano's stance as a male chauvinist. Damasco takes issue with this last point, asking "what's there to redeem?" and challenging the idea that Chicana/os are "deficient" in some way (76). Here Damasco doesn't dispute the importance of reporters—Galeano or Salazar—but she does suggest that Galeano's approach, that Chicana/os are in need of redemption, is a faulty premise that leads to unhealthy actions. This conversation happens in the context of Kenyon explaining why he thinks Galeano murdered Mando. From this perspective, Galeano's rigid militancy does little to help some of the most vulnerable Chicana/os such as Mando, who, despite his gang affiliation, is a young man and is never shown to commit any crimes in the course of the novel. For Galeano, Salazar becomes a figurehead around which he can illustrate his own mode of political engagement. Damasco is careful to never endorse this approach or attribute it to Salazar himself; in fact, her questioning of Kenyon's narrative suggests that there is more than one perspective on Chicana/o "problems" and their attendant "solutions." Furthermore, her earlier disparagement of masculine posturing displays her acute understanding of the impact of gender, specifically masculinity, on social and political interactions and her skepticism regarding the efficacy of Galeano's tactics.

Salazar continues to be mentioned throughout the text and often in scenes involving Galeano, again allowing the violent, misogynist Galeano to be contrasted with the murdered reporter. When Damasco agrees to try to record Galeano confessing to Mando's death, she wears a wire and mentions Salazar's death as part of the tragic three days they have all lived through (81). Thinking that Galeano will be interested in new information about Salazar, she repeats what she'd learned from Kenyon, that the LAPD would institute an inquest into the killing (82). But this conversation only provides the opportunity for Galeano to lament his failed career, the fact that he wanted to "write for a newspaper [and] make a living as a photographer" but was never able to make enough money to satisfy his wife and his mother-in-law (82). Galeano expresses his frustrations in a sexist manner, referring to his wife more than once as a *cabrona* and then to her and Damasco as both *traidoras*; "You, too, Gloria. *Traidoras. Todas.* You women are all traitors" (85). Accusations of "traitor" were leveraged against Chicana women during this time for a myriad of perceived infractions against the movement, including lesbianism, feminism, and not being sufficiently supportive of men or male-led initiatives. Scripting Galeano as a sexist reporter allows the novel to simultaneously affirm the importance of Chicana/o media workers to Chicana/o communities and movements and point out the damaging effects of sexism and its function as a divisive element. Although Galeano is a criminal, in a manner typical of Corpi's detective mysteries, he is not brought to justice by the criminal justice system but rather side-steps responsibility for his actions by committing suicide.

Emblematic of her intersectional feminism, Damasco does not propose a narrow perspective on Chicana/o peoples or Chicana/o politics. Her character actively explores how to remain politically and morally aligned with the causes she feels strongly about and is up front with herself when potentially faced with the necessity of taking a contradictory stance. She thinks carefully, for example, about cooperating with police to implicate Galeano in Mando's murder, wondering if her actions would be for the greater good. She explains to readers that she and her best friend Luisa "treaded on a quagmire of the conscience" (65). She realizes the complexity of the situation she is in and doesn't purport to offer simple solutions. Rather, utilizing Chela Sandoval's concept of differential consciousness that functions like a "clutch," to shift gears when necessary, she considers the specifics of whatever political decision faces her (75). The multiple perspectives she holds are reflected in her own version of Chicana/o community. She describes the Chicana/o Moratorium: "Young and old, militant and conservative, Chicano and Mexican-American, grandchild and grandparent, Spanish-speaking and English-speaking, *vato loco* and college teacher, man and woman, all 20,000 of us had marched down Whittier Boulevard in the heart of the barrio. . . . to protest U.S. intervention in Southeast Asia and the induction of hundreds of young Chicanos into the armed forces" (17). Her Chicana/o community is diverse and inclusive and implicitly incommensurate with Galeano's ideology. Galeano may be representative of certain strands of Chicano movement activists, but Damasco rebukes any temptation to assume he stood in for all activists, then or now.

This struggle over what kind of activist is representative of the larger movement has much to do with the portrait of Salazar in the text. As Ralph Rodríguez points out, the novel is largely concerned with the memory of the movement—a concern highlighted by the fact that the narrative takes place in two distinct years, 1970 and 1988. In the latter part of the novel, Damasco is involved in both revisiting the events of 1970 in order to get to the bottom of Cisneros's murder and reconciling her own memories of the period and her understanding of its impact on her current life and the US state of affairs more largely. By the end of the text, Galeano is dead and seldom mentioned. Salazar, however, continues to be mentioned, and his name is invoked as a significant part of Chicana/o history, an index of the losses that Chicana/o people have endured, and a marker of what the movement and its activists might have gone on to achieve. As such, Salazar becomes a figure around whom other characters engage in negotiation about the state and trajectory of Chicana/o activism.

Two murders—one historical, one fictional—open the novel, but whereas one is solved, the other remains unsolved. Both murders gesture toward the loss of innocence. While Chicana/o protestors may have intuited that they were taking on state power through their mobilization, the murder of Salazar drove home just how high the stakes were. His death, as both Corpi's and Acosta's books suggest, was a transformative moment for many activists. But while in *Revolt* Salazar's murder is used to justify the continuation of militant politics, in Corpi's text his death represents the end of a particular kind of politics, provoking political soul-searching and mourning. The final time he is mentioned, Salazar stands in for a lost hope not only for Damasco but for a larger people and movement. Aside from a plaque near Laguna Park bearing his name, Damasco writes, "there is little to remind people of the events that at the time we thought would shape our political future in California" (131). According to Ralph Rodríguez, Damasco's comment underscores that "Salazar, once a central voice in Chicana/o struggles, no longer marks a specific moment in history or even in the everyday geography of Laguna Park. His efforts, like his presence, exist in some unspecified space" (61). Rodríguez also concludes that in this and other ways the text reminds us of the constructedness and creativity of memory, such that Damasco's own memories "challenge traditional understandings of US history and shape-shift into her own construction of Chicana/o identity and community" (61). While Damasco's memories illuminate the lack of telos, Salazar's status as a public figure bears further scrutiny. Damasco is commenting on the lack of a marker not just within a US social space but within a specifically Chicana/o space. Moreover, her reference to "people" is an evocation of a Chicana/o public. By "people" she does not mean all of humanity or all citizens of the US: she's calling on a smaller group; at the same time, her allusion is not to a nameable group of people, for example Chicano elected officials. This at once personal and impersonal reference is a reference to, in Michael Warner's words, "a self-organized relation among strangers," in other words, a Chicano counterpublic ("Politics" 1). Recall the "we" referenced by Galeano when speaking of Salazar's murder at the start of the novel. While Galeano wanted to claim Salazar as part of his understanding of what he thought Chicana/o activists could or should be, Damasco's return to the time and place of Salazar's death reminds us that this vision of a Chicana/o counterpublic is itself contested and a site of negotiation. Moreover, via its scripting within a specifically Chicana feminist text in which Damasco must contend with racist white police and misogynist Chicano men, the role of both race and gender in this negotiation is made explicit. Interestingly, in terms of the rest of Damasco's statement—that there is little to remind the Chicana/o public of that period—she is wrong. For one, the plaque that adorns Laguna Park serves as such a reminder. And of course this text as well as the many other texts that document the Chicana/o movement function as important reminders. Nevertheless, Damasco's comment exhibits the continued resonance of Salazar's death and the relationship between Salazar and a Chicana/o public.

Where *Eulogy* aligns with *Revolt* is in its scripting of Salazar into an explicitly Chicana/o political context. Where the two novels depart is in their specific portraits of these Chicana/o politics. Whereas *Revolt*'s world is one in which the Chicana/o movement is led only by men who use sexual power and masculinist politics to advance their personal and political goals, *Eulogy* speaks of a community of specifically Chicana feminist activists committed to sexual and racial liberation. Both texts lay claim to Salazar, suggesting that the characters want to claim his relevance to their specific modes of political organizing. In contrast to Brown's individual, masculinist Chicano political rhetoric and actions, Damasco puts forth a collective Chicana feminist vision. And rather than portray herself as the hero of her own story, Damasco underscores her place within a larger and heterogeneous community. Perhaps most importantly, in Corpi's text the process of contestation and negotiation continues; there is no character who has the final word on the state or trajectory of Chicana/o politics. Even Damasco herself can only speak of her own experiences, hopes, and expectations while making it clear that she does not know precisely what is to come or even how future activists will regard her and her contemporaries. This indeterminacy is hopeful and gestures to possibilities, with Damasco inviting readers to continue the journey with her, rather than stating a definitive ending. This invitation to collaboration, conversation, and speculation is indicative of Damasco's and Corpi's feminist praxis, which is not prescriptive or teleological but open-ended and continuous.

## GENDER, JOURNALISM, AND THE CHICANA/O COUNTERPUBLIC

Both Acosta's and Corpi's texts evidence a robust and long-standing investment with questions of access to media representation that in many ways predate more contemporary discussions about Latina/

os and media. Here we have evidence of not only what we may term *Chicana/o media* but also an understanding of the stakes of this media in relation to Chicana/o political power and community formation. They also illustrate how Chicana/o authors and activists link Chicana/o publics to journalists, specifically Salazar, and comment on the relationship between media and a subaltern counterpublic. Many aspects of these works' depiction of Salazar depend on some amount of prior knowledge of the reporter and the significance of his murder as well as aspects of *Chicanidad*—Spanish language and Chicana/o slang, suspicion of the police, and so forth—such that these texts may in fact gesture toward a counterpublic. Like US feminist subaltern counterpublics of the late twentieth century that brought into existence new terms to name and theorize the social reality of women (i.e., *sexual harassment, marital rape*), the Chicana/o counterpublic put forth its own lexicon of terms—*la raza, el movimiento, la causa,* and even *Chicana/o* (Fraser 67). As Michael Warner and others have pointed out, publics are dependent on, and created through, the circulation of texts. Warner clarifies that no single text itself creates a public; rather, "the concatenation of texts through time" does so (*Publics* 90). By the 1970s, and possibly earlier, a sufficient number of texts by and about Chicana/o peoples had contributed to the Chicana/o counterpublic. Terms such as those designated above circulated in Chicana/o media: independent presses, university journals, as well as, thanks to journalists such as Salazar, mainstream presses. The proliferation and adoption of these terms allowed Chicana/o and Latina/o peoples to name and theorize the reality of their lives and histories as well as to formulate a cohesive ethnic and political identity. As such, they illustrate how the Chicana/o counterpublic was also an arena "for the formation and enactment of social identities" (Fraser 68). The importance of journalists such as Salazar to the identity formation that took place within the Chicana/o public sphere is evident in the characters' feelings of intimacy toward him and with their despair over his death. Both novels recognize that Salazar, and Chicana/o journalism largely, was/is one of the extra-state mechanisms through which the Chicana/o counterpublic organizes and addresses itself through discourse (Warner, *Publics* 68). As evident in how characters speak of Salazar, he was a formative part of the Chicana/o movement and of their own identities as Chicana/os. That the texts are set during the movement (which was a significant, but not the only significant part of Salazar's life) further endorses the relationship between media, counterpublics, and social justice movements.

Overall, via their engagement with Salazar's life, death, and legacy, these novels attest to the importance of Salazar as a media worker and an important part of shaping and contributing to a Chicana/o public. At the same time, the differing portraits of Salazar and his relationship to other characters in the text remind us that ideas of a Chicana/o counterpublic are not monolithic, uncontested, or unchanging. Rather, they affirm the multiple investments in a Chicana/o counterpublic; the continued importance of gendered debates, concerns, and perspectives; and the importance of literary works as venues in which these deliberations may be showcased and digested. In *Revolt,* Zanzibar's murder is further evidence of Brown's own approach to politics, which sees no place for institutional actors—cops, judges, police—and places all faith in individuals and community-controlled organizations. From this perspective, his murder is further evidence of the relentless war against the cockroaches and necessity of resisting through extralegal and violent means. In *Eulogy,* Salazar's murder is likewise evidence of police repression and the inability of Chicana/os to receive justice through Anglo-controlled institutions. But he is also explicitly contrasted with a strand of Chicana/o masculinist nationalism via Joel Galeano that is violent, disparaging of women, and, ultimately, ineffectual at achieving justice. To be clear, Corpi's characters are no less committed to *la causa* then Acosta's, no less invested in justice and representation for Chicana/o peoples. Remember that despite being consulted, the police in Corpi's books never end up solving the crimes, and this institution is never held up as a source of justice. Corpi's characters are no less opposed to racist, patriarchal, Anglo-controlled institutions than Acosta's, but they also propose a different solution than an equally patriarchal, male-controlled Chicano leadership that Acosta's characters are so invested in.

And while Acosta's militancy would seem to present a hard line, within the span of his works, it is unsustained. At the end of *Autobiography* the narrator escapes to Mexico. *Revolt* concludes similarly, with Brown declaring that he is taking off for "the bright lights and white women of San Francisco" (258). Despite his brave language and actions, Brown voluntarily exits the geographic space of the movement. Damasco, while she mourns the loss of lives and potential, doesn't actually leave politically. Rather, as her life and subsequent books in Corpi's series testify, she remains part of a Chicana/o community, and future cases exhibit her seeking justice for others wronged during the movement and other periods. Corpi's characters present a different methodology for political engagement, one that is perhaps more quiet, more subdued, but also more invested in long-term, sustainable, community-based work. That Salazar is absent at the conclusion of both novels in some ways engenders these disparate visions. Absent a real-life referent, the other characters are able to script him in to the legacy they desire, a legacy that fulfills their own perspectives on political action and social change—masculinist militancy in the case of Acosta's texts, community-based egalitarianism in the case of Corpi's.

While the texts present different visions of Salazar, what neither can account for is change over time or how the reporter himself did, and would likely have continued to, evolve as a thinker, writer, and, possibly, Chicano activist. In both texts, Salazar is fixed in time, unable to fulfill the hopes and dreams of the protagonists and of the Chicana/o movement largely. As Ralph Rodríguez points out, Corpi's novel is highly invested in the plotting and shaping of historical memory; the two periods in which the text takes place—1970 and 1988—indicate that Damasco "wants to impose a linear historical construction on the development of Chicana/o history and identity" (61). That the plaque bearing Salazar's name is located "somewhere around Laguna Park" indicates that Salazar's "efforts, like his presence, exist in some unspecified space" (61). While the plaque rightfully gestures to the enduring importance of Salazar's life and legacy, Rodríguez correctly points out that the specificity of this legacy is yet to be determined.

Ultimately, neither Acosta's nor Corpi's novels can offer a definitive statement on what Salazar meant to the Chicana/o movement, largely because they cannot account for what he *might have come to mean*. That is, they cannot account for the ways in which Salazar's life and career would likely have continued to shift in the coming decades. We can see in his career as it existed, however, several large shifts, including his decision to join a Spanish-language station. Some of his publications from the last months of his life indicate similar changes. In a *Times* article published in April 1970, the journalist reports on a conference he attended regarding "the image of Spanish-speaking people in the media" (García 248). Notably, he speaks about the attendees of the conferences, writing, "the 15 of us—Chicano newsmen, educators, consultants" (248). In a mainstream, English-language newspaper, after scores of columns devoted to the growing "militancy" of Chicana/o peoples in California and elsewhere, Salazar emphatically assumes the identity of "Chicano." Two months later, in an article in June of that year, he describes a "vato loco" as "a zoot suiter with a social conscience" and contextualizes the growing frustration on the part of Chicana/os (260). He goes so far to write that the "mood" expressed by MAYO [Mexican American Youth Organization] leader José Ángel Gutiérrez, that violence is inevitable, "is not helped by our political and law-and-order leaders who are trying to discredit militants in the barrios as subversive or criminal" (260). This comment indicates a subtle editorializing that marks some of the last columns that Salazar published. These comments also indicate Salazar pushing the boundaries of the journalistic norm of objectivity, a particularly salient issue for journalists of color, who are often called on to fulfill "diversity" through their very presence yet are "expected to 'act' like journalists, not like minorities" (Nishikawa et al. 245). In some of his last columns, Salazar displays a determination to be a "Chicano journalist," with emphasis equally on each of those descriptors. Ultimately, however, we do not know how Salazar would have continued to cover the Chicana/o movement or his own place in the movement and the periods that were to come.

Rather than understand this lack of a definitive perspective on Salazar as a lack of the texts, however, we should view it as one of their most significant contributions. As Warner and others point out, a counterpublic "does not simply reflect identities formed elsewhere [but also] is one of the ways its members' identities are formed and transformed" ("Publics" 87). It is in regard to this last point, transformation, that questions of gender and sexuality play out most explicitly, so that we can see how these different texts participate in different imaginings, inaugurations, and mobilizations of a Chicana/o public, defined and expressed through masculinist vanguardism, on the one hand, and feminist intersectionality, on the other. Here both novels remind us that for these authors a Chicana/o public sphere was, and remains, integral to political discourse and organizing as well as one whose orientation and affiliations, particularly in regard to gender and sexuality, was and remains contested. What these novels capture is the dynamic interplay between media actors and social movements. The Chicana/o movement made as much of an impact on Salazar as he did on the movement, and the various perspectives on the reporter illustrate this multifaceted exchange. In this way, both *The Revolt of the Cockroach People* and *Eulogy for a Brown Angel* capture incredibly well the process involving the formation and negotiation of a Chicana/o counterpublic. The role that gendered differences—including in terms of how gender impacts political posturing and strategic engagement—play in this counterpublic validates the multiplicity and heterogeneity of counterpublics. Moreover, the negotiation that takes place among Salazar and other characters illustrates how ideas are not only formed *in* the public sphere, they are formed *out* of it: "preferences, interests, and identities are as much outcomes as antecedents of public deliberation" (Fraser 72). Finally, their greatest contribution to understandings of literature, media, and a Chicana/o counterpublic is to implicitly, but forcefully, argue for the role that literature plays in the shape and content of a Chicana/o counterpublic.

CHAPTER 2

# The End(s) of Representation

*Media and Activism in Cherríe Moraga's*
Heroes and Saints

NEAR THE END of act 1 of Cherríe Moraga's play *Heroes and Saints* (1994), Father Juan Cunningham and Cerezita Valle discuss the importance of visibility for Chicana/o social justice movements. Speaking of a recent rally in support of campesinos protesting pesticide poisoning, Cere approves of Juan's idea to join a fast. "People like to see priests and celebrities sacrificing," the young protagonist opines. "I'd do it, too, if anyone would notice me. The trick is to be noticed" (45). Juan agrees but underscores how mass media creates the necessary conditions for being noticed when he says "that's the very thing that brought me here . . . to the Valley" (45). Cere asks for clarification, and Juan explains: "I saw this newspaper photo of Cesar Chávez. He had just finished a thirty-three-day fast . . . So I came home" (45). Juan's return to the Valley because of activism he learned of via mass media echoes Acosta's return to LA after hearing about the Chicano movement. Both figures reference landmark moments in Chicana/o history, with Juan alluding to Chávez's 1968 fast, which ended with him taking communion next to Robert Kennedy in front of network news cameras. The event was both "a private and spiritual statement" by Chávez and "a public and telegenic way" of publicizing the UFW's work (Hondagneu-Sotelo 84). As Randy Ontiveros explains, this moment was important not only for the Chicana/o movement but also for the movement's relationship with television news broadcasts. Ontiveros calls the coverage that inspired Juan "the most prominent example of Chávez using the camera for the benefit of *la causa*" (905). While the priest is understandably impacted by this image of religious-based activism—he explains that Chávez "looked like a damn saint, a veritable" Gandhi—he is also impacted as a working-class Chicano (Moraga, *Heroes* 45). His reference to this highly circulated image affirms not only the power of media but the power of a media focused on Chicana/os and Chicana/o movements. Cere, however, points out that particular people are favored for media coverage: "People like to see priests and celebrities sacrificing. I'd do it, too, if anyone would notice me" (45). Here the young protagonist acknowledges that she does not occupy a position that would garner media attention while also suggesting that aspects of her identity—as a differently abled, female, working-class Chicana—make her less noticeable. This exchange between Juan and Cere grounds the characters and their activism in historical events while also establishing a relationship between the play's primary concerns and media coverage. As this chapter demonstrates, *Heroes and Saints* evidences a sustained engagement with mass media and questions of race, class, gender, and activism with regard to media production and representation. Looking in depth at the play's single named media representative, journalist Ana Pérez, allows us to appreciate how the play negotiates the links between media representation, visibility, and social change within the context of a youth- and female-led Chicana/o social movement and puts forth a vision of community-embedded journalism.

While issues of gender, visibility, and activism are central to the plot and its characters, little attention to date has been paid to one important mechanism by which characters and the town of McLaughlin gain visibility, the reporter Ana Pérez. This chapter examines Pérez and in particular her interactions with the townspeople to understand how the play uses her character to develop a nuanced and multifaceted perspective on media representation and visibility in relationship to Chicana/o social justice movements. Pérez's character highlights the paucity and limits of existing mainstream media coverage of Chicana/o communities and issues, in particular the cancer clusters and pesticide poisoning on which the play centers. Not only does Pérez grant specific attention to working-class Chicana/os; she highlights the voices and stories of Chicanas. At the same time, her status as a Latina reporter working on a Latina/o-oriented program challenges ideas about the positive correlation between media representation and power. When Pérez abandons her status as a reporter to join protests in the play's concluding scene, her character acknowledges that media access does not ensure political power, illustrating what Hector Amaya calls the "Latina/o public sphere paradox." This move raises questions about the limitations of the potential power of media representation for Latina/os and especially Chicanas. However, Pérez's transformation from journalist to activist offers a model of a new kind of relationship between communities, publics, and media and affirms the play's insistence on the importance of direct action and the voices and lives of Chicanas.

This chapter reads the play in relation to its sociohistorical origins, Chicana/o and Latina/o feminist literary scholarship, and Latina/o media studies. It begins by situating *Heroes and Saints* within the social, political, and geographic context of its genesis and, in particular, within its media context to pinpoint how Pérez's reports depart from mainstream media representations of McFarland, California, the town on which McLaughlin is based. This context demonstrates that, in contrast to broadcasts on the cancer cluster in McFarland that aired on major networks, Pérez's coverage highlights issues of race, gender, and activism. The play's Latina reporter, then, fills gaps in terms of representation and content that persist in mainstream news coverage to this day. The second section considers how Pérez develops the play's themes of voice, visibility, and action. While early scenes such as the conversation between Juan and Cere referenced above point to the power of media representation to inspire activism and bring change to the town, as the narrative progresses Pérez moves further and further away from her role as a journalist and explores a different relationship with the townspeople. This movement is manifested in the play through her changing forms of communication: she moves from an intercultural and interlingual translator to an intracommunal source of information and finally to a character who speaks not individually but only collectively with other activists. In her role as a translator, the character invokes the historical figure of La Malinche. In this way the play embeds Pérez, and Latina/o journalists in general, within a larger Latina/o and Chicana/o cultural context. Her evolution mirrors that of the play's principal character, Cere. That is, Cere spends considerable time exploring the importance of speech and linguistic representation but falls silent in several scenes before making one final speech in which she evokes and mobilizes the collective. When Pérez likewise stops reporting and joins the protestors, we can see the play's insistence on exploring the limits of linguistic and visual representation and the importance of direct, collective action. In the last lines of the play, Pérez joins the townspeople in following the leadership of a young Chicana, abandoning her role as a journalist and translator to become an activist. This last scene is illustrative of the Latina/o public sphere paradox, as Pérez acknowledges that an increase in the quantity of Latina/o-oriented media may not necessarily further Latina/o social justice concerns. But it also affirms the possibility of a different kind of journalism that is directly integrated in and accountable to the needs of a Latina/o public. The play thus calls on us to reconsider the limitations of a Latina/o media produced within a mainstream, Anglo-dominated market while also providing a portrait of what a mass media attuned to the significance of race, class, and gender might look like.

Existing criticism on *Heroes and Saints* has foregrounded questions of injustice, activism, and visibility. Yvonne Yarbro-Bejarano and Mary Pat Brady both contextualize the play within Chicana/o theater, discussing the work in relation to Luis Valdez's *The Shrunken Head of Pancho Villa*.[1] These critics focus on an extensive history of Chicana/o protest literature and Chicana/o farmworker activism and the possibilities that the play poses for both terrains. For Yarbro-Bejarano, the significance of "in-between" characters such as Mario and Father Juan allows the work to productively expand the idea of "Chicano." Brady's reading engages with the landscape of the play to argue that the work "denaturalizes California's economic dependence on conditions of exploitation and inequality" and "makes visible those who labor to produce the landscape, those who work the fields and gather the harvest" (169–70). While Brady explains how the play grants visibility to land and labor, other critics focus on how the work stages social protest. Linda Margarita Greenberg argues that the crucified bodies of chil-

---

1. Valdez's best-known play, *Zoot Suit*, includes significant rumination on the role of mass media in the accusations against and defense of the main characters. The play also emphasizes the diversity of media, including the character of "Press"—representing corporate-controlled mainstream media—and Alice Bloomfield, a reporter for the left-wing *Daily People's World*. However, because the media figures in the play are non-Latina/o, the play does not fit within the contours of this project.

dren lost to cancer that initially attract Pérez to McLaughlin indicate how the work explores "death and injury as potentially productive of social protest" (164). Irma Mayorga similarly stresses the ends of the staging of death in the play to argue that the work "[theatricalizes] violence in order to enunciate visibility" and that "visibility and violence work hand in hand to endow and enfranchise" (158, 163). The following analysis concurs with the importance of questions of violence, visibility, and justice while arguing that Pérez plays an important role in developing these themes. Through Pérez we can see and trace evolving ideas of speech and visibility and arrive at a more nuanced understanding of how the play views these modes of interaction to encourage direct action. Bringing Pérez to the foreground allows for a slightly different understanding of the play's engagement with questions of gender, labor, visibility, and justice; allows us to place the work within the larger context of Latina/o media; and offers another example of engagement with mass communication on the part of contemporary Chicana/o and Latina/o writers.

Focusing on the text's portrayal of the reporter yields important questions and insights that develop, continue, and challenge ideas about the relationship between media representation, visibility, political power, and social change. The play's inclusion of Pérez serves as a counterpoint to the very limited number of Latina/o reporters or newscasts that focus on US Latina/o individuals and communities in mainstream, English-language media. At the same time, when the play charts Pérez's evolution from journalist to activist, it fails to fully endorse the idea that more media representation by and/or about Latina/os will further Latina/o social justice concerns. The play thus challenges commonly held ideas about the relationship between representation, power, and social change. These ideas pertain not only to questions of media representation but also to linguistic representation. The play, then, asks us to understand and recognize the limits of linguistic representation and affirms the significance of direct action.

## McFARLAND AND MEDIA COVERAGE

The setting of *Heroes and Saints*—the fictional town of McLaughlin, California, in 1988—evokes in place and time the town of McFarland,

California. Like McLaughlin, McFarland made headlines in the late 1980s when it was designated a "cancer cluster" as a result of the disproportionate rates of disease suffered by residents. Pérez's description of "the sudden death of numerous children, as well as a high incidence of birth defects," directly references occurrences in McFarland (Moraga, *Heroes* 4). While her coverage of McLaughlin calls to mind the attention given to McFarland and issues of farm labor and pesticides in the late 1980s and early 1990s, Pérez's reporting diverges from historical broadcasts. A brief survey of mainstream broadcast news segments on pesticide poisoning in the San Joaquin Valley illustrates that such broadcasts were primarily composed of two threads.[2] The first thread focused on the tragedies and losses suffered by residents and their accusations or speculations that the illnesses were the result of environmental factors such as pesticides and pollutants in the water. The second thread consisted of discussions of "inconclusive" studies and/or interviews with "experts" who did not affirm residents' accusations. For example, an *ABC World News Tonight* segment broadcast on December 3, 1987, opened with correspondent Tom Schell explaining: "McFarland, the town of 6,000 is surrounded by fields that are regularly sprayed with fertilizers and pesticides. Residents believe those chemicals have seeped into the community's water supply" ("World News Tonight"). Similarly, when *48 Hours* ran a story on the town on April 18, 1990, correspondent Erin Moriarty spoke to a town resident, Donna Rose, who had lost her son and who stated: "It's in our water" ("'Growing Concern'"). These accusations by townspeople are "balanced" by discussions of inconclusive studies and experts who do not verify residents' beliefs. In the *ABC* segment Schell says, "A 1985 study by county health officials failed to come up with any cause of the cancers. And now the state of California is taking a new look, but preliminary reports say they haven't found a cause either" ("World News Tonight"). Likewise, Moriarty speaks to Dr. Stewart Segal, who says, "At

---

2. Of the three broadcasts I discuss, two—*CBS This Morning* and *ABC World News Tonight*—report directly on and from McFarland. The third—*48 Hours*—names the San Joaquin Valley, of which McFarland is a part, as its location. I discuss these broadcasts to offer a context for the newscasts featured in the play, not as a way to argue for their representativeness of the coverage of McFarland in general, the scope of which is outside this chapter. Furthermore, since readers do not have access to the visual staging of Pérez's broadcasts, I analyze the texts of these broadcasts only, as opposed to their use of camera angles, framing, and so forth.

this point in time, I think we have to say that without knowing what the cause—we don't know whether it's the environment, whether it's other factors outside the environment. We can't answer that question without really having more information that points to a specific cause" ("Growing Concern"). These broadcasts do spend significant amounts of time interviewing town residents and especially inhabitants such as Rose who have lost children. However, they set up the discussion of the cause of the children's deaths as a disagreement between two sides: town residents, who are primarily working-class farmers, and "experts," such as medical doctors and nameless people, organizations, or governmental agencies who conduct studies. These broadcasts illustrate a strain of "unreflective journalism" that represents "'both sides' of a case, even when the merits of the case do not warrant it" (Romano 231–32). While the broadcasts may seem to offer a balanced view of the topic in a way that is commonly accepted as "objective," they fail to account for unequal power relationships between the residents and agribusiness, journalists, and government agencies, or for the financial ties between corporations and news networks.[3]

In contrast, Pérez spends no time interviewing nonresident experts or citing studies that contradict residents' accusations that pesticides in the water are to blame for the cancer and deaths. Her opening report focuses on the deaths of children and on the subsequent activism. What has drawn her to the story and what makes the scene newsworthy, her broadcast suggests, are not only the deaths but also the town's response to the deaths. She reports: "One of the most alarming recent events which has brought sudden public attention to the McLaughlin situation has been a series of . . . crucifixions . . ." (Moraga, Heroes 4). Thus, if there are "two sides" to Pérez's story, they are the deaths and the town's response to the deaths, not differing explanations for the cancer. The religiously influenced protests and Pérez's coverage of them call to mind César Chávez's activism during the grape boycotts in the 1960s. Chávez and the United Farm Workers drew heavily on Catholic symbolism and rhetoric in their actions; the organization "innovated a

---

3. For more on the ways in which corporate control compromises media networks, see Croteau and Hoynes. Randy Ontiveros also points out that the relationship between news networks and the government is fraught: "television has historically been highly sensitive to executive power, largely because it is FCC appointees who grant licenses to private interests seeking access to public airwaves" (917).

way of seamlessly blending religious ritual, spirituality, and labor advocacy" (Hondagneu-Sotelo 82). Contemporary campaigns by social-justice-oriented religious organizations to support immigrant workers borrow from the UFW's actions as well as those from the sanctuary movement of the 1980s and the civil rights movement of the 1950s and 1960s (85).[4] Highly visible actions such as the 1966 march from Delano to Sacramento, CA (a 340-mile journey) resulted in landmark media coverage of Chicana/o issues. However, the religiously tinged activism along with the networks' propensity to offer coverage without much context or depth played into a "media dialectic" of Chicana/o activists as "suffering saints" or "dangerous revolutionaries" (Ontiveros 909). When Pérez is drawn to McLaughlin by the crucifixions, she evokes the attention given to the activism of the 1960s and 1970s. However, her broadcasts differ markedly from those cited by Ontiveros in the attention given to women and to a wider number of activists. In fact, while Pérez does interact with Father Juan, her interviews in front of the camera occur exclusively with female characters—Amparo, Dolores, and Yolanda. These interactions contrast with mainstream journalism that often gathers information from political and economic leaders to the extent that "women and a range of ethnic and other minorities . . . [are] overlooked and underutilized as the sources of information or topics for stories" (Romano 235). The attention given to women may reinforce the idea that the death of children is primarily a "woman's concern"; nevertheless, her interviews with a range of female residents correct the historical record that has downplayed or ignored Chicana activism while also moving beyond the familiar focus on a single, charismatic, and male civil rights leader.[5]

---

4. For example, CLUE (Clergy and Laity United for Economic Justice), a Los Angeles–based organization, holds an annual Holy Week–Passover Procession down Rodeo Drive in which participants pressure luxury hotels to sign union contracts with their workers and offer positive recognition of those that have already done so. Utilizing symbols from the Bible and the story of Passover, members of CLUE have left milk and honey at hotels that have signed contracts and bitter herbs at those that have not (Hondagneu-Sotelo 91).

5. Ontiveros explains that television coverage tends to "exacerbate what is always a danger in social movements, namely, the establishment of top-down leadership structures centered on a charismatic individual" (907). These single charismatic figures—best exemplified by César Chávez and Martin Luther King Jr.—are invariably male.

Pérez's reporting also departs from mainstream coverage of the cancer clusters in its foregrounding of race. Remarkably, neither the *48 Hours* nor the *World News Tonight* reports ever mention this very salient issue. The ethnic makeup of McLaughlin, however, is fundamental to Pérez's broadcast, as she announces that she is reporting for the program "Hispanic California." The title of the program solidifies the existence of a stable, sizable "Hispanic" population in the state and suggests that this population faces unique circumstances and experiences. Pérez's role as a journalist for the show would of course not be possible without the existence and interest of a "Hispanic" constituency, and thus the name of the show reflects how "the creation of a commercially viable Hispanic audience is what makes Latino-oriented journalism possible" (Rodríguez, *Making* 5). The name of the show, which uses the US-government-created term *Hispanic*, fulfills Arlene Dávila's assertion that, following intensifying global competition in the 1990s, advertising agencies emphasized "the abstract ideal of 'Hispanics' as an undifferentiated reality" (qtd. in Castañeda 60). The use of the title *Hispanic* speaks to the extent to which this audience is very much created and establishes a tension between Pérez as a character with ties to both Latina/o peoples and Anglo-dominated media interests. Still, the show is dedicated to recognizing questions of race, and Pérez enacts this dedication when she speaks with residents who bring up the issue. In her first segment, she interviews Amparo, who says that the cancer deaths have brought attention from white folks. "The gabachos, s'cuze me, los americanos always coming through McLaughlin nowdays. Pero, not too much change" (Moraga, *Heroes* 6). Suggesting that the presence of gabachos, or Anglos, is notable characterizes the town as majority Mexicana/o or Chicana/o. Amparo's reference to outsiders may also be an invocation of representatives of government agencies or directors of medical and public health studies, those experts interviewed in the broadcasts cited above. When Moraga's work only allows such individuals to appear in the dismissive comments of Amparo, the play privileges the words and perspectives of a Chicana activist. Pérez's reports thus draw attention to race and favor marginalized individuals and voices.

Featuring a Latina reporter who calls attention to racial differences and inequities, the play suggests that the identity of journalists is important. Pérez's discussion of race is more in line with a segment from *CBS This Morning* that ran on December 30, 1997. The segment is hosted by respected LA-based, Latino correspondent Manuel Gallegus. Like Pérez, Gallegus foregrounds race and interviews activists. He notes after speaking with activist Marta Salinas that McFarland is "94% Latino" ("McFarland"). Gallegus also includes a quote by Salinas who, in explaining why the cancer deaths remain unsolved, opines: "They didn't care about how many children died. Why? Because we are just poor brown people" ("McFarland"). Thus, of the three major national reports on the cancer deaths examined here, only the one with a Latino reporter mentions race, and only this one foregrounds Chicana/o activism. This report offers a more comprehensive view of the situation in McFarland that includes the relevance of race and an organized community response. Unlike the other two national broadcasts mentioned earlier, Gallegus's report does not center on "two sides." Rather, the report focuses on activists and a new EPA study that will include water samples and continue for two years. While the ethnicity of the reporter is significant, so is the period. This report was aired more than a decade after the cancer cluster gained national news and several years after *Heroes and Saints* was published. The report therefore may be a product of the kinds of cultural and social intervention that Moraga's play was attempting to make and a testament to the importance of having reporters who understand and appreciate the significance of race and community activism.

These reports suggest the lack of quality and in-depth coverage by and about Latina/os, an implication borne out in studies of national news coverage. For example, Otto Santa Ana has documented the gross underrepresentation of US Latina/os by network news programs, revealing a 1:100 ratio of news stories featuring Latina/os to the US Latina/o population. While Latina/os make up 14 percent of the US population, less than 1 percent of network evening news stories address Latina/o issues (Santa Ana 1). Pérez offers a corrective to this dearth of coverage while simultaneously failing to fully remedy the situation. Her reports are at times complicit with the state and engage in a commodification of "Chicana/o events as mainstream entertainment" (Greenberg 169). As such, the play does not facilely suggest that an increase in Latina/o media will lead to an increase in political and social power. Rather, Pérez's evolution from reporter to activist foregrounds the importance of direct action.

## VISIBILITY AND SOCIAL CHANGE

Throughout the first act, Pérez fulfills her role as a reporter by transmitting information about McLaughlin to her camera crew and, by extension, to her viewing audience. Her newscasts follow a three-part story structure consisting of an opening, body, and closing (Santa Ana 27). For example, in the first scene in which she appears, act 1, scene 2, she begins by introducing her story: "Today I am speaking to you from the town of McLaughlin in the San Joaquín Valley. McLaughlin is commonly believed to be a cancer cluster area, where a disproportionate number of children have been diagnosed with cancer in the last few years" (Moraga, *Heroes* 4). She then speaks with Amparo about the latest crucifixion and finally turns back to her camera: "That concludes our Hispanic hour for the week, but watch for next week's show where we will take a five-hour drive north to the heart of San Francisco's Latino Mission District, for an insider's observation of the Day of the Dead, the Mexican Halloween" (7). The three-part structure of the broadcast establishes Pérez's work as following a model commonly used by newscasters. Furthermore, the declaration that the station devotes only one hour per week to "Hispanic" issues echoes the results of Santa Ana's study in terms of the time spent on US Latina/os. The "Hispanic hour," in both title and temporal span, affirms that the segment offers attention to Latina/o people in a contained and packaged manner that is easily assimilable within a market invested in "multicultural" content as opposed to justice-oriented material.

The content of her broadcast reflects Pérez's status as a reporter for a mainstream program but nevertheless opens up the possibility for challenging a hegemonic framing of the events. Pérez translates the crucifixions into media terms when she calls them a "publicity stunt," indicating her inability to see them as "a valid means of resistance" (Greenberg 169). This language, along with Pérez's employment by a show titled "Hispanic California," situates her firmly within the mainstream and even as complicit with state powers that would criminalize Chicana/o protest (168). At the same time, the play's use of Pérez situates audience members as spectators, allowing the play to "[highlight] reading as a way of enacting citizenship" (168). Considered within the context of the play, the use of Pérez to broach the possibility for enacting a different kind of citizenship calls to mind Tiffany Ana López's concept of "critical witnessing." For López, playwrights enact critical witnessing in creating not just audience viewers but co-witnesses that may participate in enacting social justice (33). Pérez's initial framing of the protests references a hegemonic perspective on Chicana/o activism while broaching the possibility for a collaborative transformation involving media producers and viewers.

Highly visible from the start of the play, Pérez affirms the effectiveness of the children's protest and the potential for media coverage to bring some change to the town. The children's dramatic demonstrations exhibit a keen understanding of the power of spectacle as well as the importance of media coverage. The play's opening scene describes the crucifixion of the bodies of dead children, acts that "counter state interpretations of those bodies—as unintelligible, as public commodity, and as invisible" and that "make death visible and meaningful" (Greenberg 164, 165). Pérez's first lines confirm that the crucifixions have indeed achieved visibility for the town. She explains that the town is the site of "crucifixions, performed in what seems to be a kind of ritualized protest against the dying of McLaughlin children" (Moraga, *Heroes* 4). These lines affirm the efficacy of the actions; Pérez correctly interprets the crucifixions as protests against the use of pesticides and a request for public attention. Pérez's presence in and reporting from the town illustrates the efficacy of the protests and her own willingness to discuss the interventions of working-class Chicana/o children. From the start, then, she (and the play) presents the children as subjects in their own right, challenging coverage that would merely infantilize or sensationalize such activism and signaling that Pérez has already begun to negotiate a different kind of relationship between her subjects and her viewers. Calling attention to visibility in this way marks the play as one that is attuned to the importance of visibility so far as it furthers justice; the work's opening and closing scenes attest to how *Heroes and Saints* "seeks to make the violence against a community visible through strategic images that stage their violation" (Mayorga 161). Pérez's presence in McLaughlin confirms that the violence against town residents has been seen while also contributing to its visibility. These opening scenes, then, establish a relationship between the protestors and Pérez in which the former are able to communicate effectively to and through the latter.

Of course, Cere and the other protestors want more than visibility; they want visibility that leads to change, and media coverage of the crucifixions does lead to concrete, although minor, changes in the lives of townspeople. In act 1, scene 3, Father Juan and Amparo bring a five-gallon tank of spring water to the Valle home; Amparo explains that Arrowhead donated the water. Juan credits not simply the newscast but the person featured, Amparo: "Thanks to Doña Amparo. Last week's newscast stirred up everyone!" Amparo defers: "It wasn' me. It was la crucifixión. That's what brought the newspeepo here" (Moraga, *Heroes* 14). Here, we see the result of the relationship between the protestors and the media, with an added component—the public ("everyone"). Amparo is correct that the crucifixions brought the newscasters to the town, but the newscasters fulfilled their obligation to the public, who in turn pressured the corporation to offer a remedy, albeit a temporary and insufficient one. These two early scenes signal that the coverage of the children's actions by media can result in concrete change in the lives of town residents.

Pérez's coverage of the protests, the donation of bottled water, and Juan's decision to return to the valley reflect the role that media may play in granting visibility and inspiring action and change. However, the play does not stop there; at the same time that it argues for the relationship between media visibility and change, it shows how characters consider questions of voice and representation in effecting change. Cere and Pérez in particular move from speaking many lines in the play to near silence by the end. The following section reads closely Pérez's interactions with townspeople and charts her change throughout the play, comparing her own relationship to speech and voice with that of Cere's. This discussion shows how Pérez moves from an intercultural and interlinguistic translator to an intracommunal voice and finally to an activist with no distinguishable voice. This transformation occurs alongside that of Cere, who also speaks less and less as the play develops, until, after one final speech, she silently martyrs herself. The evolution allows the play to thoughtfully ruminate on the complex questions involved in questions of speech and representation. Considering these questions within Chicana feminist literary and scholarly work, and in particular in relation to representations of La Malinche, illustrates how the play stages an intervention in ideas about gender, speech, language, and translation and calls on us to consider the ends of linguistic representation.

## TRANSLATION

Looking more closely at how Pérez engages with the townspeople during her first broadcast, we see that she specifically functions as a translator. Her opening monologue, in which she explains to viewers the situation and activism that has brought her to McLaughlin, can be read as an act of spatial, cultural, and political translation, but she quickly engages in more explicit linguistic translations as well. In this first broadcast she attempts to speak to Dolores, who rebuffs her; she is offered an explanation by Amparo: "she [Dolores] says es como un circo." Pérez then turns to the camera: "a circus" (Moraga, *Heroes* 5). Pérez's translative act has a clear purpose—to make Amparo's words intelligible to the presumably monolingual viewing audience. However, for bilingual readers the line offers some humor: by simply repeating the word *circus*, Pérez contributes to the image of unruly noise that Dolores is describing. Moreover, Pérez's translation is not precise; she doesn't clarify that the city is now "like/as a circus" but rather only repeats the noun phrase, supporting Dolores's description. By functioning as a linguistic translator, Pérez serves a particular purpose within the play and for its readers while also calling forth a longer history of Latina/o journalism. Early Latina/o journalists such as those who had Spanish-language columns within privately owned newspapers in the period immediately following the Mexican–American War functioned largely as translators (Rodríguez, *Making Latino News* 15). Their work was often seen as accommodationist to Anglo cultural and political interests. Pérez's translations may be read as a reference to this larger history of Latina/o journalism and a mechanism by which she is contextualized as a Latina journalist.

The historical relationship between translation and accommodation has a much larger context within Latina/o and Chicana/o culture and history such that Pérez's translations also place her in relationship to La Malinche. Malinche, also known as Malintzín, Malinalli, and Doña Marina, translated during Hernán Cortés's conquest of Mexico. In her essay "A Long Line of Vendidas," Moraga explains the heteropatriarchal understanding of Malinche: "Malinche sold out her indio people by acting as courtesan and translator for Cortéz, whose offspring symbolically represent the birth of the bastardized mestizo/mexican people" (108). While Malinche has long been regarded as a symbol of betrayal, her life and psyche has also become a rich source of Chicana feminist explorations of cultural and linguistic hybridity and the legacies of colonization, sexism, and patriarchy. At the same time, Chicana feminist interpretations do not reduce Malinche to her reproductive role but rather "[subsume] her reproductive activity into her political and strategic identity" (Pratt 869–70). As an evocation of Malinche, Pérez's character calls to mind the complicated role that interlinguistic and interethnic translators have played in Mexican and Chicana/o history. Her translations, which do more than recreate but also help to create an activist community, contribute to a significant tradition of feminist reappraisals and appreciation for Malinche's legacy.[6]

Along with her contemporary Chicana feminist writers and scholars, Moraga is deeply invested in Malinche, and this figure appears in several of her works. In her play *The Hungry Woman: A Mexican Medea* (2001), the principal character Medea also overtly invokes Malinche. Patricia Ybarra explains that in "layering Malinche's story upon Medea's," *The Hungry Woman* "combines various losses and betrayals between women, men and women, and women and their children" (69). In both plays, Malinche is invoked within a queer context. In act 1, scene 8 of *Heroes and Saints,* Cere and Father Juan discuss at length—and not without sexual innuendo—the significance of tongues, the body part with which Malinche, as Cortés's translator, is highly associated. This conversation between Cere and Juan, two queer characters, alludes to the fact that Malinche is indicted for being sexually unfaithful to her race in a way that queer men and women are perceived as sexually unfaithful to heteronormative Chicanidad. Moraga's consistent linking of Malinche to queer characters exemplifies her own and her plays' "queer sexual politics" (Ybarra 69). The connection between Malinche and Pérez, through the latter's translations, places Pérez, and by extension Latina/o journalists, in a complicated but important position. Pérez as Malinche offers a new understand-

---

6. For more on Chicana feminist reappraisals of Malinche, see, among others, Del Castillo, Alarcón.

ing of Latina/o media representatives that situate them in relation to the vexed history of translators while also calling on us to reconsider the historical figure of Malinche. This reconsideration is founded on a renewed understanding of the importance of the public; just as we understand Pérez as a cultural worker tasked with creating and contributing to a Latina/o public, so too may we reconsider Malinche as neither a traitor nor a visionary but as a woman whose translations, like Pérez's, inaugurate a social body.

Pérez's Malinche-like status connects her to the larger field of Latina/o journalism while also portraying her as an "in-between" character. Yarbro-Bejarano discusses how several characters function as "in-between" due to questions of race, location, and sexuality. She explains that Father Juan's "'in-betweenness' echoes his own locations and desires (valley/city, white men/brown men)" (71). Cere's brother Mario is a similarly in-between character whose desires seem to be unrealizable within the space of the Chicano family and the rural hometown (71). Like Mario and Father Juan, Pérez's gender performance and geography mark her as in-between. She does not live in McLaughlin but frequents the town in order to report on the goings-on. She works for an English-language television station but has clear linguistic ties to Spanish-speaking peoples—evidenced by her bilingualism. Her gender performance is in-between, as she dons the markers of heteronormativity while simultaneously pushing against the pressures to remain a passive woman on the sidelines of political action and social change.

While these markers of in-betweenness connect her to Juan and Mario, they also reinforce her status as Latina journalist. America Rodríguez explains that Latina/o journalists of the "1.5 generation" are positioned "as translators and mediators between their audience and the dominant majority society . . . this 'inbetweenness' is activated daily in tension between objectivity and ethnicity" (5).[7] Rodríguez's perspective offers us a new way of reading Pérez's early lines, when she interviews Amparo but then remarks to her crew that they will "edit her out later" (Moraga, *Heroes* 7). Pérez's desire to silence Amparo may not be caused by her own inability to read the crucifixions as anything

---

7. Mario T. García offers yet another example of describing Latina/o journalists as "translators" when he uses this term for the pioneering journalist Rubén Salazar, situating Salazar as likewise in between community and corporate interests (30).

other than a publicity stunt but rather may reflect a struggle between her own competing desires to represent Latina/o people while meeting the calls for "objectivity" heralded by her profession (Greenberg 169). Rodríguez reminds us that "objectivity is the dominant ideology and practice of U.S. journalism" and that remaining true to ideas and standards of objectivity bestows legitimacy on ethnic minority journalists (86). Mari Castañeda similarly notes that "mainstream outlets have criticized Latino media producers for often working as advocates for the community and taking a subjective perspective on stories" (63). That Pérez is in fact struggling internally at this point is affirmed by stage directions explaining that she concludes her broadcast after Amparo has walked away "with false bravado" (Moraga, Heroes 7). This description suggests that Pérez has been impacted by Amparo's words, even if she finds them inappropriate for broadcast. The false bravado exhibited by Pérez indicates her gendered position as a Latina journalist; "objectivity" is a trait that is not only called for on the part of Anglo-dominated media but often heralded as a trait that comes "naturally" to men. Thus, Pérez's actions in this scene show how she shares traits of in-betweenness with Juan and Mario and reflect the pressures and challenges that she faces as a Latina journalist.

These early scenes illustrate that Pérez stands in relation to historical figures such as La Malinche as well as other in-between characters such as Mario and Father Juan. Where Pérez perhaps departs from these other characters is that her in-betweenness has a specific, bridgelike, function. That is, while Mario's sexuality may place him in between white and brown spaces, sexualities, and desires, he never brings these different sites together. Neither does Father Juan. In fact, as Yarbro-Bejarano points out, both characters "[desert their] people in their time of need" (72). In contrast, Pérez's in-betweenness is an essential part of her profession as a journalist as well as her role in the play. She literally explains and translates what is happening in McLaughlin to viewers of Channel Five as well as to readers or viewers of the play. Furthermore, while questions of fidelity and betrayal haunt all of these characters, the play's use of Pérez to evoke Malinche opens up the possibility for a deeper exploration that moves beyond binary understandings of us/them. Martha J. Cutter argues that Malinche's command of several languages (Nahuatl, Maya, and Spanish) means that she herself may help us to move beyond these questions and to think outside a binary "between voice and silence, colonizer and colonized" (2). While *Heroes and Saints* references Malinche early on, Pérez herself does not remain a translator but rather engages in different and more complex forms of communication between herself, townspeople, and viewers. The evolution of Pérez in relationship to translation encourages us to place her as a character and the play as a whole within a larger context of cultural and linguistic translation. That is, while she translates lexically between Amparo and her camera crew, she also, as stated above, engages in visual and spatial translations for readers and viewers. These functions offer up the play itself as a cultural translation, affirming Adam Versényi's assertion that translation can be understood to be a defining component of theater in the Americas. When Pérez translates for individual characters in both literal and nonliteral ways, she fulfills Cere's urging for visibility while connecting herself and other characters to a larger history and context. The play then places Pérez in relationship to Chicana/o history and literature, while also opening up the possibility for different, and changing, communicative and translative acts.

As the play progresses, Pérez's broadcasts offer more attention not only to the spectacle of the protests but to the protestors themselves. Her report that opens act 2, scene 3 foregrounds women who have been organizing to demand an appropriate response to the loss of their children's lives. The journalist names the organization—"the Mothers and Friends of McLaughlin"—and explains the mothers' demands, which she describes as "quite concrete" (Moraga, *Heroes* 77). These demands include federal money to relocate to an environmentally safe community, the closing of the well that has been providing tap water to the town, and the establishment of a free health clinic for those affected. In describing the demands as "quite concrete," Pérez suggests that the requests are reasonable and achievable and that the protestors themselves are an intelligent and organized group. Moreover, she offers brief explanations of the demands, explaining that the request for federal money to relocate is based on the fact that the protestors currently live on federally subsidized land. This detail again portrays the demands, and, by extension, the protestors, as rational and reasonable. Pérez's broadcast further develops her early focus on the protests themselves, giving more space to activists, particularly female activists.

While this monologue is in line with her earlier broadcasts that focused on the protests and protestors as opposed to giving "equal time" to government or health officials, this scene also includes a transformative moment for Pérez. Following her broadcast, the play stages a moving protest which consists of mothers who have lost children holding up a photograph of their dead child and declaring the child's name, date of death, cause of death, and age at death. A group of protestors nearby shout "¡Asesinos! ¡Asesinos! ¡Asesinos!" (78). A young child who is with the group slips, and Amparo steps out of line to pick her up; as she does so, a policeman begins to beat Amparo. Pérez shouts out with shock and concern: "She's been struck! Amparo Manríquez ... oh my god! the policeman!... Stop him! Jesus! Somebody stop him! No! No! Stop him!" (79). Amparo's husband, Don Gilberto, throws his body over his wife, the protestors scatter, and the scene ends. Reading this scene with attention to Pérez, we can see how she has been brought into the community of protestors. She shouts Amparo's full name, indicating familiarity with the town and with one of its prominent figures. Moreover, her shouts evidence her stepping out of her role as a journalist; she is no longer reporting from outside the town but attempting to change a situation unfolding in front of her. This scene also highlights a transformation regarding Pérez's understanding of the power of voice. In terms of aiding Amparo, Pérez's verbal protest is ineffectual: her shouts do not stop the policeman from beating Amparo; only Don Gilberto's body is able to do that. Pérez is confronted with the idea that directing her voice at an unnamed public may not inaugurate the change that the town needs. Evidence that Pérez slowly accepts this idea can be found in subsequent scenes, in which she speaks less and less to her viewing public in favor of greater communication with and between townspeople. Here the play offers commentary on the transformation that translation brings to the translator as well as an endorsement of intracommunal communication and the importance of direct action. As Pérez comes to play a more significant role in the lives and goals of the townspeople, her individual voice takes on less and less importance, until it becomes indistinguishable from that of other characters. While this movement may appear to undermine the play's emphasis on the importance of voice, Pérez in fact recasts voice from an individual to a communal sound.

Affirming her dedication to offering complex portrayals and reappraisals of Malinche, Moraga's Malinche-like figure in the play does not remain static but shifts in her relationship to the townspeople. This shift is best evidenced through her changing communication. Whereas at first she offered translations between the townspeople and her viewing audience, in act 2 she begins to communicate more directly with the town. Act 2, scene 11, the final scene of the play, opens with Pérez functioning as a traditional reporter. "This is Ana Pérez, coming to you live from McLaughlin, California. Today is the funeral of Evalina Valle, the tenth child to die of cancer in this small Valley town" (Moraga, *Heroes* 103). Here we can see a shift from spectacle to justice—these lines are focused not on a protest or even on the ritual of the funeral but on the death of Evalina. The characters are observing the funeral of Yolanda's infant daughter—Evalina—and Cere's transformation into the Virgen of Guadalupe and eventual martyrdom. Pérez attempts to speak to Yolanda and is rebuffed; she then justifies her intrusion by telling the grieving mother "the priest asked me to be here" and then adds, "he said there was to be a crucifixion" (104). This last sentence provides Yolanda with shocking and tragic information, as she immediately understands Cere's intent. The scene is notable because for the first time Pérez provides a character in the play with information gathered from another character—that is, she provides a communicative bridge between characters of McLaughlin, rather than between them and those outside the town. In conveying information to Yolanda, Pérez begins to transform herself as a translator and evidences traits of public journalism. Her transmission of information fulfills one of Judith Lichtenberg's descriptions of public journalism as a way "to connect with citizens . . . and not just merely provide a one-way flow of information to consumers" (qtd. in Romano 17–18). What she tells Yolanda does nothing to further the needs of Channel Five or her own job; rather, she is fulfilling a utilitarian function within the community. While the actual words she speaks to Yolanda transmit information as opposed to translating words, her action remains deeply related to the act of translation. That is, we may read the change in Pérez's relationship with Yolanda and Father Juan as one product of translation itself: the ability of translation to impact the translator. Rather than translating one character's words to another, in her act of communication between Juan, herself, and Yolanda, she is translated from an outsider to a member of the McLaughlin community.

Evidence of this transformation in Pérez's relationship with the residents is emphasized when, for the first time, Pérez is invited to bear witness and act as a spotlight on the townspeople's tragedies. Dolores, who had in the first scene refused to speak to Pérez, now calls out to her: "Come, señorita. Come see how my baby se vuelve a santita. Come show the peepo" (Moraga, *Heroes* 106). Dolores's words also evidence a shift from a reliance on voice to a request for visual representation. Here, Dolores demands a visual interpretation rather than a linguistic translation. She does not want Pérez to translate her words (and Pérez doesn't) but wants her to use her camera and her position to offer representation.

Dolores's specific desire to utilize the journalist for visibility reflects a stark change in her understanding of the power of seeing. Not only did Dolores initially refuse to speak to Pérez; she also spends a large section of the play keeping Cere out of sight. Earlier scenes explain how Dolores believes that visibility poses a threat to her daughter; she articulates a fear of Cere being seen by a ridiculing public. The first time Father Juan visits the Valle home, Dolores "quickly pushes Cerezita out of sight, drawing a curtain around her" (13). Later, when Cere protests her mother removing her from beside the window, where she was watching Juan distribute pamphlets, Dolores claims "You don't need to see," and then warns "You think you're so tough, go on. But we'll see how you feel the first time some stranger looks at you with cruel eyes" (39, 41). For Dolores, the danger in seeing is in the potential of the seer to be seen. To protect Cere from the scorn of outsiders, she is willing to attempt to prevent her from seeing. Cere refutes her mother's fears, and links seeing to knowledge, saying "I am smart" and "I'm old enough now to go out!" (40, 41). Yolanda also suggests the futility of Dolores's attempts, saying early on that "[Cere] sees" (15). When Dolores asks Pérez to film Cere, the play suggests that the contested issue of visibility has been resolved and that the mother has acknowledged, and herself been influenced by, the power of the sight of her daughter. Dolores's calling forth to Pérez indicates the mother's shifting understanding of visibility in general and the journalist in particular.

The final scene of the work brings together the play's central themes of speech, visibility, and direct action and marks the culmination of Pérez's transformation from outside observer to community-embedded activist. After refusing to speak for some time, Cere offers a speech to the assembled protestors. Her speech, however, does not call for more protests or demonstrations. She does not even exhort the people to take action but rather affirms them, telling them that they are, in one of the most memorable lines of the play, "the miracle people" (106). The young woman's speech provides a deliberative moment, in which characters undertake consideration of their circumstances and possibilities before taking action (Romano 3). After her speech, Cere turns and enters the fields. Her brother Mario shouts "Burn the fields," and the people echo him in Spanish: "Enciendan los files!" Then: "They all, including Ana Pérez, rush out to the vineyards, shouting as they exit. '¡Asesinos! ¡Asesinos! ¡Asesinos!'" (107). Here we see the culmination of the transformation that began earlier in this act. Whereas before Pérez had shouted for someone to stop the policeman while the protestors shouted "murderers," here she joins her voice and body with the people.

## THE ENDS

There are several ways we can read the last lines of the play. From one perspective, Pérez's joining of the protestors may be a culmination of their success—the creation of a mobilized public. The children have successfully caught the attention of the public, represented by Pérez, and the public has joined their cause. Another reading may reflect the opposite—the abandonment of any dialogue with the public. Read this way, we can see Pérez as commenting on the failure of news sources to adequately take Latina/o people and/or Latina/o issues seriously. Reflecting on his year-long study of network news, Santa Ana concludes that "the single major finding is their [network's] gross disregard for Latinos" (15). Thus, Pérez may be turning her back on a media industry that has turned its back on Latina/os.

Considering Pérez in relationship to Latina/os and media, we may also understand her actions as a cynical acknowledgment of the Latina/o public-sphere paradox. The public sphere is the realm in which citizens can come together to deliberate and exert positive influence on the nation-state.⁸ Mass media, or the fourth estate, can help to create this space, thus contributing to the public sphere and, by extension, to greater democracy.⁹ The idea undergirding this relationship is that access to media engenders political power; that is, once citizens have access to media, they can participate in the public sphere and help to shape political thought, opinion, and processes. Of course, this ideal of democracy is constrained by dominant notions of citizenship that "give preeminence to white, middle-class producers and contributors to a political body defined in national terms" (Dávila, *Latinos, Inc.* 142). Moreover, one of the oft-unquestioned statuses of public participants is that of the citizen, a status that may not be conferred upon Latina/os and other marginalized peoples in either the political or the social sense (Amaya 18–19). This brings us to what Hector Amaya terms the Latina/o public sphere paradox: Latina/os contradict the idea that more access to media translates into more power. In fact, Latina/os have great access to mass media, particularly Spanish Language Media (SLM): "Latina/os struggle to get access to ELM (English Language Media) but have access to SLM," requiring us to rethink the relationship between access to media and access to the public sphere; "with Latina/os, more access to a public sphere equals less political power" (42). Moreover, within Spanish Language Media the "range of what is accepted and promoted as 'Latina' on the airwaves" may be as limited as it is in English Language Media (Dávila, *Latinos, Inc* 157). Pérez's abandonment of her role as a journalist can thus be read as both an acknowledgment of this paradox and a refusal to continue to perpetuate this inverse and unequal relationship between Latina/o media presence and Latina/o political and social power.

Read within Latina/o literary and media studies, *Heroes and Saints* has much to offer our understandings of the relationship between media access and political power. The focus of several broadcasts of a show that is itself devoted to "Hispanics," the characters in *Heroes and*

---

8. Nancy Fraser describes the public sphere as "a discursive realm that allows for making the state accountable to the citizenry" (qtd. in Amaya 44).

9. Mass media are considered to be the "fourth estate"; following the legislative, judicial, and executive branches, they are the fourth and no less essential section of government within liberal, modern democracies. The concept of the fourth estate holds that media play a fundamental role in regulating these other branches of government.

*Saints* do not lack access to media, even English Language Media. At the same time, the use of code-switching, bilingualism, and nonstandard English by the characters indicates how issues of multi- and bilingualism impact their efficacy: as marginalized peoples, they are not easily able to convert their cultural capital into political capital (Amaya 49). Where Pérez most firmly reflects the Latina/o public sphere paradox, and where she intervenes, is in her turn away from journalism. She and the townspeople recognize that more media access will not create more access to the public sphere or help them achieve their political goals. Here the play also coincides with Chon Noriega's exhortation to be wary of "the numbers game." Noriega warns that "the statistical substantiation of discrimination [will not] reform the film and television industries" (103). We must keep in mind that representation does not equal power: "What numbers 'mean'—that is, the impact they have—depends on the power relations within which they are asserted" (103). Moreover, in a neoliberal environment in which multiculturalism is "reduced to issues of representation," we can see that "diversity" and "numbers" have little to do with empowerment (Dávila, "El Barrio's" 153). Pérez's apparent turn to silence reflects an acknowledgment of this numerical paradox, gesturing toward the existence of Amaya's paradox as well as Noriega's analysis of the fallacy of assuming that more media will engender either more comprehensive coverage or more access to the public sphere and political power. This silence connects her to her role as a journalist as well as to her relation to Malinche, bringing to mind Moraga's explicit reference to Malinche as a translator as well as the potentially sinister effects of intercultural translations (Moraga, *Xicana* 150). Here Pérez fulfills the doubts many have about issues of translation, bringing them to bear explicitly within the realm of media and communication.

The play astutely recognizes the difficulties inherent in Latina/os effectively harnessing access to the public sphere to achieve political goals, but it does not find journalism or media ineffective or unnecessary. In fact, when the final stage directions specify her by name as joining the other protestors, they highlight that Pérez is an important member of the community. What the play presents, rather, is the idea that media access in and of itself is not sufficient; it calls on us to separate the too-facile, and andro- and Anglocentric idea, that access equals power. As such, the play grants attention to Latina/o media and encourages us to understand the challenges it faces. When Pérez joins the protestors, she acknowledges the Latina/o public-sphere paradox while modeling a community-embedded journalism. Her character and the play overall, then, point to the power of Latina/o media while encouraging the further development of a Latina/o media that remains connected to and supportive of direct community engagement.

While Pérez doesn't offer us any linguistic cues—besides her own voice joined with that of others—for how to interpret her actions, we can understand her final actions as engaging in a particularly raced and gendered negotiation with the public sphere. In her discussion of the relationship between precarity, performance, and gender, Judith Butler explains that subjects do not necessarily precede politics; rather, politics may in fact create the terms of who may be considered a subject ("Performativity" iii). Using the 2006 marches in favor of comprehensive immigration reform, Butler describes the participants in the demonstrations as people who articulated their right to freedom of expression and assembly even though, as noncitizens, they were not necessarily understood as being recipients of these rights by the US Constitution (vi). Building from Hannah Arendt and speaking specifically of demonstrators who sang the US and Mexican national anthems in English and Spanish, Butler points out that the protestors exercised their rights even in the absence of the recognition of their rights (vii). Butler's take on the 2006 marches is useful not only because they bring a specifically Latina/o context to questions of agency, articulations, and politics but also because they are the same occasion that spurred Amaya's articulation of the Latina/o public-sphere paradox. But where Amaya is understandably disappointed in the lack of concrete political action as the result of the protests—and thus seeks to understand this lack of change through his theory of the Latina/o public-sphere paradox—Butler finds in the manifestations an articulation of agency that is closely linked to sexual and gender performativity. Acting in the political sense is akin to gender performativity, because just as the latter does not "presuppose an always acting subject," the former is performed "within a set of norms that are acting upon us" (xi). In other words, our very modes of performing—whether they be in terms of gender or political action—are always determined for us by a larger social, cultural, and political landscape. Butler's discussion of precarity, politics, and gender helps us to understand the political stakes of social movements that seek legibility and visibility in the public sphere. For her this is very much about "how the unspeakable population," or vulnerable and precarious populations, "speak and make [their] claims" (xiii). The public sphere must be a part of these considerations; again following Arendt, she argues that the exercise of a right (e.g., freedom) "has to be an action with others, and it has to be public" (vi). Both Butler and Amaya allow us to understand the stakes of Pérez's (and the townspeople's) actions. Butler suggests that political activism must take place in the public sphere, while Amaya argues that US Latina/o access to the public sphere has not been sufficient, although he would agree that it is necessary. Butler allows us to understand how the townspeople in the play are demanding the same kind of legibility that other marginalized populations have demanded—specifically queer men and women and racial minorities. While Butler's discussion of precarity only spells out the stakes of political activism and its relationship to gender performativity, her earlier work on gender is not unhopeful. In her groundbreaking essay, she concludes by suggesting that if we understand the performativity whereby gender is "put on," we may be able to "expand the cultural field bodily through subversive performances of various kinds" ("Performative Acts" 531). We may thus view Pérez's actions as such as a subversive act—one that both responds to the lack of political power that Latina/os have in the play and that recognizes the relationship between the necessity of performing particular political acts—equality, access, assembly—in order to constitute them.

## CONCLUSION

Through Pérez, including her early reports from/on the protests and her later joining of the protestors, *Heroes and Saints* portrays how a Latina reporter engages in gendered negotiations of the Latina/o public sphere. Pérez's status as a reporter for "Hispanic California" indicates that she and her journalism exist in relation to Latina/o communities; she is thus actively involved in the creation and dissemination of a Latina/o public sphere. But the play does not present a static portrait of this relationship, suggesting instead that Pérez negotiates her status and identity within both an Anglo-dominated mass media and a larger Chicana/o social justice movement. Rather than suggest an unchanging or linear relationship between Latina/o reporters and the Latina/o public sphere, Pérez and the play engage in questions about the kinds of publics that Latina/o journalists reflect and create. Pérez, like her fictional counterpart Lyla Rodríguez from *A Day Without a Mexican,* engages in a negotiation concerning her role as a Latina reporter covering an issue that is pressing for US Latina/os. And, like Rodríguez, Pérez is transformed by her own work, eventually abandoning her position as a network reporter to work directly with people impacted by the crisis. This transformation spurs a break with her network but the forging of closer links with the people of McLaughlin. In addition, Pérez's near exclusive attention to the voices and experiences of female activists reflects a highlighting of a particular kind of Latina/o public— one that will center the lives and experiences of the disenfranchised and marginalized, even within an already largely marginalized population. Here the journalist negotiates her status vis-à-vis mainstream mass media and the specific community in which she works, eventually choosing to join the latter. The play then portrays a Latina reporter who affirms and solidifies the relationship between Latina/o-oriented media and Latina/o publics, portraying the means by which each forms the other.

# PART 2

# TRANSNATIONAL NEGOTIATIONS

CHAPTER 3

# Femininity, Journalism, and the Necessity of a Transnational Public in *The Long Night of White Chickens*

IN LATE 2014 mainstream media reports in the US began to talk about a "crisis" on the US–Mexico border. The border had been undergoing heavy militarization for decades and had become increasingly difficult and dangerous to cross, leading to thousands of deaths as migrants pursued treacherous paths through adjacent deserts. The "crisis" these reports referred to, however, was not these deaths or the related cases of mistreatment of migrants by border patrol agents, but rather an increase in the numbers of Central American migrants appearing at the border and, specifically, the growing number of unaccompanied minor children.[1] Referred to frequently as a "surge," the number of children attempting to cross into the US had nearly doubled from 2013 to 2014 (from 35,000 children to almost 66,000). As the radio program *Latino USA* pointed out, little was new about this phenomenon: children (mostly from Mexico) had been crossing into the US for decades, and the US had seen heavy migration from Central America in previous decades. In a September 2014 show dedicated to the

---

1. Whether those appearing at the border in recent years, or today, should be considered "migrants" or "refugees" is a matter of contention. For the purposes of this discussion, I use the language employed by the media outlets analyzed, which is "migrant."

topic, host María Hinojosa and her staff offered a valuable brief history of US intervention in Central America and ensuing migration from the region while also critiquing the framing of the current situation in mainstream media outlets. Words such as *crisis* and *surge* suggest a catastrophe instigated by a singular powerful force, obscuring the root causes of the issue, in particular US foreign policy. The language also others and racializes migrant children, suggesting that they are a threat to the US nation. Delving into the history of US intervention in the region, including the role that the US prison system played in fomenting the powerful gangs, or *maras*, that threaten many peoples' safety, *Latino USA* attests to the importance of a transnational perspective that exposes the origins of migration and links conditions in foreign countries to recent US policies and actions. The reporting by *Latino USA* exists in relationship to a diverse US Latina/o public increasingly hungry for media coverage that accurately captures and speaks to their lives while offering information that can place lived experiences (of racism, migration, family separation, etc.) in historical and political perspective. In their turn to the US-backed wars of the 1970s through 1990s to explain the current migration phenomenon, the staff of *Latino USA* offer information about a period that continues to be understudied within the US but is vital to understanding our current moment. Seeking to analyze how the relationship between the US and Central America raises questions not only about political and economic ties but also about issues of social expression and identity, this chapter turns to a novel set during the US-backed Guatemalan Civil War that includes important portrayals of mass media and media workers. Written by a former correspondent, Francisco Goldman, *The Long Night of White Chickens* pays particular attention to the role of the press and the way in which a Guatemalan reporter must negotiate Guatemalan and US contexts. The novel offers a historical portrait relevant to our current situation and an example of media workers operating binationally. As such, it offers a valuable portrait of media operating in a militarized context, while emphasizing the gendered dimensions of power and the necessity of a transnational understanding of Guatemalan, Central American, and Central American–American politics and migration.

Published in 1992, Goldman's debut novel remains one of the few US Latina/o novels to take up the Guatemalan Civil War from a transnational perspective. Written by the binational Goldman, the text is remarkable for its ability to combine elements of US and Guatemalan history and culture within a narrative that is personal as well as historically and politically situated. The novel tells the story of Rogerio Graetz, a young man who, like Goldman, is the son of a Guatemalan mother and Jewish American father. Raised in Massachusetts but with close ties to his mother's homeland, Rogerio finds his life changed forever when his family "acquires" a Guatemalan maid, Flor de Mayo Puac. Rogerio and Flor grow up together, and she functions as an older sister to him throughout his childhood. After graduating from college, Flor decides to return to Guatemala, where she becomes the director of an orphanage. During one of the bloodiest periods of the Guatemalan Civil War, in 1983, Flor is found murdered in her bedroom in the orphanage. When the novel opens, Rogerio and his father, Ira, have flown to Guatemala City to recover Flor's body. There they discover that she has been accused of facilitating illegal adoptions, and most suspect that her murder came at the hands of her criminal associates. The rest of the novel consists of various backstories, as Rogerio recalls memorable moments in his childhood and youth with Flor, alongside several more recent stays in Guatemala as he attempts to solve the mystery of her murder. In his pursuits, he is joined by his childhood friend, Luis Martínez Moya, who goes by Moya in the text and is a Guatemalan journalist who was briefly Flor's lover. By the end of the novel, Rogerio has found no evidence that the rumors about Flor's activities and reason for her murder are untrue, and Moya has had to flee to the US for asylum.

As a reporter who wrote about conflicts in Central America throughout the 1970s and 1980s, Goldman was well positioned to write a novel that takes place during the Guatemalan Civil War. *Chickens* may therefore be read as a novel in which the young writer attempts to come to terms with the years he has just spent living in the war-torn country of his mother's birth as well as the first foray into literature by the former journalist. It is this latter point, and the text's use of journalism and journalists to reflect the multiple layers of corruption and injustice within Guatemala, with which this chapter is concerned. The chapter begins by situating the novel historically as well as within Goldman's own career as a journalist. This section is followed by an analysis of how journalism and journalistic inquiry is treated in the novel via the characters Rogerio and Moya. A focus on questions of gender, race, and sexuality reveals that Moya, the principal journalist in the text, is constructed as a feminine figure. As a result, the larger state of journalism in Guatemala is feminized. This femininity is expressed in three ways: sexual and emotional dependency, a subordinate status in relationship to men and male-controlled institutions (the government and military), and forms of discourse. The powerlessness and subordinate status of Moya and Guatemalan journalism at large align them with the primary victims of the civil war: Guatemalan civilians, women, and the country's majority-Maya population. The latter two groups were explicitly targeted in gender- and sex-based ways. Thus, journalism in the novel is closely aligned with a public that is under attack by state institutions, namely the military and government. As Moya finds himself dependent on a US-based audience for safety when his life is threatened, the novel illustrates the important role that transnational US Latina/o journalists, including Goldman himself, have played in creating a specifically transnational Latina/o public sphere where questions of democracy, human rights, and war may be discussed and contested.

The final section of this chapter considers the novel in relationship to Central American–American transmigration. While Rogerio, the binational Guatemalan American Jewish protagonist is often considered the work's principal Central American–American character, we would do well to consider Flor de Mayo Puac as an exemplar of this identity. Focusing on Flor presents a new understanding of how questions of national identity, gender, and media coalesce in the novel that have implications for our current social and political moment. The development of Flor as a character, as a woman overdetermined by media discourse, gestures to the extent to which Central American and Central American–American subjects are gendered in mainstream US media as well as the relative overrepresentation of this population in mass media, as opposed to in the literary, cultural, or political realms. Acknowledging this phenomenon calls us to appreciate the role of transnational journalism in creating a specifically transnational US Latina/o public sphere and the significant role that Central American–Americans and Central American–American women play in this sphere.

## HISTORICAL BACKGROUND

*Chickens* is both Goldman's debut novel and one of the first novels to address the Guatemalan Civil War from a Guatemalan American perspective. Goldman's protagonist manages to represent both the in-betweenness (of language, nation, and culture) that characterizes so much of US Latina/o literature and a committed investment in recent Guatemalan history and US–Guatemalan relations. This knowledge and intimate relation is refracted through a cynical and often morbid humor such that the work is marked by both a denunciation of US-backed human rights abuses in Guatemala and a depressing lack of hope for the future.

The novel centers on Rogerio Graetz, the son of a poor Boston Jew and a wealthy Guatemalan *mestiza*. At a young age, Graetz contracts tuberculosis, and his Guatemalan grandmother responds by "sending" the Graetz family a *muchacha* to help care for Rogerio and perform housework in the Graetz home.[2] In the US, Flor de Mayo Puac fulfills a number of roles; for Mr. Graetz she is a daughter, for Mrs. Graetz she is a housekeeper, and for Rogerio she slips between sister and object of intense emotional affection. Flor attends high school and college in the Boston area and then returns to Guatemala City, where she runs an orphanage, *Los Quetzalitos*. A few years after returning, when she is in her early thirties, Flor is found mysteriously murdered, stabbed in the throat in her bed in *Los Quetzalitos*. When the narrative begins, Flor is dead and Rogerio and his father have flown to Guatemala to bring her body back to the States. The subsequent narrative consists of a mix of Rogerio's memories of his childhood and life with Flor, juxtaposed with his own present-day travels to Guatemala and inquiries into Flor's life and death.

The text engages with civil and "post"–civil war Guatemala and US intervention in the region through the focus on Flor's murder and the narrative perspective. The story jumps around in time and place, narrating Rogerio's childhood in suburban Massachusetts, his teen and college years, adult visits to Flor in Guatemala, and present-day inves-

---

2. See chapter 2 of *Understanding Francisco Goldman* (Vigil) for more on the autobiographical elements of the novel.

tigations into his friend's death. However, most of the action and the most significant events occur within a five-year span, 1979–84, which includes the year that Flor returns to Guatemala City (1979), when she is found murdered (February 1983), and when Rogerio and Moya take up the investigation into her death in earnest (1984). These years represent some of the most bloody and brutal in modern Guatemalan history and occur during the nation's thirty-six-year civil war (1960–96).

The Guatemalan Civil War and US role in the conflict is broached in the novel through references to violence and repression as well as through Rogerio's own binationality. As a Guatemalan American he is well positioned to view and understand the history between the two nations, and he occasionally alludes to his own family's role in significant historical events. For example, Rogerio references the 1954 coup, in which the CIA overthrew the democratically elected president Jacobo Árbenz Guzmán, by explaining that his upper-class grandmother welcomed the change in power. He writes that Abuelita had helped to overthrow Árbenz by "defying the government-imposed blackout of the capital by lighting charcoal in a pit in her patio and fanning it while she stared up at the sky" (201). Rogerio explains that his grandmother was cheering the country's liberation from "Communism" and was unaware of the CIA's role in that moment, although she would not have minded much had she known. He also tells readers that he educated himself on his mother's country by reading a range of books. These books have a decidedly leftist perspective because, according to Rogerio: "Four hundred years of repressing the Indian majority, dictatorship after dictatorship, one decade of democracy ended by a US-sponsored coup that issued in the current thirty years of military rule—understandably, the Rightist Latinist is likely to find more that interests him in, say, Cuba" (186). Rogerio's binationality and his ties to upper-class society through his mother's family allow the text to comment on the role of US military intervention as well as Guatemalan racism and classism.

The Guatemalan Civil War included severe repression in urban centers as well as genocidal campaigns against indigenous communities in the country's rural highlands. Peace accords were signed in 1996; two years later, in 1998, the Human Rights Office of the Archdiocese of the Catholic Church released an extensive report on the violence, published in English as *Guatemala: Never Again!* The report, known also by its Spanish acronym, REMHI (*Recuperación de la Memoria Histórica*), consists of testimony covering the thirty-six-year civil war. The report explains that most human rights violations occurred between 1980 and 1984 and attributes the vast majority of abuses to the US-backed Guatemalan military. Estimates indicate that over 200,000 people were killed and millions were displaced. Recent scholarship has traced the continuing violence in the region from the 1954 coup through the civil war period and into the post-conflict period, emphasizing the ongoing state of impunity that exists.

The ostensible cause of Flor's death, retribution for her role in an illegal adoption ring, also references the civil war. For Marc Zimmerman, the subject of adoption is an excellent way to approach civil war and post–civil war Guatemalan society, insofar as "no other theme [than that of the supposed selling of Guatemalan babies for organ transplants] can better encompass this period of intense war in the highlands or the continuing efforts to find a base for social peace in the 1990s" (652; my translation).[3] Zimmerman's reference to "the highlands" points out how the text broaches the Guatemalan genocide of indigenous peoples, most of whom are located in the highland regions and who were brutally targeted during the war. That Flor oversees international adoptions also allows the text to comment on social relations between Guatemalans and North Americans and Europeans. These social relations remained strained for decades and led to several violent attacks on (and in one case a murder of) foreigners by Guatemalan locals who suspected the individuals of trying to steal babies. (Guatemala halted international adoptions in 2007.) Through Flor's activities, the text broaches the genocidal campaigns against Guatemala's Mayan people, the continued lack of security and social cohesion in the nation, and foreign intervention.

Mass media, including print journalism, was heavily depreciated during the war. In addition, journalists and newspapers were subordinated to the interests of political and economic elites and forced to obfuscate information via the use of euphemisms. In the late 1970s, as the Sandinista victory in neighboring Nicaragua was about to come

---

3. Original Spanish: Ningún otro tema [que la supuesta venta de bebés guatemaltecos para trasplantes de órganos] puede abarcar más el periodo de guerra intensa en el altiplano ni los continuos esfuerzos por encontrar una base para la paz social en la década de 1990.

to fruition, Guatemalan elites and the army initiated a campaign of aggression against the free press, resulting in the closure of many media outlets and the exile of many journalists (Barrera Ortíz 37). Journalists and owners of newspapers were targets of political violence by both the state and armed insurgents, although violence was disproportionally committed by the state and army. According to Byron Barrera Ortíz, newspapers during the war engaged in "disinformation," whereby reports did not provide adequate information, distracted public attention, and minimized or overstated the importance of facts and events (24). Because of pressure from the government and army, newspapers also engaged heavily in "self-censure." The REMHI reports that although there were some who raised their voices in spite of risks, most adhered to the norms of self-censure such that Guatemala came to be a "silent country" (qtd. in Barrera Ortíz 35; my translation). As covert threats to freedom of the press became overt, newspapers actually grew in value, evidenced by the kidnapping of newspaper editors by revolutionary groups to force periodicals to publish their demands (Barrera Ortíz 37–38). When newspapers met the demands of kidnappers by publishing what was demanded, they defied government law, illustrating the ways in which newspapers and journalism became a site of violence and contestation during the civil war.

Newspapers could not avoid publishing accounts of violence, but they negotiated political pressure by engaging in sensationalism and euphemism. Both are well reflected in the novel via Rogerio's descriptions of newspapers that ran "photographs of a house full of crowded cribs" in the wake of Flor's murder and his discussion of how the dailies covered the results of General Efraín Ríos Montt's "counterinsurgency campaigns" (itself a euphemistic title, of course; 4). Ludmila Damjanova explains that the use of euphemisms "is well known in repressive regimes or dictatorships," and that, "on the one hand, euphemisms obscure comprehension. On the other, they utilize a sophisticated language that prevents the reader from facing a violent reality" (590; my translation). Newspapers in Rogerio's estimate go a step further than engaging in euphemism; they traffic in mistruths and deception. In his characteristic sarcastic humor, Rogerio tells readers that newspapers in Guatemala "have to be read to be believed" (7). This perspective again encourages readers to doubt the veracity of reports about Flor's baby-smuggling campaign. Of course, the newspapers are protecting themselves as much as their readers; by not discussing issues such as state-backed violence or political corruption directly, they are able to continue operating.[4]

Living and working within this context of corruption and impunity, Goldman sought other ways to reflect political and social realities. According to the author, the novel was "an interrogation, through story-telling of all the ways we try to figure out and express 'the truth'" (qtd in Coppedge). Given the compromised state of Central American journalism, it makes sense that Goldman would turn to fiction to try to express the "truth" of Guatemala. Journalism provided a means of measuring the political status of Central America and exploring new modes of communication. He continues: "In the wars in Central America, journalism proved a central example, or metaphor. I realized the war wasn't just over bodies and bullets but over words, over which description of the events and the reasons for those events would carry the day, not just locally but abroad in the US and elsewhere" (qtd in Coppedge). Goldman's use of journalism in the novel demonstrates how the author drew on his own writing career as well as his understanding of Guatemala to tell a historically grounded story.[5]

His work as a novelist and journalist evidences Goldman's breadth as a writer while also placing him within a specifically Latin American tradition. Some of the most critically and commercially success-

---

4. M. Gabriela Torres's study of newspapers during the years that precisely coincide with Flor's return to Guatemala and death (1979–84) finds a clear bias in favor of the government and military and a similar lack of the attribution of crimes to specific individuals or entities. In an attempt to piece together the "paper trails of the counterinsurgency," Torres looks at how the Guatemalan government sought to increase public support for its position, including through the use of mass media. Torres studies what she terms "cadaver reports," or reports about victims published frequently in mainstream periodicals such *Prensa Libre*. She finds that cadaver reports in *Prensa Libre* increased in the periods 1978–81 and 1983–84, a time that coincided with Ríos Montt's presidency and an increase in political violence in the countryside. These cadaver reports are specifically "non-political," in that they fail to discuss motives or perpetrators, leading Torres to speculate that perhaps their increase signals an attempt to draw attention away from the politically—and often racially motivated—crimes taking place in the indigenous, rural areas of the country.

5. Although the author eventually earned fame and success as a novelist, journalism was and continues to be an important part of his writing. Before, during, and after publishing his fictional works, he has published long-form journalism in magazines such as *Harper's* and *The New Yorker*. Most of his journalism has focused on Central America and US–Central American relations.

ful Latin American writers, including Gabriel García Márquez, Mario Vargas Llosa, and Elena Poniatowska, also worked as journalists. For Goldman, these writers didn't simply move from one genre to the next but rather transformed the meaning of journalism, suggesting that it could be an extension of creative work, and vice versa. Goldman recalls: "García Márquez is always saying that journalism—he means narrative journalism—is just another branch of literature, and he's completely right" (qtd in Coppedge). Goldman's work merges this tradition with an emerging US Latina/o one; several of his most successful contemporaries—Guatemalan American Héctor Tobar, Cuban American Achy Obejas, and Peruvian American Daniel Alarcón—also worked and work as both journalists and novelists. Goldman, Tobar, Obejas, and Alarcón illustrate the important role of journalism and journalists in US Latina/o letters and encourage us to see journalistic and creative work as existing on a continuum.

The next section looks in depth at how precisely journalism and journalists are characterized in *Chickens*. In addition to offering a portrait that coincides with the compromised state of journalism in relation to state and government forces discussed here, newspaper and newspaper reporters, specifically Moya, are distinctly gendered in relation to powerful Guatemalan military, government, and economic forces.

## JOURNALISM IN *CHICKENS*

Within the novel, journalism plays an important role in character development, plot progression, and the establishment of a context for events and characters. All of the information readers have about Flor come from Rogerio's memories, Moya's memories (including those he speaks about with Rogerio), and newspaper accounts of her life and death (related via Rogerio). The latter two sources are explicitly linked to journalism, as Moya himself is a reporter. Journalism and journalistic discourse serve as a vital source of information and as an adversary for Rogerio. The first conflict established in the novel is that between Rogerio and accounts of Flor's death in the Guatemalan papers, whereby Rogerio seeks to disprove the papers and clear Flor's name as an alleged baby-thief/seller. Even when they do not contain information that he wants to believe, Rogerio relies on newspaper accounts of Flor's death to understand her life and actions since returning to Guatemala. Likewise, Moya is indispensable as he offers information and aids Rogerio in his travels and investigations. The portrait of mass media given via newspaper headlines, Moya's reports, and Rogerio's comments on the state of the press all provide readers with a sense of the social, economic, and political state of the nation.

Readers are introduced to the compromised state of Guatemalan journalism almost immediately in the text, when in the opening chapter Ira and Rogerio arrive in Guatemala City to recover Flor's remains. It is through the Guatemalan newspapers, "two major Guatemala City dailies," that Flor's alleged crimes are first presented to the reader. Rogerio informs us that these papers report the discovery of a *casa de engordes*—an illegal "fattening house" where orphans illegally acquired (kidnapped?) await adoption by foreign couples in Europe and the US. This fattening house, discovered by the national police, provides the motive for Flor's murder. Rogerio's description of the newspapers includes emphasis on sensational tactics as well as superfluous information. He tells us that one article includes a "close-up" photo of the frightened face of a nursemaid employed by *Los Quetzalitos*, a paper's description of Flor as a woman with "few scruples," as well as papers that highlighted the murdered woman's beauty and her US citizenship. These last two details make clear the papers' investment in questions of gendered nationality; they paint Flor as a woman corrupted by her time in the US and corrupting of others through her physical charms.

Later, Moya sheds light on a mechanism by which biased or contrived reports are published: the *fafa* system. Moya explains that *faferos* are journalists who take *fafas*—bribes. Rogerio has never heard the term:

ROGERIO: What? What the fuck's a *fafero*?
MOYA: What's a *fafero*!
ROGERIO: What's a *fafero*! C'mon Moya, don't dick me around!
MOYA: *Ay no.* It's a reporter who takes *fafas, vos*—bribes. (229)

Moya goes on to explain that there is "*un cierto tipo*" [a certain type] of journalist who survives in Guatemala from bribes; some are even on the payroll of the army. Moya cynically offers his version of the *fafero* oath: "*Fear, ignorance and* fafa *are my shepherds, I shall not question or want*" (231–32). *Faferos* index the level of corruption in the media and civil society in Guatemala as well as the subordinate status of the press—as Moya suggests that some rely on bribes simply for survival.[6] Moya's shock that Rogerio is unfamiliar with the term/practice indicates how widespread the *fafa* system was in Guatemala at the time.

While these characterizations focus on how media is produced and disseminated within Guatemala, the interactions between characters and media point to a larger, transnational circuit of power and discourse. Referring to the attention focused on Flor's US citizenship, the narrator explains that many in the Guatemalan military and press remained offended by the cessation of US military aid to the nation in 1978. The opportunity to publish information about crimes committed by a US citizen allowed these injured parties to highlight the US's own hypocrisy. Thus, readers see how political relations between the two countries influences the Guatemalan press. Moya's perspectives and position also underscore transnational connections. He seems to delight in opening his friend's eyes to the *fafa* system, and his tone suggests that he understands how shocked his North American friend is with this practice that violates both Guatemalan and US norms of journalistic integrity. Moya's ability to remain connected to powerful Guatemalan and US peoples and institutions is also crucial to his survival. Thus, the principal journalist in the novel relies on his knowledge and understanding of two different national and political contexts, moving among and between them in order to continue to do his work.

---

6. M. Gabriela Torres corroborates Moya's assessment with historical information, explaining that large newspapers such as *Prensa Libre* did not pay journalists salaries but rather offered payment after accepting an image or story for publication. Journalists were then highly incentivized to find other ways to support themselves, including through taking *fafas* from the army or other institutions. These institutions, in turn, benefited from the placement of certain information in the papers. Torres explains: "Because of the financial instability experienced by many journalists, the main mechanism used by the political right to direct news content was the *fafa* (bribe-for-headline) system. All journalists interviewed described the pervasiveness of the *fafa* while vehemently denying their own involvement" ("Art and Labor" 17).

## MOYA AS FEMINIZED

While Moya expertly and necessarily exploits his transnational connections, he is forced to do so because of the subordinate status he occupies. In fact, the novel portrays Moya as occupying a traditionally feminine status, marked by financial, emotional, and sexual dependence on both women and men. Moya is dependent on his employer, Celso Batres, for physical and financial safety. Batres "discovers" Moya when the latter is a student at the public university where Batres came to give a talk. During the question-and-answer period, Moya responded to Batres's speech: "It's true, what you say, *Licenciado* Batres, that here in Guatemala there is a fundamental respect for freedom of expression. Here, anyone is free to say whatever he wants. And if someone doesn't like it, then he's free to kill you" (253). The quip ended up earning Moya a weekly column, "The University Student's Point of View," at *El Minuto*. This anecdote illustrates Moya's wit and boldness and suggests that Batres knows talent when he sees it. But the event also underscores Batres's power, as we're told that with his decision to hire Moya he "pluck[ed] Moya from an unknown fate" (253). He was able to make a unilateral decision that altered Moya's life. In fact, Rogerio suggests that Batres may have saved his friend's life: "By the end of 1980 *La U* was a shell of its former self . . . as many student leaders dead or in hiding up in the mountains and much of the faculty dead or in exile" (262). Rogerio speculates that because Moya has worked for Batres, Moya's name has been tossed into police files marked "journalists" as opposed to those marked "students," thereby removing Moya from a "deadly lottery" (262). Batres's family owns two newspapers, and both are used to protect Moya. Rogerio explains: "Moya writes for *El Minuto*, a low-circulation broadsheet of never more than twelve pages . . . but [the Batres family] really makes their money from *Dónde?* by far the most popular 'newspaper' in the country, . . . and the Batres name appears nowhere in its pages" (178). Rogerio's descriptions establish the varying qualities of newspapers in Guatemala City, descriptions he bolsters with the novel's typical humor when he quips "to say that [*Dónde?* is a Guatemalan version of] *National Enquirer* is definitely an offense to the editorial standards of the latter" (178). Despite its questionable standards, *Dónde?* provides a useful cover for Moya when he oversteps his editorial boundaries. At that point, when the reporter begins to receive death threats or even just phone calls from "curious military officers and prominent rightists seeking clarification," Batres sends Moya to write under a pseudonym at *Dónde?* (178).

When Moya relies on the protection that Batres's power and influence offers him, he is placed into a gendered relationship with his boss. As Iris Marion Young explains, the security state itself, best exemplified by the US post-9/11, assumes a masculinist protectionist role toward its citizens. For Young, the sex/gender of either individual government actors or citizens does not matter; the gendering of the security state is masculine and of the citizenry is feminine. Thus, women can embody masculinist protectionism, and men can be figured as needing protection by the state. Moya's need for protection from a man aligned with powerful economic, social, and political interests aligns him with a larger, feminized citizenry. This situation positions Moya as a citizen/journalist/feminine character in relation to Batres as an emblem of government/protectionism/masculinity.

Broaching both his subordinate/feminine status and his relationship to Guatemalan and US power brokers, Moya also relies on the US political scientist Sylvia McCourt for protection. Rogerio describes Sylvia McCourt as a capable, ambitious, and successful figure in both the US and Guatemala. Although she is roughly the same age as Flor, by the time she meets Moya she is "already a tenured professor of political science" at Harvard. Her area of specialty is Central America, and she is "prominent outside of academic circles too: a frequent contributor of editorials and articles to influential newspapers and journals, invited to appear on televised panel discussions, a member of prestigious foreign policy councils and so on" (252). Her close ties to government garner Moya his introduction, as the two meet though the US embassy's press attaché. Also present at the party are the head of the Guatemalan Army's public relations and the owner of Guatemala's largest newspapers. The party's guests indicate the close relationship between US and Guatemalan government, military, and media forces, again underscoring that power and influence function between and across the two nations. According to Rogerio, Moya is motivated to meet McCourt both because he wants to influence her perception of the country (which might otherwise be biased in favor of government accounts) and because he knows that people like her can offer him protection. "Some time before his exile, [Moya] had begun to suspect and hope that the army had finally begun to regard him as a relative untouchable because of his having been seen at so many events befriending the likes of Sylvia" (255). Lest readers be unclear about what McCourt might be protecting Moya from, the narrator continues: "That is, the army might have come to regard him as someone better left alone or even chased into exile than as someone to snatch, torture, rip open for his secrets, and then kill," actions which could raise "outcry in the editorial and opinion pages of American and European newspapers" (255). To drive home Moya's gendered, subordinate status in the country, the text employs the derogatory adjective *mariconcito* (roughly: faggoty) to describe Moya's work, writing that surely the army found Moya's "*mariconcito* propaganda dinners" less threatening than potential responses to his death (255). Like its English counterpart, the epithet denotes not just a sexual identity but a gendered one, alluding to the degraded, feminine status of homosexual and heterosexual men who fail to embody proper masculinity.[7] Moya's gendered relationship to powerful people and institutions does not preclude his own agency—he clearly understands the risks he runs and works to garner the protection he needs. Still, he lacks the power that a closer affiliation with a patriarchal nation would offer him, forcing him to rely on people with those affiliations such as Batres and McCourt. These relationships, based on the protection they offer him, contribute to the gendering of Moya as female and to his status as a journalist who lives and works within transnational spaces.

## NEWSPAPERS AND THE FRAMING OF FLOR

Although Moya is the novel's only named journalist, Flor's relationship with mass media is also significant. In fact, her character is developed and mediated through journalistic accounts. The novel juxtaposes two main sources of information about Flor: Guatemalan government

---

7. Although Moya may be viewed as opportunistic, this doesn't discount his subordinate status. Cornelia Gräbner describes Moya as a "slightly callous Latin American *macho* lover" concerned with his own vanity (57). However, this view of Moya is put forth by Rogerio, and Moya's own descriptions of his relationships with Flor and Dr. McCourt largely lack the marks of an egoistic, hypermasculine lover.

and media and Rogerio's own memories and anecdotes. While these sources may at first appear to be polar opposites, with Rogerio's memories influenced by his love and affection for Flor, which the Guatemalan media and government lack, the novel in fact creates several parallels between these sources of information. We learn that both are compromised sources of information, both are heavily influenced by gendered and racialized ideas, and both illustrate multiple allegiances, or goals, in their framing of Flor.

Rogerio's early framing of Flor takes on overtures of a *cuenta de hadas,* a fairytale in which she and he are the main characters. When Flor arrives in Namoset, Rogerio is five years old and she is thirteen (her passport says sixteen, but she is "pretty positive" that she is younger). Rogerio is excited at Flor's arrival and already has a knowledge of *muchachas*—"which just means girls and is what maids are called"—from his time at his grandparents' house in Guatemala (43). He recalls the *muchachas* who "plucked chickens in the courtyard; helped me lure my fat palomino rabbit out from under the oversized sepulchral furniture"; and "wore the native skirts and *huipil* blouses of the Indians" (44). As this description indicates, Rogerio stood poised to welcome Flor into his life in a predetermined way; he already had a sense of the role that a *muchacha* could play in his life. He continues: "I loved you from that instant on, loved you almost as if not for yourself at all but as if you were a girl in a storybook that we both had a part in" (46). Flor arrives toward the end of Rogerio's year-long quarantine, and her arrival represents not only a tie with Guatemala but a tie with a world outside of his house that he has barely experienced. Her presence means that he can leave the house and thus marks an important beginning for him; the adult narrates: "The world that I still live in begins for me then and there, with you stepping in from the breezeway so that we could be infiltrated in it together" (47). In this description, Rogerio moves from referencing himself, "I," to referencing Flor, "you," and then ends with the two of them joined: "we . . . together." This sentence as well as Rogerio's other descriptions capture the importance of Flor in Rogerio's life, the impact her arrival had on his development, and the extent to which their lives were intertwined.

For the Guatemalan media, Flor's story fulfills another genre—a sensationalistic story about a corrupt(ed) woman. Rogerio explains that after Flor's death the newspapers ran pictures of "a house full of crowded cribs"—the supposed *casa de engorde* that Flor was running (4). The newspapers are heavily invested in the power of a story about a woman whose crime appears to go so against feminine nature; rather than nourish and protect children as women are thought to naturally aspire to, Flor allegedly neglected and exploited the orphans in her care. The framing of Flor is built upon the ideas of her as a woman who does not fulfill her feminine/maternal responsibilities, as well as upon ideas of her as a woman who does not fulfill her specifically Guatemalan responsibilities. The text several times refers to Flor as a *gringa chapina*, an American Guatemalan, and the adjective suggests that she is simultaneously both and neither, neither fully/sufficiently American nor Guatemalan, or perhaps a degraded/Americanized Guatemalan woman. In the context of her alleged crime, the double adjective is meant to offer some sort of explanation: only a *gringa chapina*, experienced and aware of Guatemala but with an American sense of entitlement and hubris, could have become as involved in this crime as she. The double adjective suggests that Flor's status as a woman has played a part in this hybrid, corrupted identity, as women are more susceptible to be *agringada* or Americanized. This specific but in-between nationality that Flor is given is also a reflection of her indigeneity; as a woman of indigenous heritage, she will never be fully accepted within Guatemala's *ladino* elite; thus, her racial otherness is invoked through a reference to a "foreign" nation.

Both Moya and Flor are individuals who move in and between two nations and are characters developed via their relationships to mass media; thus, the text engages with transnational migration and movement and journalistic discourse simultaneously. Linking these two phenomena pushes the boundaries of US Latinidad, showcasing the necessity of a more expansive understanding of a US Latina/o public and the important role that the Central American diaspora has played and will play in revising our understanding of a US Latina/o public sphere. At the same time, if we understand Flor as the text's principal Central American–American figure, we can read the novel as commenting on the significance of mass media—specifically newspapers—in presenting Central American–American figures.

## FLOR, CENTRAL AMERICAN–AMERICANS, AND A TRANSNATIONAL LATINA/O PUBLIC

That journalism plays such an important role in a novel about a murdered Guatemalan American woman reflects the importance of journalistic representation for Guatemalan American, Central American, and Central American–American populations. *Chickens* is set during some of the bloodiest years of the Guatemalan Civil War. During this time, "a popular president," Ronald Reagan, "sought to mobilize support for his policy by framing US military intervention in Central America as a response to a communist threat." But Reagan's policies lacked substantial public support "because of the existence and prevalence of an alternative frame. . , heavily promoted by a transnational social movement and transnational public diplomacy campaign by Central American revolutionaries" (Perla 163). This alternative frame was present in mainstream media outlets such as the *New York Times* and *ABC News*. Leveraging this perspective, the faith-based and human rights groups that worked alongside and in support of Central American peoples were particularly successful at preventing what many thought was the inevitable invasion of Nicaragua by US troops.[8] This history reflects Antonieta Mercado's observation about the importance of access to a public sphere, as she explains that "communicative participation in the public sphere" is linked to "the formation of social capital" (240). Social justice organizations used access to mass media to temper US intervention in the region, as significant and disastrous as that intervention was.[9]

Similarly, the binational status of Rogerio and Flor and the movement between the US and Guatemala of Moya underscore the sig-

---

8. The US military did of course play a large military and economic role in the counterrevolution that sought to overthrow the democratically elected Sandinista government; however, an all-out invasion of Nicaragua by US troops never occurred.

9. For an extensive discussion of US Latina/o cultural production in support of Central America and opposed to US intervention in the region in the 1980s, see Vigil's *War Echoes* (2014).

nificance of transnationalism in the lives of the text's characters. This transnationality is an important hallmark of Central American and Central American–American studies. Ana Patricia Rodríguez has proposed the trope of the "transisthmus" as a means through which to understand and study the Central American diaspora, arguing that the transisthmus captures the "constant discursive shifts, reconfigurations, and reassemblages in historical context" that marks Central American cultural production (104). To the cultural production on which Rodríguez focuses, we might add mass media as a technology that operates in the transisthmus that marks Central American peoples. While Rodríguez's trope proposes a way of situating Central America transnationally, Arturo Arias suggests that foregrounding indigeneity may similarly trouble national boundaries and contribute to much-needed knowledge on immigrant communities. Noting that "the Central American wave of immigrants to the US is far from ending," he laments that "there is still little work on immigrant indigeneities, despite the high percentage of Central American immigrants of indigenous origin" (99, 100). Indigenous migrant subjects bring a different set of issues to the forefront, seeing as they are both "more vulnerable to not only US sovereign power but also to its deployment by racialized others" and that racism and colonialism view indigenous peoples as "residual nonsubjects . . . abandoned by law . . . bereft of legal protections of citizenship" (100). The focus on an indigenous protagonist in the novel requires us to think beyond and through categories of national identity and to acknowledge the ways that certain transnational subjects such as Flor are not recognized as full citizens of any country. As an indigenous woman, Flor, the *"gringa chapina,"* is denied recognition of belonging in either the US or Guatemala.

Arias's invocation of the ongoing migration from Central America (especially Honduras, El Salvador, and Guatemala) to the US reminds us of the continuing salience of a transnational frame for understanding diasporic communities today. In addition, we must place gender and sexuality at the forefront of this framing. One of the reasons the post-2013 migrants referenced at the start of this chapter drew increased national attention was that they, more than previous groups, were composed largely of unaccompanied minors and women. Furthermore, girls and women face particular danger in their countries of origin as well as near-pervasive sexual assault on the migrant trail. In late 2018, a caravan of thousands of Central Americans, mostly Hondurans, were attacked as they attempted to cross into Mexico from Guatemala. That same year a caravan of LGBT migrants made its way across Mexico to the US–Mexico border, where one migrant, the transgender woman Roxana Hernández, died while in the custody of US Border Patrol. These events call attention to the particular dangers faced by women and LGBT peoples in their countries of origins, on the migrant trails, and in the countries where they seek asylum. As right-wing politicians and news outlets portray such people out of historical and political context and as dangerous threats, we must maintain a transnational and gendered perspective on Central American migration, taking local and national media to task for incomplete and narrow perspectives while appreciating the relationship between migration, media workers, and a transnational Latina/o public sphere.

As the characters in *Chickens* emphasize, a comprehensive understanding of past and present Central American diaspora requires that we look not only at migrants themselves and the conditions they flee but also at US policies and investments in the area. Furthermore, Central American–American issues in particular emphasize the necessity of making Latina/o Studies and approaches to a Latina/o public sphere soundly transnational. Not only does the movement of ideas, people, and information within migratory networks contribute to a transnational public sphere, but a dialogue between counterpublics "contributes to the diversity of voices and dialogue in the public sphere" (Mercado 253). This diversity, and attention to questions of gender, indigeneity, nationality, and class, is imperative for an understanding of the current US Latina/o public sphere, both those whose voices are included and those whose voices are excluded. Continuing in this vein, the following chapter continues an analysis of a transnational Latina/o public sphere but turns to photojournalism to explore more fully the mechanisms by which populations outside of the US are brought into or excluded from the Latina/o public sphere.

CHAPTER 4

# Photojournalism, Militarized Conflict, and the Boundaries of Latinidad in Graciela Limón and Ana Menéndez

IN MAY 2014 Subcomandante Insurgente Marcos, an enigmatic political and social figure who had long served as the spokesperson for the Zapatista Army of National Liberation (EZLN, or Zapatistas), declared that he "no longer exists" ("Mexico's"). While this shift marked internal reorganization within the Zapatistas, it also continued decades of press releases and communiqués from the spokesman about his own lack of importance. Marcos became a figure of fascination despite, or perhaps because of, his position as the voice of a movement who seemed to continually undermine his own stature. For example, Marcos often attributed ideas and lessons he had learned not to his own intellect or experiences but rather to Don Antonio, an indigenous man he befriended in the Lacandón jungle. (Whether Don Antonio exists/ed is a point of speculation.) Marcos's discourse was matched by his own comportment, in which he spoke under a pseudonym and only ever appeared wearing a black ski mask over his entire face. The ski mask, often accompanied by a pipe attached to Marcos's lips, was used by many Zapatista combatants; other members of the movement frequently covered the lower half of their face with red or red and black bandanas. In the 1998 documentary *Zapatista!* Marcos explains the use of the mask: "We will take off our masks when the governments of the world take off theirs," he says, referring to the fact that behind the "masks" of such governments are not the interests of citizens but those of corporations and global capital. Thus Marcos and the Zapatistas simultaneously sought attention from media to bring support to their cause, while also seeking to manipulate the press and coverage they received. Tactics such as mask, pseudonyms, and pointedly lower ranks (the non-indigenous Marcos is not a commander in the indigenous-led army, but a subcommander) illustrate the movement's understanding of, and attempt to intervene in, the complicated ways that revolutionary movements are covered and co-opted in an age of media conglomerates. That Marcos and the Zapatistas often refuse to be seen by the cameras that seek to cover their struggle indicates their understanding of the power of images as well as their dedication to intervene in how their movement is covered in the press.

Marcos and the Zapatistas intervened in how their revolution was covered visually and textually at a moment when the shape and scope of war coverage was undergoing drastic change. The increase and proliferation in military technology, including infrared sensors, night-vision goggles, and drones, has changed how citizens look at war. Nightly news reports that offer perspectives on bombings from the viewpoint of cockpits and soldiers on the ground allow viewers to see war from the perspective of combatants and to visually compare such violence with other kinds of violence enacted on screens, specifically the violence depicted in video games and movies.[1] This shift in how war "looks" brings with it the necessity of understanding how non-combatants "look at" war as well as examining the production, circulation, and impact of visual images of warfare and military intervention. We might ask: what kinds of images are circulated, by whom, where, and to what effect? Using Wendy Kozol's terminology, do the images of atrocities or human rights abuses reproduce colonialist logics—locating violence "over there," and reinforcing the abjection of non-Western subjects? Or might they have the potential to shift the consciousness of viewers and challenge hierarchies and policies? What kinds of images, and what kind of photographers, can intervene in discourses of nation,

---

1. This shared visuality of course also speaks to the shared technology between militaries and video game producers and the growth of the "military-entertainment complex." The US military uses video games to train soldiers, and civilian enthusiasm for military-inspired games such as *Call of Duty* remains strong.

self, and other in ways that advance, rather than exploit, assimilate, or sensationalize human rights worldwide?

This chapter considers these questions and how they are taken up within two contemporary Latina novels. *Erased Faces* (2001) and *The Last War* (2009) both focus on Latina photojournalists who live and work in, or on the edge of, war zones. The first novel takes place in Chiapas, Mexico, in the years leading up to and just after the Zapatista uprising in 1994. The second takes place on the eve of and just after the 2003 US invasion of Iraq, although the narrator remains in Istanbul, Turkey, throughout the narrative. Both of the female protagonists use their status as photojournalists to engage in the social and political world around them, places that bear the mark of US intervention. The novels narrate the protagonists' time in Mexico and Turkey, respectively, and consider how the experiences shape their own ideas of self in relationship to their "home" communities, specifically their families. Like *Chickens,* both novels engage with psychic explorations as much as political ones, and equal time is devoted to narrating characters' internal processing and scenes of war or violence. The texts, then, offer us an opportunity to analyze how these photojournalists align with or resist normative logics of Western spectatorship in their work. Do they, for example, figure the people and places in a state of otherness and abjection, necessitating foreign intervention? Or do they offer portraits that resist a Western gaze in favor of a more complicated, agentic one? That both narrators are young Latinas living outside the confines of the US allows us to consider their work and journeys in light of their race, nationality, gender, and sexual orientation. While both novels focus on photojournalists living and working within, or near, sites of military conflict, neither of the texts includes photographs. As readers, then, we are unable to analyze the images that the photographers, Adriana and Flash, produce. What we can do, however, is analyze the conditions that underlie their work. Following Judith Butler's exhortation to understand framing not as a passive device but as a structuring device, this chapter considers Adriana's and Flash's social, physical, and psychological locations to be part of the larger structuring device through which their photographs are framed. Butler explains: "The frame is always throwing something away, always keeping something out, always de-realizing and de-legitimating alternative versions of reality" (*Frames of War* xiii). Analyzing the characters' reactions to the world around them, and looking closely at how they and other characters discuss their photography, offers us an important perspective on the kinds of images they are producing and not producing.

Through a close reading of the novels' description of the protagonists' work, alongside analyses of their social, political, and psychological explorations, this chapter argues that the two women engage in disparate journeys. Limón's Adriana mines the depths of her own connections to the people and places she photographs to arrive at images that question a Western gaze and Western spectatorship. Her work among the Zapatistas, specifically her photographs, prompts a revisiting of childhood trauma such that her own subjectivity is brought to bear in her work. The result is pictures that, according to the subjects she photographs, offer accurate, or "true" portraits of the Zapatistas. Menéndez's Flash, however, refuses the personal interrogation that Adriana accepts. Although the narrator discusses aspects of her home and family life, she does not engage with this history in a substantive way. This lack of engagement is reflected in her work, which evidences a focus on surface images. Considering both protagonists in light of questions of ethical engagement, Orientalism, and the framing of war, we can see that Adriana produces ethical co-participant photography whereas Flash produces only spectatorship. The result of this analysis is an understanding of how contemporary Latina literature takes up questions of viewership, spectatorship, and agency within a context of militarized conflict, allowing us to appreciate how these issues are impacted by race, class, nationality, gender, and sexuality and how they may (or may not) extend the bounds of Latinidad.

This chapter begins with a discussion of photojournalism within the context of war. After briefly reviewing literature on war photography and its importance in the public sphere, I turn to an analysis of each text. Both novels are contextualized within their literary landscape as well as within their political context: specifically the ways in which the US has been involved in supporting the Mexican state in its low-intensity warfare against the Zapatistas, and how Turkey has figured in the US war on terror. Close readings of the discussion of the protagonists' journalism, relying on theoretical work from feminist media studies and Latina/o studies, explain how this work is figured in relation to their personal psychological explorations. After looking at the texts separately, the chapter considers a significant way in which the two works align—the visual overlap between the photographers and the indigenous inhabitants of the lands where they are working. This section reads the last pages of each novel in conjunction with each other to consider how the different orientations of Adriana and Flash as inward and outward, respectively, offer different approaches to a transnational Latina/o public. The chapter concludes by arguing that the different approaches to the people and conflicts in which they are working reflect the extent to which concerns with the Zapatistas and concerns with the Middle East have, or have not, been taken up within the Latina/o public sphere.

## WAR PHOTOGRAPHY, SOCIAL JUSTICE, AND THE PUBLIC SPHERE

For several centuries, photography has played an important role in the staging and reception of war. In the US, the aftermath of the American Civil War was heavily photographed, and these photographs shaped how the war has been remembered and understood (Apel x). For many in the US, the US war in Vietnam is synonymous with Nick Ut's photograph of Phan Thi Kim Phúc, running naked after being burned by napalm. For Robert Hariman and John Louis Lucaites, images such as this one, which are themselves traumatic, have likely contributed to the ways in which the American war in Vietnam has remained significant in a country whose media in other respects exhibits a "short-term attention span and near-total historical amnesia" (172). Iconic war images do more than just illustrate a particular story or narrative; they shape the script itself (172). In more recent years, images of the toppling of the statue of Saddam Hussein and US soldiers torturing Iraqi detainees at the Abu Ghraib prison have come to shape how the 2003 invasion and occupation of Iraq has been understood and represented. The fact that the toppling of Hussein's statute in Firdos Square in April 2003 was likely manipulated by US forces to suggest Iraqi civilian support for the US invasion—Robert Fisk called it "the most staged photo-opportunity since Iwo Jima"—underscores that participants in war are hyperaware of how their actions may be recorded and disseminated.

Of course, a photograph's meaning depends on how it is received and interpreted. In 2014 an image of hundreds of Central American children held in overcrowded detention centers was leaked by the alt-right website *Breitbart News* in an attempt to illustrate how President Barack Obama's policies had led to US border forces being "overrun." The image of young children in inhumane conditions, however, galvanized support for more resources for newly arrived migrants, many of them fleeing violence and gang warfare, as opposed to calling for the "border security" that *Breitbart* supported. For Hariman and Lucaites, who point out that prior to the picture of Phan Thi Kim Phúc, published in 1972, there were plenty of print and visual reports of the death and destruction in Vietnam, the achievement of "iconic" status for a photograph depends as much on the society that receives it as on the image itself. According to the authors, this picture activated public conscience because it contained "important features of moral life," namely "pain, fragmentation, modal relationships among strangers, betrayal, and trauma" (175). But the photograph also stimulated ideas of liberal individualism important in the US, specifically articulating the tension in public memory between "a liberal-individualist narrative of denial . . . and a mode of democratic dissent" (175). The image of a naked young girl running toward the viewer with arms outstretched reflects a violation of individual rights to physical safety and autonomy while activating gendered sympathy for victims of war. Again, the meaning of a photograph depends on the context—military, political, social, sexual—in which it is received. For Wendy Kozol, pictures of gendered suffering may not resist, but rather encourage, military intervention. Images of crowded train cars full of refugees from Kosova from 1999 invoked for many in the West the Nazi Holocaust and were articulated "within a Western framework that unquestioningly champions U.S. and NATO intervention" (37–39). Furthermore, photographs don't necessarily "achieve" what they can or should; Kozol points out that despite their wide circulation, the photographs of Abu Ghraib did not change US policy in Iraq (17). Judith Butler agrees that an image can't necessarily "free anyone from prison, or stop a bomb" but may "nevertheless provide the conditions for breaking out of the quotidian acceptance of war and for a more generalized horror and outrage that will support and impel calls for justice and an end to violence" (*Frames of War* 11). Thus we would do well to neither underestimate nor overestimate the potential impact of any image or set of images, and to remain attuned to questions of mediating and framing.

As the above history indicates, photography's relationship with social justice is a complicated one. Photojournalism specifically can easily straddle the line between exploitation and advocacy and may both challenge issues of privilege and reify hierarchies of power. That is to say, photography remains embedded in "a visual apparatus of power" built upon racial, sexual, and gender-based objectification as well as voyeurism and spectacle (Kozol 17). For Susan Sontag, photographers can be akin to both tourists and colonizers. As she explains: "The camera is a kind of passport that annihilates moral boundaries and social inhibitions, freeing the photographer from any responsibility toward the people photographed" (41). The camera may in fact facilitate this lack of responsibility; when capturing people, the photographer is not "intervening in their lives, only visiting them" (42). In this way, the photographer may become the "supertourist," a person present only for fleeting moments who "brings back" visual records of the people and lands they have visited (42). The idea of a tourist who "collects" or "brings back" ideas or objects gestures to the relationship between colonialist anthropology and photography. Indeed, early anthropologists used photography to fix native subjects in particular moments and discourses, including ones that sought to denote a racial type (Poole 165). War photography, for Sontag, is not free from this limitation, although it involves the combination of voyeurism and danger (39). However, neither the subjects of photographs nor their viewers are fixed in time. In fact, for Deborah Poole, while anthropological photographs illustrated the colonial gaze, they also illustrated the "instability of the photograph as ethnological evidence" (165). This instability creates the possibility for an "unsettling" that may be productive (160). Similarly, Kozol acknowledges that the ability of photojournalism to embody ethnocentrism does not discount the potential for it to "activate witnessing practices" that do not rely on appropriation (19). Acknowledging the inequities that war photography may reproduce, not the least of which is a Western gaze that situates violent people and processes "over there," Kozol nonetheless contends that "ethical spectatorship" may emerge "*through*, not despite, encounters with spectacles of violence" (17). While Kozol examines various uses of war photography that achieve ethical spectatorship, this chapter argues that *Erased Faces* adds to this discussion by illustrating how photojournalism, and a particular photojournalist, works to enact ethical spectatorship or, rather, solidarity through photography.

Despite, or perhaps because of, their complicated situation within larger social, political, and cultural milieux, photographs, particularly iconic ones, remain an important form of mediating relations between strangers in the public sphere. It is precisely because a public is a relation between strangers that publics are "in need of images" (Hariman and Lucaites 198). The photo of Phan Thi Kim Phúc "provides figural embodiment of the concepts of political innocence, human rights, third world vulnerability and victimage," while those discussed by Kozol may embody maternal care, vulnerability, and dangers posed to religious and ethnic diversity (199). That the individuals in the photographs are strangers in fact helps to place them within the larger public; we do not know them, just as we do not know other members of the public sphere (199). In this way, photos and their circulation become an aspect of public life—a document to be contested, discussed, criticized—as well as a means for "remaking the public world." The many different interpretations/meanings of one image suggests that photographs offer up the opportunity for in fact making different kinds of public worlds (207). Likewise, Butler encourages us to consider the ways in which the public sphere is "constituted by the visual technologies of war" (*Frames of War* xii). Within the context of this chapter, we can see that the different kinds of photographs taken by the narrators engender different kinds of publics. Specifically, Adriana's photographs, and the way in which she harnesses her own identity and experiences to frame them, are images that may transform the Latina/o public sphere, expanding it to include indigenous Mexicans and the Zapatistas. Flash's photographs, on the other hand, are produced via a deliberate avoidance of engagement with her own position and privilege and thus lack the potential to bring the people and places that she captures into the relation among strangers that is the US Latina/o public.

## ERASED FACES

Graciela Limón's *Erased Faces* focuses on a young Afro-Latina protagonist, Adriana Mora. As a child, Adriana witnessed and survived the terrifying murder-suicide of her parents; her mother shot her father and then herself. Adriana then spent time with a foster family, where she experienced racist mistreatment and abuse. She eventually set off on her own, and her work as a photojournalist brought her to Chiapas, Mexico, prior to the 1994 uprising. In Chiapas she is asked to join the community of insurgent indigenous people and to photograph their cause for wider dissemination. Narratively, her story is interspersed with those of two other protagonists—the Zapatistas Orlando Flores and Juana Galván. Adriana is also deeply moved by dreams in which she witnesses the mistreatment of indigenous peoples by the conquering Spaniards. These dreams suggest a transhistorical connection between Adriana and an indigenous woman, solidifying her belonging among the Zapatistas. She participates in the January 1, 1994, uprising alongside her lover, the Zapatista combatant Juana Galván. The timing of the uprising, the day that NAFTA went into effect, marked the Zapatistas' keen understanding of the relationship between neoliberal economic policies and the social and political realities of Mexico's indigenous communities. Shortly after taking control of several towns in Chiapas, the Zapatistas retreated and have at several points in the last two decades attempted to negotiate with the Mexican government. Limón's novel interweaves some of this history, although the work concentrates on the organizing efforts of several fictional characters prior to the 1994 uprising. Each of the principal characters comes to the rebellion from different circumstances, highlighting the heterogeneous identities and political viewpoints that characterize the Zapatistas and suggesting that "social movements are made up of individuals with diverse motivations" (López-Calvo 70). Their individual circumstances notwithstanding, Limón's novel scripts the Zapatista movement as a place where characters come to understand and act upon their personal and political subordination while unequivocally pointing to the role of colonialism in the establishment and perpetuation of oppressive systems. After the uprising, Adriana and Juana remain in the area, but Juana is murdered in the Acteal massacre in 1997. Adriana then returns to the US.

## US MILITARY INVOLVEMENT, THE ZAPATISTAS, AND SELF-REFLECTION

Although Adriana is a fictional character, she alludes to a larger context of US military and civilian involvement with the Zapatista conflict.

While the conflict between the EZLN and the Mexican government was a domestic/internal one, the US played an important role in bolstering the Mexican government's strength. In 1995 President Bill Clinton arranged for a multibillion-dollar credit bailout to Mexico to help the nation stabilize after billions of dollars had fled the country following the January 1994 uprising (Fineman). The bailout served to strengthen the Mexican government's position vis-à-vis the Zapatista rebellion, and in the next month the Zedillo government launched an offensive against the Zapatista communities, which included torture and rape (Davison; *Zapatista!*). Adriana's participation in the Zapatista uprising then reflects US involvement in the conflict while also gesturing to the ways in which the rebellion inspired and influenced US Latina/os.

Much of the novel is devoted to Adriana's explorations of her past trauma as a way to understand herself and her role in the Zapatista community. Her Tzeltal lover, Juana, suffers abuse at the hands of a patriarchal community that sells women for the price of a donkey and that fails to recognize marital rape. In the vocabulary of the novel, Juana and Adriana are connected via their experiences of suffering. When Juana asks Adriana to join the movement, Adriana protests "I am not one of your people," but Juana assures her that "soon you will be" and then adds "besides, you, too, have suffered, haven't you?" (38). Adriana's time with the Zapatistas, coupled with her dreams and role as a photographer, proves integral to her understanding of her own suffering and integration into Juana's life and the Zapatista movement. Tim Libretti explains that the novel suggests that "the suffering and loss [Adriana] endures in her individual life are conditioned by larger historical processes of colonization and labor exploitation" (99). For Limón, Libretti argues, "individual psychotherapeutic disalienation requires revolutionary social transformation" and "revolutionary social transformation . . . requires a psychotherapeutic decolonization" (101). Libretti's reading explains the role that Adriana's dreams play in her self-discovery and *concientización*; the young woman's connections to indigenous women living during the Conquest spurs a confrontation with her own traumatic past that culminates in her understanding and acknowledgment of her personal and political connections to the Zapatista rebellion. More than a merely linear process whereby personal change prompts social and political commitment, the transformations modeled in the novel stress that psychic and political change are mutually constitutive. While Libretti's analysis explains the connections between Adriana's personal and political change, this chapter focuses on a key *mechanism* in that change, her photography. Photography facilitates access to her past and past lives, explorations that lead her to understand her relationship to the Zapatista rebellion. But her political consciousness also informs her explorations into her past, as it is only after living with the Zapatistas that she confronts her mother. This change is both spurred by and evidenced in her photography, which grows more sophisticated throughout the novel. When Adriana returns to the US at the conclusion of the novel, she demonstrates that the psychic and political transformations she has undergone remain with her as she continues her work as a photographer in the US.

Throughout the text, mirrors signify the splitting of Adriana's subjectivity and help to illustrate the relationship between photographic imagery and her psychological growth. Early in the story, Adriana awakes from an intense dream in which she is among an indigenous group of people fleeing from invaders during the Conquest. Focusing on the woman at the center of her dream, she exclaims out loud, "She didn't look like me!" (3). The character then takes a small mirror off her wall and goes outside to examine herself in the moonlight. As she runs her fingers along her body, she remembers incidents from her childhood, specifically abuse she suffered that resulted in a scar on her forearm. Running through memories that span from childhood to adulthood, filling readers in on significant times in her life, Adriana is overcome: "a nagging sense of loss forced Adriana to shut her eyes . . . ever since she could remember, she had felt lost, separated, alone" (4). Looking into the mirror forces Adriana to confront the separation from the indigenous women with whom she is connected. But the loss that she suffers is multiplied, as it recalls both the loss of both her parents and the alienation she felt as a child. Adriana's recollections are prompted by visual cues, linking her photographs to earlier experiences when she was forced to recognize her difference from those around her.

Some time later, Adriana recalls an incident from her youth that was also focused on mirrors. She remembers contemplating her body in the bathroom of her foster family's home. There she considers her Afro-Latina features: "skin the color of coffee with cream . . . a broad forehead, full, wide lips . . . tight [curly hair]" and "almond-shaped" eyes "flecked with green" (46). Here Adriana's mirrored reflection specifically notes the separation, racially, from those around her, a Latino family with mestizo features. She also feels the first tinglings of sexual desire. Her distant memory joins with her recent dreams when the door of the bathroom breaks open and "something [comes] at her, forcing her to run" (47). She awakes, drenched in sweat, in the arms of Juana. In this instance, Adriana's memory of seeing herself in a mirror becomes incorporated into a dream that aligns with recent dreams she has been having. These dreams speak to Adriana's belonging with the inhabitants in Chiapas as she seeks to recover that which she and they have lost.

Mirrors provoke a memory of earlier times in Adriana's life and align with photographs within the novel. That is, the moment in which Adriana looks into a mirror and is reminded of her childhood and adolescence is paralleled at later points in the narrative. At these later points, however, what prompts the retreat into memory is not a mirror but rather a photograph. One day, she finds herself fixated on a young mother nursing a baby. She is particularly struck by the woman's age: "*Chispas!* The girl can't be more than thirteen!" (30). Adriana's photograph is a popular trope of war photography; the nursing baby contributes to a picture of idealized femininity (Kozol 45). This easily recognizable image calls out to viewers to acknowledge a shared humanity as viewers, and the subject of the photograph may coalesce around shared values—a respect for life, and so forth (45). The recognition of shared humanity, however, is built on "fictive unity" that is only an "empty" quality (Sontag 110–11).[2] Moreover, while images of mothers and children may gesture to a universal humanity, they have often been militarized in specific ways. For example, images of gun-toting, nursing mothers have been widely disseminated by various nationalistic and revolutionary movements to align motherhood with a nation that needs protecting or is in revolt. Pictures of feminine vulnerability may also justify protection in the form of US or Western military intervention (Kozol 45). For Adriana, the image of the mother and child does in fact call to mind motherhood more largely. But rather than meditate

---

2. "When Cartier-Bresson goes to China," Sontag writes, "he shows that there are people in China, and that they are Chinese" (111).

on questions of femininity or vulnerability, Adriana considers her own maternal relationships. After taking a few shots of the young mother and child, Adriana sits down and begins "jotting down her impressions . . . including not only the details of her subjects, but her own feelings as well" (31). Taking pictures of and thinking about the mother and child pushes Adriana into a complex set of emotions about her own childhood, including "envy because she was not the child sheltered in those arms, sadness at having been robbed of love, [and] fierce desire to discover the reason for her mother having murdered her father" (30). Suddenly, Adriana is mentally transported to her childhood in Los Angeles, and readers are taken with her as the narrative fills in the story of Adriana's adolescence. While Adriana's stance as a photographer at first positions her as distant from her subject—her surprise at the young age of the mother highlights her outsider status—her meditations on her subjects facilitate her own exploration into her past. While her guide/mentor Chan K'in tells her that dreams are mirrors "in which we can see our past lives" (14), the narrative suggests that photographs also function in this manner.

For Adriana, photographs/still images provoke a feeling of desire and loss, specifically the loss of her mother. But Adriana is on a dual journey to understand/recover what she has lost (her mother, her indigenous past) and what she *will have* lost. By the time the novel concludes, Adriana has lost her lover Juana, who has been killed by a homophobic and racist Mexican soldier. The mirror scenes in the novel drive home the fact that Adriana is dealing with transhistorical loss (indigenous identity and sovereignty) that plays out in the contemporary moment via her relationship with Juana and the Zapatistas. While Adriana's photographs allow her to explore her past, they also have clear consequences. Specifically, the novel suggests not only that her photographs prompt earlier memories but that these earlier memories allow her to produce better, truer photographs. Here, Adriana's psychological journey allows her to become an ethical co-participant, based on Wendy Kozol's discussion of "ethical spectatorship."

Adriana's photography continues to prompt her psychic explorations. Later in the narrative, when she has joined the Zapatistas and is documenting their organizing efforts, she is again thrown into a memory of her past. This time, Adriana has a vivid dream in which she is photographing the drafting of a declaration. Suddenly government forces attack the camp and Adriana finds herself taking pictures of a battle, until she herself is struck by a bullet. As she loses consciousness, she meets her mother and is able to ask her why she [the mother] murdered her father and killed herself (197). Adriana expresses her sense of abandonment; just before waking from her dream, she asks her mother "What about me?" (197). Here, photography takes place within a dream that facilitates a necessary conversation between Adriana and her mother. In her dream, photography places her in danger and leads to her meeting with her mother on her deathbed. Like the previous instance in which Adriana's pictures prompt her to remember her childhood, this instance affirms the relationship between Adriana's photography and her return to her past.

These two scenes figure photography as a kind of reflective mirror; Adriana looks into a camera lens only to find herself looking into her own psyche. An indigenous friend informs Adriana that dreams are like mirrors. In a conversation with the elderly Chan K'in, Adriana is told, "a dream, though imperfect, is a mirror in which we see our own past lives" (14). When Adriana's photography prompts her vision into her past, the narrative suggests that photography functions similarly to dreams—as an imperfect mirror into a character's past. In this equation, the novel scripts a positive, productive relationship between indigenous and Western epistemologies. Adriana's photography functions not as a means to objectify the indigenous people but rather as a way for her to explore her own experiences and her connection to the Zapatistas.

Adriana's intellectual and ethical growth is indexed in the narrative by the quality of her photographs. Juana directly challenges Adriana on this point and suggests that for the photographer to contribute actively to the revolution, she must learn how to create pictures that accurately reflect the situation, a learning that comes about through direct experience. In their first encounter, Juana challenges Adriana's assumption that she is able to capture "truth" in her pictures. "Why do you take pictures of our women, what is it that you are looking for?" (37). Here Juana echoes one of photography's imperatives, that of truth-telling, an imperative that comes from a scientific legacy and one that is predicated on a notion of value-free truth (Sontag 86). While Juana uses the word *truth,* she also pushes back against ideas of a freestanding value because she embeds truth within the particularities of the female Zapatistas. Her words claim collective possession of the women in the community and signal Adriana's outsider status. Adriana replies, naively, that what she hopes to find is "the truth." Juana calls Adriana's pictures "empty" and explains:

> When you take the face of a woman with your camera, and her expression reflects misery, it is not enough to have that image on paper only. You must also capture her spirit, and the reasons for its anguish. (37)

Rather than feeling chastised, Adriana feels that Juana understands perfectly what she wants but cannot at that moment accomplish with her photography. Juana then offers Adriana the chance to join the Zapatistas as a photographer. Seeming to reverse her earlier articulation of Adriana's distance from the community, she insists that the people have already accepted Adriana and that the Zapatistas' actions need to be chronicled in writing and pictures "for all the world to see" (39). Seeking to understand more fully the people she has been filming, Adriana agrees.

Once Adriana joins the Zapatista rebellion and explores her own past and the current realities of the indigenous struggles, her photography does indeed begin to reflect truth. After the 1994 uprising, Adriana stays in Chiapas and continues to organize with Juana. Reflecting the use of first-world technologies and labors in the service of the third world (Olguín 163), the two women are able to live off the sales of Adriana's work.

> [Adriana] knew that with her photography she had a special way to be part of the struggle. Hers was a unique way of alerting the world to the anguish that was tormenting Chiapas. She had no doubt that the portraits she brought forth were a graphic and undeniable testimony of truth . . . she wired and mailed her work from San Cristóbal de las Casas to publishers in New York, Houston, Chicago and Los Angeles . . . all of which resulted in stipends on which she and Juana were able to live. (239)

After living within the Zapatista communities and taking part in the struggles of the people, Adriana is able to capture "truth." While Adriana's reliance on the descriptor "truth" bears scrutiny, passages such as the one above offer an argument for the ability of photography to engage in testimony and specifically to reflect trauma. Noting the ways in which postcolonial studies and contemporary trauma have coalesced in contemporary criticism, Katherine Baxter explains how the representation of trauma in literature has been unable to move beyond "event-based" models to account for ongoing trauma such as living under apartheid or prolonged experiences of domestic violence or poverty (20). She writes: "Psychoanalysis and European trauma literature have prescribed acceptable modes of presenting trauma within literary and therapeutic frameworks [that] potentially [close] off other modes of presenting trauma" (19). Considering the representation of trauma in media journalism, on the other hand, may offer "other modes." Baxter suggests that photographic representations of trauma may create in viewers what Dominic LaCapra terms "empathic unsettlement," a condition in which the subject's realization of her own alienation from the traumatic event mimics the traumatized, alienated subject in the photograph (25). The result is a "failure of empathy" wherein the reader (or viewer) "is excluded and alienated from the pathos of the subject" (25). Adriana's early photographs of the young mother illustrate her empathic unsettlement and highlight her distance from her subjects. However, these encounters force Adriana to explore her own past via dreams and memories in a way that alters her relationship with the Zapatistas. Thus, the narrative demonstrates Adriana's empathy as well as exotopy, Bakhtin's term for the process by which a reader imagines herself in the position of another but then importantly returns to her original position, with a new consideration of that position (Nance 2006b 12). This "round-trip journey," as Kimberly A. Nance calls it, is evident in the eventual creation of "true" photographs by the protagonist as well as in her physical return to the US at the conclusion of the novel (Nance 2006a 62). When Adriana and others claim her photographs as "truth," they affirm the ability for photographs produced in tandem with psychic and political exploration, and with empathy and exotopy, to represent trauma such as war in productive ways.

In her stance as a photographer, Adriana subverts the male gaze and disrupts the binary of male = active / female = passive. Moreover, the narrative actively breaks the reader's identification with the spectator by quickly making Adriana not simply a lens through which to view the indigenous women but a character to be scrutinized as well. That Adriana's photography is integral in this shift reflects the narrative's interruption of the relationship between gender and visual technology in which woman functions only as the object of the spectator/male gaze (Mulvey). Adriana does not simply become the object of her own gaze; turning her lens inward, as it were, produces not a static image but a psychic terrain to be explored. As Libretti explains, Adriana's psychic healing is necessary for her to be able to connect to the indigenous movement (100). However, her psychic healing is *also* necessary for her to mature as a photographer. Here photography becomes both an instigator of, and a beneficiary of, Adriana's self-exploration. Adriana's use of visual technology and the ways in which both she and her photography transform throughout the narrative deconstruct the male gaze while nonetheless gesturing to the political and psychic possibilities inherent in the camera's lens.

*Erased Faces* presents a nuanced perspective on the relationship between photography, knowledge, identity, representation, and solidarity. Adriana's photography, rather than creating still images through which she presents static, exotic pictures of "others," spurs her to explore her own past. The novel presents photography as both the means to and the product of self-exploration. Photography prompts Adriana's return to and reckoning with her past, a step necessary to her creation of accurate representations of the people whose struggle she is documenting. In a decidedly anti-imperialist move, the novel suggests that knowledge of the other begins with knowledge of the self.

As the narrative draws to a close, the novel cements Adriana's role as a witness-in-solidarity, rather than an appropriator of others' experiences and identities, by having her return to the US to continue her work. After Juana's death at Acteal, Adriana places a photograph of the two of them on her lover's dead body and then makes her way back to the US. When she goes through customs, she declares to the agent "I'm a photographer" (257). Remaining a photographer in the US, Adriana illustrates her commitment to contributing to a global struggle from her particular position and assures readers of the ability of her work and experience in Chiapas to transform both herself and the US. By having Adriana return to her life in Los Angeles in order to participate productively in the revolution, the narrative illustrates how the Zapatistas "solicit information from the First World for the benefit of the Third" (Olguín 163). Bringing her work with her to the US, Adriana moves toward transforming a US Latina/o community. She literally brings Zapatista concerns and methodologies to the US nation-state. In this way, her character answers the Zapatistas's "*doble llamada*," or double call: for people in solidarity with their cause to look for ways to resist multinational power, racism, and injustice in their own communities. Adriana's work as a photojournalist has transformed herself and has the potential to transform the US Latina/o public.

## THE LAST WAR

Ana Menéndez's *The Last War* was published nearly a decade after *Erased Faces*, in 2009. The novel is Menéndez's second, following *Loving Che* (2003); however, the author is best known for her debut collection of short stories, *In Cuba I Was a German Shepherd* (2001). Most recently, she has published a second collection of short stories, *Adiós, Happy Homeland!* (2011). Menéndez has also worked as a prize-winning journalist for the *Miami Herald*. Born in LA to Cuban exile parents, she currently splits her time between Miami and the Netherlands.

*The Last War* focuses on a homodiegetic narrator, Margarita Anastasia Morales, known throughout the narrative by her nickname, Flash. Flash is the daughter of Dominican immigrants to the US and is a freelance photographer. She is frequently hired by the newspaper for which her husband, Brando, reports, and in the book the two have moved to Istanbul just before the first anniversary of September 11, 2001. She tells readers that "most Americans may not have realized that war with Iraq was inevitable by then, but we did" (7). Here Flash stresses that she is not ignorant of international politics, but rather that she is more attuned than most. This makes the lack of political reflection in her narrative, discussed later, all the more stark. In Istanbul Flash and Brando have an apartment, driver, and house cleaner, all paid for by Brando's employer.

The following spring, in 2003, Brando leaves to cover the war in Iraq, and when the novel opens, two months have passed since Flash has seen her husband. Flash explains, "I remained in Istanbul, telling friends I was waiting for my accreditation to come through. This wasn't really a lie: though I shot almost exclusively for Brando's paper now, I was still considered a freelancer and, of course, had to arrange everything for myself. But the deeper truth, of which I was only dimly aware, was that something essential had begun to give way in my marriage" (1–2). She goes on to suggest that the giving-way in their marriage has been somehow inevitable: "I understood that the disillusion we had so long been running from had finally come for us" (2). Flash's prediction soon comes true, and about twenty pages into the novel, she receives a letter informing her of Brando's infidelity. The letter is signed "mira," but Flash doesn't know anyone of that name, although she notes that it means "look" in Spanish.

She spends the remainder of the novel ruminating on her marriage, growing angry and resentful with her husband but wanting to wait to see him in person to confront him. In the meantime, she takes small assignments around Istanbul and Turkey and spends time with an old friend, Alexandra, another expat who works for Voice of America. A second significant portion of the narrative is devoted to Flash recalling several weeks of traveling in Afghanistan with Alexandra and Brando. Before she has the chance to confront Brando, he is killed by a roadside bomb in Iraq. At this point several months have passed, so the bulk of the storyline runs from the spring of 2003 through October of that year, when Brando is killed. These juxtapositions, Flash and Brando's crumbling marriage set against US imperialism and occupation, make the novel one that combines "war fiction with the domestic novel" (Kollin 132). For Susan Kollin, the text "locates the break-up of the marriage against the backdrop of two imperial powers featured in different stages of their decline" (132). Indeed, it is impossible to not understand the domestic and military catastrophes as linked. The last few chapters tell of what Flash did after Brando's death, including a year spent working for a newspaper in her hometown of Miami and a chance meeting with Alexandra in an airport in which the latter insists Brando was never unfaithful to her. At the end of the novel, Flash remains a war photographer, off to work in Delhi.

The novel mentions the narrator's given name only once; she is referred to by herself and friends as Flash, a nod to her tendency to always use a flash in her pictures. She explains:

> The other photographers in Kashmir had so baptized me for my inexperienced use of the 285. They didn't know I'd had one disastrous

shoot where, in haste and fear, I'd miscalculated apertures, and every picture was dark soup. After that, I just stuck the flash on everything. The garish shadows became a kind of signature—one of the ways that error, even the banal kind, marks us forever. (19)

What is remarkable about this passage is Flash's *lack* of engagement with the political situation in which she was working. The description is replete with language well suited to a war zone: disaster, haste, fear, miscalculations, darkness, and errors that "mark us forever." And yet these words and phrases are not used to describe Kashmir, an area in South Asia that has been besieged by conflict since the partition of India and Pakistan in 1947. Given the setting of Flash's shoot, the use of this language to describe her mistakes as a photographer as opposed to the conflict in Kashmir suggests that Flash is not simply ignoring what is going on in the areas in which she is working; she is actively *writing over* the situation with her own experiences. According to Kollin, passages such as this portray Flash as an unsympathetic narrator. As the critic notes, Flash repeatedly refers to herself as a "victim" of Brando's infidelity. The facile adoption of this identity while working on the margins of an imperial invasion and enjoying the benefits of US citizenship makes the text a commentary on "national amnesia and uncritical American worldliness" (148). Although Kollin's reading of the text is accurate, we may also question how Flash's occupation influences or is influenced by lack of self-reflection as well as the relationship between her attitude and Latinidad specifically. The aforementioned description of Kashmir is a good introduction to how Flash places herself and her work in relationship to the regions in which she is working. She doesn't simply ignore the larger political-military context, and the role of colonialism and imperialism, but she uses these assignments and locations as the setting for her own personal drama. Unlike Adriana, whose experiences in Chiapas prompt her to reflect on and engage in her own past, Flash fails to engage in self-reflection or self-scrutiny, simply mapping onto and writing over the local contexts in which she is working with her own uncritical ideas about herself. Thus, in a text about a character whose profession relies on her ability to *see,* and which has a central plot point that encourages her to look (*mira*), Flash's nickname is apt in that she overexposes her presence and does not allow other local contexts to be seen. For Kollin, the novel's illustration of the "domestic as a sphere of power" serves to "critique [ideas of] bounded identity as well as myths of national innocence that suggest 9/11 was somehow a unique or exceptional experience . . . the novel shows that the domestic is already a politicized zone" (135). While it is true that the text breaks down the supposed separation between domestic and public spheres of power, we might also explore how the work rethinks the space of the Latina/o public. Here we may focus, as in *Erased Faces,* on Flash's status as a photographer and on her location within a militarized neoliberal site. Thus, in *The Last War,* Flash's photography eschews the process that Adriana undertakes: engaging in personal and political context and histories to find a way to occupy a position of solidarity. Instead, Flash's work reflects what Wendy Kozol terms neoliberal spectatorship, engaging in exploitative work that produces little reflection or politics. The result is in fact a re-bounding of the Latina/o public sphere, and the failure specifically to integrate concerns with intervention in the Middle East into the Latina/o public sphere.

## THE WAR ON TERROR, FEMINIST ORIENTALISM, AND SURFACE IMAGERY

Flash is not working within the same context of low-intensity warfare and revolution as Adriana, but she is living and working within a militarized space. Turkey has and continues to play an important role in the US so-called war on terror waged against Middle East nations, including Afghanistan and Iraq. Although Turkey did not allow the US the use of its bases or the stationing of US troops, the nation did form part of what George W. Bush called the "coalition of the willing," or nations that supported the 2003 invasion of Iraq. The title of the novel, while certainly evoking the conflict at the heart of Flash and Brando's marriage, also explicitly refers to accounts of the US war on terror in its allusion to Dexter Filkins's *The Forever War.* Filkins published his nonfiction account of working in and reporting on Afghanistan and Pakistan in 2008, just after the conclusion of his marriage to Menéndez. The two journalists met at the *Miami Herald* in the early 1990s and married in 1995. As Filkins's career as a war journalist took off, Menéndez attempted to adjust her life around his, much as Flash does with Brando. Menéndez moved with Filkins to LA, then to India, and then to Istanbul, where he was stationed as the *New York Times* bureau chief. *The Forever War* covers the years from 1998, when Filkins was in Kabul, through September 11, 2001 (when he was in New York City), to the US invasion of Iraq in 2003. The last section of the book includes Filkins returning to Iraq to report on the 2004 elections. In the acknowledgments at the end of the book, the author notes that while working on the book he "lost the person [he] cared for most" (Filkins). The two divorced in 2005. Despite the fact that Menéndez's novel hews closely to the dissolution of her marriage, the fictional representation does not engage in "literary payback" (Bahadur). In fact, Menéndez, like Flash, received a letter alleging Filkins of infidelity. The letter arrived as Menéndez was working on the book, and although it altered the novel, it didn't fundamentally change the work's focus on the "macabre merry-go-round of reporters who have whirled in and out of Iraq" (Bahadur, n. pag.). Rather than vilify Filkins, as the plot would allow her to, Menéndez includes in the narrative the key scene in which Flash is told that Brando was "loyal" to her (221). The author likewise acknowledges her ex-husband: "And to Dexter Filkins, who showed me the whole world, my everlasting gratitude and affection" (unnumbered page). The title *The Last War* thus approaches war on several levels, placing the conflict in Flash and Brando's (Menéndez and Filkins's) marriage within the larger context of US militarism and the role that Turkey has played politically in recent/ongoing US intervention in the Middle East.

Whereas Adriana's work in Chiapas encourages her to look deeply at both her own life and the lives of the Zapatistas, Flash's work is marked by its surfaces. Throughout the text, Flash is interested only in the surface of things, and this is reflected in how she approaches the work she undertakes while in Turkey. Assignments allow her to justify to her husband that she cannot join him in Iraq because she is working (14). However, she isn't particularly interested in the work. For example, she is hired by a magazine to shoot some pictures of Ottoman tombs. Justifying taking the job as opposed to joining Brando in Iraq, she notes that the pay was good and that the "subject intrigued [her]" (13). However, when she arrives at the site, she quickly loses interest; she finds the site ugly and difficult to photograph because of its size. She does take some pictures and then reads the inscription on a tomb, which exalts the strength of a sultan (14–15). She dismisses the inscription as nothing more than words extolling an "ancient blowhard" (15). Flash's behavior at the site—not bothering to read the inscriptions on the tombs before taking her pictures—evidences a lack of engagement and interest in the work. This is contrary to her own stated interest in the assignment and also notable because this section of the novel comes after she has already received the letter alleging Brando's infidelity. Despite the letter's admonition to *look* (mira), Flash refuses to look deeply at anything around her. Rather, she remains concerned with only the superficial aspects of the city. While it's possible that she eschews deep scrutiny of the city around her in order to facilitate an introspective journey into her own history and marriage, the text doesn't support this idea. By the end of the novel, readers still know very little about Flash and her marriage to Brando, and the question of his fidelity remains ultimately unsolved. Thus, Flash's lack of engagement with the landscape around her, her refusal to learn more about the city and its context, is mirrored by her approach to her own life.

Subsequent sections of the book solidify Flash's interest in surface elements, and she links an eschewal of emotional engagement with fleeting images. Discussing her approach to her work, she explains that in her childhood "feeling became an expression on some foreign face, a frame soon to be forgotten or replaced by another greater joy or suffering" (21). Here emotional depth is related to fleeting expressions and discussed specifically in relation to photography, a "frame soon to be forgotten." She equates feelings with something inscrutable, a "foreign face," and a frame that can be quickly changed, or forgotten. She links photography with feeling and displays her desire to maintain a surface engagement with both. Flash's maintenance of distance between herself and her subjects reflects a common attribute of "photographic seeing" in which she looks at everything around her as a potential photograph, thus estranging herself from the world around her (Sontag 97).

Flash's approach to the city and country around her evidence a clear Orientalist attitude. Edward Said writes that Orientalism is "a *distribution* of geopolitical awareness into aesthetic, scholarly, economic, sociological, historical and philological texts" (12; emphasis original). This awareness is of course based on the idea that the world can be divided into two uneven halves: the Orient and the Occident. And while this discourse has clear relationships to political, military, and cultural hierarchies, Said insists, following Foucault, that Orientalism lacks a "direct, corresponding relationship with political power in the raw" but rather "is produced and exists in an uneven exchange with various kinds of power" (12). The relationship between Orientalism and cultural power as well as the lack of a direct link between discourse and political power is what makes Flash's embeddedness in Orientalism possible. As a photographer she is involved in aesthetic judgments about the value of Turkey's art and culture, a judgment she evidences through her dismissal of the landscape around her. And the uneven exchanges of powers that produce and maintain Orientalism allow Flash, herself a marginalized US citizen because of her ethnicity and gender, to nevertheless participate in cultural work that fails to question these hierarchies of taste and value.

The geographical and temporal setting of the novel, Afghanistan and Turkey after 9/11, invoke new inflections of Orientalism—ones in which Western feminism came to play an important part. Roksana Bahramitash explains how the condition of women in Muslim and Middle Eastern societies was broached by British and French colonial powers to justify domination and "civilizing missions," a history that Frantz Fanon also discussed (Bahramitash 224; Fanon 42). White women benefited culturally and rhetorically (and sometimes materially) by comparing their own situation with that of their oppressed sisters, whereas reform movements such as that of Turkey's Kemal Atatürk were often modeled on Western notions of freedom and liberation. In the contemporary moment, white feminism often continues to put forth an idea of the Muslim or Middle Eastern woman as part of what Chandra Mohanty calls the monolithic category of the "Third World woman." While depictions of Muslim and Middle Eastern women in need of saving were existent in US popular culture for many years, after 9/11 cultural production in this vein boomed (Bahramitash 227). The condition of Afghani and Iraqi women in particular became militarized as their "rights" were touted as justification for US intervention and occupation (Enloe). However, Bahramitash explains that while leaders such as George W. Bush and Laura Bush discussed bringing democracy to Middle Eastern women, the most effective propagandists for these ideas are not politicians but rather "'independent,' self-proclaimed feminists whose personal experiences with the situation of women under Islam impart an aura of authenticity to their portrayals of the primitive and misogynist nature of the religion" (227). This accounts for the problematic popularity of texts such as *Reading Lolita in Tehran*, by Azar Nafisi, and *Nine Parts of Desire*, by Geraldine Brooks.

In *The Last War*, Flash never describes herself as a feminist, although she exhibits the kind of feminist Orientalism that Bahramitash describes in her reaction to the world around her.³ In a notable scene in the novel, she beats a young Afghani boy whom she has discovered torturing a baby gecko. She blames her outburst on the country: "I shouted back in English about the gecko and all you sick bastards in this godforsaken shit country" and tells Brando that she wants to leave because "I don't understand anything, everything is disorder" (90–91). Later Flash insists that the beating wasn't about teaching the boy a lesson but was rather a part of her falling into a "preordained" order, and that her actions contradict her belief that "we knew enough to be better than we were" (122). Flash's assessment of the incident exhibits her understanding, and shame, that she has been scripted into actions resembling those on the side of "imperial rule and corrupted power instead of on the side of benevolent aid and democracy" (Kollin 141). But she also presents a false dichotomy that undergirds Orientalism and feminist Orientalism; constructions of "the Orient" as primitive and backward justify not only "benevolent aid" but also despotic rule. The characters' othering of Afghani people within a context of US imperialism reflects the relationship between white supremacy, US ethnonationalism, war, and Orientalism best captured by Andrea Smith's conception of Orientalism/war as one of the three pillars of white supremacy. Discussing how Chicana/os may be positioned in relation to these three pillars (which include slavery/capitalism and colonization/genocide), Lee Bebout suggests that Chicana/os may have been positioned in all three and lauds the schema for its focus on the "*tactics* of white supremacy" (12). With regard to the third pillar, Orientalism/war, Bebout correctly points out that "Romantic depictions of Mexico

---

3. Kollin discusses Flash's friend Alexandra as also exhibiting a Western feminist Orientalism. Alexandra describes herself as a "Great White Fixer," and her sexual dalliance with an Afghani handler leads the critic to describe her as possessing an agency that is "less liberating and radical than it is post-feminist," while her affair "connects her to a long history of sex tourists from the West—male and female alike—whose intimate desires take them on imperial treks across the globe" (142).

and a legacy of nativist discourse have combined to depict Mexico as a prosthetic frontier and Chicanas/os as perpetually foreign" (13). However, this history (and present) has not prevented Chicana/os and other Latina/os from robust participation in US wars and military interventions; nor has it, as Flash illustrates, prevented Chicana/os and Latina/os from uncritically adopting ideological complicity with the place of war and Orientalism in white supremacy. Finally, that Flash beats a young male orphan suggests the gendered dimensions of her actions—as a Western woman she feels entitled to discipline a child. That she blames Afghanistan for her actions illustrates both her refusal to take responsibility for her actions and her ideological stance that sees the country as barbaric and primitive.

Interestingly, Flash's actions are spurred not only by the boys' cruelty to the gecko and her own cultural/national entitlement to discipline others but also by the painful realization that she has misjudged the situation. Flash had in fact been watching the boys torture the lizard without knowing what was going on; she thought they were playing a game in the dirt. Her incorrect assessment of the situation actually consoled her, causing her to feel assured that "boys who had seen so much destruction could still giggle was proof that the world could repair itself" (89). The stark disconnect between what she thought was happening and what was actually happening contributed to her anger and impulsive action. This again broaches an Orientalist stance because she assumes, wrongly, that the boys are not impacted by the death and destruction surrounding them. This construction of an idealized childhood unimpacted by the trauma of war is out of touch but also dependent on an othering of the children; even while Flash herself is reeling from the things she has witnessed in Afghanistan (including a public execution), she imagines that the boys may be untouched. This suggests that as a Westerner she is more sensitive, as opposed to the inscrutable, impassive "others." The incident in Afghanistan, which Flash recalls through several memories in the novel, displays her Orientalist perspective and offers a larger history for her self-delusional and surface-level processing of the world around her. Furthermore, the novel suggests that Flash's shallow engagement and self-centeredness both enable and are enabled by her Western feminist Orientalism.

Throughout the text, Flash's preoccupation with surfaces is reflected in how she speaks of the places around her, and both are connected to images of light and darkness. She tells readers that her apartment floats on the Bosporus (76). This is appropriate as a metaphor for Flash's lack of engagement with the city around her. She also tells us that the view from her apartment is great, again illustrating her engagement with the city at only the surface, ocular level (64). While Istanbul is full of light, Kabul is depicted as dark. In a conversation with Alexandra, the latter tells Flash that Kabul "before the war" was "sparkling" (113). Earlier Flash had noted how Kabul was dark (85). Thus war has literally darkened the city. At the same time, she recognizes that there is more to the city she currently inhabits than what she acknowledges. She tells readers that Istanbul is a "city of layers" (141). This may perhaps be her justification for dwelling on the surface layer only. But light is not always associated with the lack of conflict, as Flash also suffers from migraines, which she describes as relating to light (113).

Flash also engages with images by emphasizing ideas of light. As previously stated, her nickname comes from her overuse of the flash in her work. Despite this moniker, she continues to produce photos with long exposures. She explains how, after walking around Istanbul's tourist sites, she visited the Sunken Palace. There she "discovered two Medusas floating just above the water" (11). She photographs them, but "the long exposure rendered them glowing and a little blurry in the green underwater light" (11). This section brings together images of surfaces with a sense of light—the Medusas float just above the surface of the water. And while Flash attempts to illuminate them through her photograph, she overexposes the photos, leading to a less than clearly visible image. It's as if she also only works on the surface of things, attempting to capture them by shining bright light on them, rather than taking the time to study them.

Throughout the text we can see a parallel between Flash's lack of engagement with the city and country around her and her lack of engagement with her own self and history, including her marriage. This indicates that despite the exhortation to look at her marriage, she largely refuses to do so. There are many clues in the text to suggest that Flash married Brando to escape her family of origin and that, thus, to interrogate her marriage would necessitate interrogating her own relationship with her family, which is fraught. She tells us that Brando offered a distinction from the "Latin boys" she was accustomed to, including her father. "Wonderboy wasn't like the Latin boys I had known, wasn't my father leaning back in his chair after a meal—loving him would be neither escape nor rejection but something much bigger" (38). Yet she suggests that she was indeed looking to escape an unhappy family in marrying Brando. Later she tells us how much she wanted away from her family and home. "As a child she cried when the car turned onto their street; fear of home and the familiar" (40). Brando, a successful, Anglo, international journalist, allows her a way out of both her family of origin and her hometown. Thus we can understand what is at stake in her refusal to engage and with her desire for surface-level things.

Flash's otherness is expressed in relation to her family, and specifically her father and Brando, and is something she moves away from in her marriage to Brando. In Turkey, however, her otherness is erased. (Interestingly, her marriage directly facilitates her residence in Turkey.) Given the vexed and complicated relationship between Brando, Flash, her family, her ethnic identity, and Istanbul, we can now read another layer of meaning in Flash's indecision regarding leaving her marriage and Istanbul. Would leaving Brando and returning to Miami signal a return to the "old-country bullshit" that she had sought to escape? At one point Flash recalls the years of support that Brando had offered her and discusses this in direct relationship to Istanbul. "I would not run away from this city. This was as much my home as any. Here were my books and my paintings. The rugs we had bought together in Pakistan, in India—Afghanistan . . . [Brando] had been good to me, hadn't he?" (120). Here Flash directly connects the pleasure she enjoys living in Istanbul with the good aspects of her marriage, and she seems to suggest that if she enjoys living in Istanbul, then she needs to exhibit that appreciation by staying with Brando. Flash suggests that she belongs in Istanbul and with Brando and that these two things are linked. As discussed below, Flash's sense of "belonging" in Istanbul, while not reinforced by any cultural or political engagement on her part, is something that is suggested by how others see her. Thus, we can read these lines as an acceptance by Flash that she belongs in Istanbul as well as perhaps an indication that what she has been looking for is not necessarily a place that she recognizes as home, but a place that recognizes her as belonging there.

One could argue that it is unfair to criticize Flash's lack of engagement with the society and culture around her. However, both *Erased Faces* and *The Last War* are clearly concerned with two issues—the practice of photography and the inner searchings of the protagonists. To look closely at the relationship between these two is not to suggest that there *should be* a positive correlation between them. Rather, to look at them alongside each other is to investigate what, if any, relationship between photography and introspection is apparent in the texts.

## VISUALITY AND BELONGING

Both Adriana and Flash are concerned with how things look, although their concerns are largely divergent. Adriana is interested in looking deeply to understand what lies below the surface and to understand conditions and motivations of those surrounding her and those in her past. Flash, on the other hand, is concerned with how things look but only to capture them briefly, and to use them to further her career. The texts' concern with visual representation recall *Heroes and Saints* and the work of Ana Pérez. In addition, despite their different motivations, Adriana and Flash, like Pérez, embody some commonality with the communities in which they work, and, significantly, this commonality is expressed visually. Both Flash and Adriana are repeatedly told by others around them that they *look like* they belong in the national contexts they currently inhabit.

In *Erased Faces*, Adriana's character is established via a relationship with a historical woman, Huitzilin, and the text suggests that Adriana currently embodies aspects of this woman's life, or that Huitzilin was Adriana in a past life. The text establishes their connection through Adriana's dreams and through a discussion of how Huitzilin and Adriana look. The first chapter of the book is titled "She didn't look like me." In the chapter, Adriana has and then wakes up from a dream about Huitzilin during the Spanish Conquest of Mexico. Her thought upon waking, that she does not look like the indigenous woman, betrays their obvious connection, a connection affirmed by other characters. When Adriana is asked to join the insurrection, Chan

K'in assures her that she will not be regarded as an intruder. Rather, he tells her that she will be regarded as an invited guest (41). Moreover, Chan K'in affirms her relationship to Huitzilin, so that despite Adriana's observation that they do not look alike, they are in fact alike. Other characters similarly recognize or see something inside of Adriana that affirms her place in the struggle. In a memorable scene, Juana speaks of what she can see in Adriana, namely a history of suffering that she (Juana) shares. In these examples, Adriana's belonging is affirmed through other characters seeing something that she cannot, something beyond the surface.

In *The Last War*, Flash's visual relationship with Turkey is somewhat distinct in that she is continually told that she *does* look like those around her. While Flash's marriage to Brando allows her to escape her position in the US, she becomes racially marked in a different way in Istanbul. There, the dark hair and eyes that mark Flash as a foreigner in the US suggest that she is a native in Turkey. The first night they reunite in Istanbul, Alexandra explains that when she saw Flash in Istiklal a few nights earlier, she wasn't initially sure it was her friend because "from a distance, you look like a regular Turk, you know" (66). Flash dismisses the comment, but several chapters later, when she's walking through Taksim, she notes, "no one gave me a second glance" (96). At another point she notes that she blends in, causing her to question exactly who/what she is; she asks herself "if I wasn't a foreigner, what was I?" (96). These quotes reflect a counterpoint to Flash's own attempted self-making and speak to the geographic and relational basis of racial identity; while Flash may be marked as an outsider in the US, she's marked as a native in Turkey, at least until she speaks. While these moments of (mis)recognition take place in Turkey, they nevertheless suggest the ways in which Latina/os and Middle Easterners (particularly Muslim Middle Easterners) are collectively visualized in the US. Christopher Rivera explains that the post-9/11 national security regime in the US relied on visuality, best exemplified in the Department of Homeland Security's "see something, say something" campaign, which suggested that ordinary citizens could "see" threats (read: terrorists) to the US. For Rivera, this particular regime of visuality implicated both Latina/os and Middle Easterners "because of their shared visual characteristics" (56). When Flash is "mistaken" as Turkish, Menéndez and the character reflect the ways in which Latina/os and Middle Easterners may share physical characteristics.[4]

While Adriana and Flash situate themselves very differently in relation to the subjects they photograph, with distinct results in terms of the work they produce, they share a peculiarly visual relationship with the communities in which they are located. For Adriana, the connections between herself and other, often historical characters in the novel become a destiny that she fulfills. For Flash, it is a reality that she avoids but that continues to follow her. While Flash does not work with photography in such a way as to engender ethical spectatorship, as does Adriana, the continuous comments on her "looking like" a native in Turkey suggest that the possibility exists. Flash, then, is not simply unable to enact a different relationship with the culture around her; she actively avoids doing so. As Adriana's narrative and Flash's own memories suggest, exploring more fully a different relationship with Turkey would involve or necessitate exploring a different relationship with Flash's own family and history. Nevertheless, the text's insistence that Flash looks like a native in Istanbul remind us that this opportunity remains.

## TURNING AWAY / TURNING TOWARD

The last sections of both novels are notable for the ways in which they indicate the protagonists' different decisions and orientations (literally) regarding their work and the US. In the final scenes, the protagonists are again discussed in relation to belonging, as both novels speak of the women blending in with their respective environments. But they make radically different choices—Adriana chooses to return to the US to work there, and Flash decides (after a brief time in Miami) to take

---

4. Anouar Majid mentions the murder of two Latina/o men who were killed because they were "mistaken" for Muslims. A Colombian man was killed in Florida, and a Brazilian man was killed in London. For Majid, "it is clear that the two had the right (or is it wrong?) profile" (142). The gender of the victims supports Rivera's contention that "the Brown Threat primarily hinges on the ideological constructions of Latinos and Middle Eastern Muslims as social deviants and as cultural problems because of their non-white and non-black, male bodies" (46).

another foreign assignment. This is consistent with the choices they have made throughout the text, because Adriana wants to return to her homeland to interrogate it further while Flash wants to avoid her family.

When Adriana returns to the US, she does so as a changed person and one determined to bring the work that she has done with her, integrating a transnational awareness in her photography. In many ways, her return to the States is itself the best reflection of her integration of Zapatista ideology, as she does not remain in Chiapas to paternalistically work *on behalf of* indigenous communities but exhibits resolve to work *in solidarity with* these communities. Thus she harnesses her photography to enlarge the concerns of a US Latina/o public. Flash engages in a different kind of work. She returns to the US, but only briefly, and there is no discussion of how her work may at all question US ideas. Rather, when the end of the novel has her leaving on yet another assignment, this time to India, she appears to continue to rely on spectatorship as a detached foreigner. Finally, it is clear from the narration of their journeys in what directions the two women travel.

*Erased Faces* ends with an image of arriving; *The Last War* ends with an image of leaving. Speaking of Adriana in the Los Angeles airport, Limón tells us: "[Adriana] took a deep breath, adjusted the bag on her back, and disappeared into the crowd" (258). Flash also narrates a moment of disappearing into a crowd, but this is one that is leaving the US: "A few minutes later, my flight was called, and after a moment's hesitation, I rose to stand in line with everyone else" (225). The description of Adriana is one of resolve as she walks out onto the streets to continue her work; the description of her adjusting her bag, which carries her photography equipment, emphasizes that this work will include photography. Rather than make her own way into a crowd, Flash appears to be absorbed by one. The most important difference, however, is that Adriana is arriving in the US whereas Flash is leaving. In an anti-imperialist move, Adriana literally brings Zapatista concerns and methodologies to the US, thereby potentially transforming the US Latina/o public sphere. Flash, however, continues to eschew the potential to alter her personal or political landscape, choosing only to take yet another assignment, which, if her history is any indication, will fail to move beyond surface engagements with self or politics.

## PHOTOJOURNALISM AND THE LATINA/O PUBLIC SPHERE

Adriana and Flash model distinct kinds of photojournalism in which Adriana turns inward and Flash outward. The texts also suggest the impact of their different perspectives and thus broach how they may or may not offer a new way of approaching a Latina/o public. Adriana's work is concerned with expanding a Latina/o public; her memories and experiences broach antiblack and anti-indigenous sentiments within Latina/o communities and seek a full accounting with these aspects of Latinidad. She likewise seeks to use her camera to expand these boundaries, to raise consciousness. She does so through a psychic exploration that occurs alongside her photographic work. Flash is unconcerned with these things—since her childhood she has sought to evade Latinidad, specifically male Latinos, and she continues this without fully questioning or seeking to understand why. Her photography is similarly escapist and doesn't really engage with the world around her.

The disparate approaches to the people and places around them evidenced by Adriana and Flash illustrate solidarity versus spectatorship, respectively. That both characters engage in these actions via photography speaks to the important, but not singular, role that photography may play in these endeavors. The two texts also suggest a different relationship between a more expansive Latina/o public sphere, mainly one that can draw connections between colonized and occupied peoples outside the US, and one that remains within the confines of the US nation-state. Here the two texts largely evidence recent social and historical developments, or their lack thereof. That is to say, the Zapatista uprising was largely positively received within US Latina/o communities. Particularly for US Latina/os of Mexican descent (who make up a majority of the US Latina/o population), their linguistic, cultural, and familial ties to Mexico made that conflict relevant. But Chicana/os and Latina/os, as marginalized peoples within the US, also largely understood and sympathized with the indigenous uprising. While this redrawing of Latina/o political affinity to include the Zapatistas might seem intuitive, it followed several decades of activism and scholarship that asserted the distinction between Latina/os and Chicana/os and

Latin Americans. Thus, Chicana/os did not automatically see themselves reflected in Mexican social and political movements. Furthermore, while they may experience political and social marginalization, non-indigenous Latina/os and Chicana/os do not necessarily share ethnic, cultural, or linguistic commonalities with indigenous Mexican peoples. What, then, facilitated this expansion of the US Latina/o public sphere to incorporate the Zapatista cause?[5] Chicana/os and Latina/os also engaged in solidarity work with the Zapatistas by spending time in Chiapas, sponsoring speakers' tours, and purchasing and selling products such as coffee and Zapatista dolls to aid the cause. Alisa Valdés-Rodríguez's novel *The Dirty Girls Social Club* includes the character Amber, for whom knowledge and support of the Zapatistas is one way that she realizes her Xicana identity. Amber, who renames herself Cuicatl, is transformed through a summer spent crisscrossing the US Southwest and Mexico on a "Free Chiapas" tour. As Debra Castillo explains, Amber/Cuicatl "comes to this sense of ethnic identity through a transnational experience, one very much in accord with the larger aims of the EZLN to make translocal changes from a defined and narrowly localized geopolitical space. In this narrative, Chiapas offers access to Aztlán" (52–53). While Valdés-Rodríguez's character is the butt of many jokes in the text—after asserting that Chicana should be spelled with an *X*, as the Aztecs did, her friend Lauren points out that the Aztecs didn't use the Roman alphabet—she nevertheless reflects the ways in which the Zapatista uprising and continued organizing and governing structures have transformed Chicana/os in the US. No doubt one of the appeals for Chicana/os was their explicit recognition by Zapatistas. Former spokesperson Subcommander Marcos, upon being asked if he was gay, famously replied: "Marcos is gay in San Francisco, black in South Africa, an Asian in Europe, a Chicano in San Ysidro. . . ." (qtd. in Lingis 33). Given that the identity "Chicana/o" is often illegible and unrecognized within the US and Mexico, Marcos's

---

5. A plethora of Chicano cultural production indicates the extent to which Chicana/o peoples adopted the Zapatista cause as their own. Rage Against the Machine, for example, released a hit single entitled "People of the Sun," in 1997. The song was written immediately after their lead singer, the Chicano Zack de la Rocha, had visited Chiapas. In the late 1990s and early 2000s (and to some extent today), it was not difficult to find Chicana/os sporting the Zapatista-inspired red-and-black handkerchiefs, exhibiting Zapatista "dolls" on keychains or T-shirts, or drinking fair-trade Zapatista coffee.

explicit invocation of the term, and his expression of solidarity with Chicana/os, facilitated Chicana/o-Zapatista identification. In addition, the Zapatistas, and Marcos, were largely lauded for their ingenious use of the internet, which included websites and blogs, as well as tongue-in-cheek communiqués sent out regularly to supporters and detractors alike. Such communication no doubt facilitated the way in which Chicana/o and Latina/o peoples incorporated Zapatista ideas and cultures, thereby transforming the Latina/o public sphere. *Erased Faces* suggests an alternative, but corollary story and path, by which the circulation of images, via the product of self-interrogation, may alter the Latina/o public sphere. In this way the novel largely reflects this expansion of the US Latina/o public sphere to include the Zapatista conflict while homing in on a different mechanism, photojournalism, as opposed to internet communication, by which this expansion was / could be achieved.

In the case of *The Last War,* there is also a relationship between the perspective and action of Flash and that of a US Latina/o public sphere; in this case Flash reflects that the US Latina/o public has largely not engaged substantially with Middle Eastern conflicts and identities. This lack is actually less intuitive than it might seem, as Latina/os and Middle Eastern peoples (in particular Muslim Middle Easterners) share linguistic and political histories as well as a contemporary social reality. Spanish is filled with words whose origins are Arabic, as a result of the Moorish occupation of Spain in the fifteenth century. US Latina/os have also experienced occupation, conquest, and colonization by many of the same imperial powers that have been active in the Middle East, including Britain and France. And US policies between the two regions has had much in common in more recent years.[6] Even closer to home, the border wall that forms part of the increasingly militarized border with Mexico is composed of recycled army materials from the Persian Gulf War. Rivera considers US Latina/os and Middle Eastern Muslims as they collectively form a "Brown Threat" in post-9/11 US government

---

6. As I discuss in my book *War Echoes,* there is a direct carryover between and among US military intervention in the Middle East and Latin America. In the 2003 invasion and occupation of Iraq, the Bush administration sought to implement the Salvador option—this was a tactic used in the US-backed civil war in El Salvador that created and relied on paramilitary groups and death squads to ensure that US interests were met and detractors punished.

and media representations. Rivera's idea of the Brown Threat explains that Latina/os and Muslims are "potentially interchangeable in the post-9/11 American imagination" and is based on "interconnected histories of Muslims in Spain and the Spanish in the New World; the legal treatment of these two minorities as white (at various points throughout American history)[; and] their ideological status as neither white nor black but specifically brown(ed)" (46, 48). Importantly for this discussion of *The Last War*, Rivera uses the example of Turkey's unsuccessful application for European Union membership as an example of how the Brown Threat works outside the US; despite the "Europeanization" of Turkey—culturally, politically, and economically—it is not recognized as European (62). Thus, US Latina/os have many reasons to understand themselves in relation to Middle Eastern nations and peoples, in particular those that have played a strategic role in the US war on terror. Flash's lack of engagement with the landscape around her echoes a particular situation: that the US Latina/o public sphere has not grown to include Middle Eastern peoples and contexts. Despite its setting outside the geographic boundaries of the US, Flash's narrative is largely "still firmly located in a politics of nation" (Caminero-Santangelo 39). What her story may suggest to us is that a serious interrogation of US Latina/o positioning and privileging, along with a dedication to looking below the surface, is necessary to achieve this new understanding.

## CONCLUSION: PHOTOGRAPHY, LITERATURE, AND THE PUBLIC SPHERE

This chapter has looked closely at how *Erased Faces* and *The Last War* use photojournalism to raise questions surrounding the relationship between war photography, the framing of militarized conflicts, identity, and the Latina/o public sphere. Both novels narrate the extent to which the protagonists' journalistic work is tied to, and dependent on, their personal psychological journeys. The texts thus stage an encounter between personal and political travel, offering the geopolitical sites of US military intervention as locations where these encounters take place. While both works acknowledge the interrelatedness of these journeys, they offer different portraits of their outcomes. Adriana is able to engage with her family trauma and to understand how it impacts her experiences in Chiapas, harnessing this knowledge of self and other to produce work that reflects the reality of the Zapatista communities. Flash, on the other hand, eschews serious engagement with the situation around her, seeking to fully separate herself from her family life, and, as a result, fails to produce more accurate representations of the spaces she inhabits. Rather than view these two characters as emblematic of simplistic accurate/inaccurate or successful/unsuccessful journeys, this chapter considers their relationship to the Latina/o public sphere. Although both texts acknowledge the importance of which and how images circulate, they also point to how the different contexts (cultural, political, military) have differently impacted the Latina/o public sphere. That is, Adriana's journey reflects the extent to which the Zapatista struggle has been integrated into US Latina/o identity and politics, whereas Flash's work reflects the ways in which Middle Eastern, Muslim, and Arab experiences and movements remain largely figured as outside the Latina/o public sphere.

As literature, the texts themselves provide an important opportunity for these considerations. When we are forced to consider Adriana's relationship to Juana and the Zapatistas, we confront her status as a US Latina and how her photography foments her relationship. Flash's myopia similarly calls on us to place Latina/os in relation to her and to question the Latina/o public sphere in relation to the Middle East. These novels then reflect certain relationships (or lack thereof) between US Latina/os and occupied and colonized peoples in the Middle East and Mexico, suggest the importance of photojournalism to realizing and problematizing these relationships, and provide the opportunity for readers to reflect on their content.

CONCLUSION

# Publics Unbound

*Undocuqueer Activism*

NEARLY TWO DECADES into the twenty-first century, we cannot discuss mass media and cultural production without talking about digital platforms and social media. Indeed, when it comes to journalism, the internet is transforming, and threatening, standard forms of news and reporting. Considerations of internet-based news sources, whether referring to online versions of print newspapers and magazines or to blogs and journals that only exist on the web, often speak about the simultaneous democratization and denigration of mass media. Web-based sources, many of which provide free access via a medium easily available to millions of people, may promise the greater circulation of information and ideas. The proliferation of a larger variety of news sources, particularly ones not tied to media conglomerates, may open up the field of news and information to more diverse perspectives. At the same time, audiences may be self-selecting, choosing only to receive their news from sources that reflect their own viewpoints or ideologies. Michael Warner points to the contested relationship between social movements and new media when he explains that "the question for debate . . . is to what extent the environment for critical social movements is becoming more undemocratic, 'refeudalized,' or colonized by changing relations among the state, mass media, and the market" ("Publics" 50). One of the greatest potentials for democratization is that many internet-based outlets regularly rely on guest columnists who are not professional journalists. Such columnists are not paid and may undercut the labor of professional journalists, posing a potential threat to the profession, but there is no doubt that these opportunities open up space for a multiplicity of viewpoints and voices. In fact, the potential for guest columnists to offer new perspectives is contingent on the fact that they are *not* professionalized.

As a conclusion to this book's analysis of journalists and journalism in contemporary Latina/o literature, this section looks more broadly at mass media and Latina/o cultural production. The following pages consider internet-based media produced and disseminated by nonprofessionals. These nonprofessionals are not employed full time as journalists, although some, like Julio Salgado, have college degrees and experience in the field. Combining this book's focus on questions of cultural production and a Latina/o public sphere, the ensuing analysis suggests that such media blurs the boundary not only between "new" and "old" media but also between art and news. The discussion focuses on content produced by queer undocumented Latina/o cultural workers, or "undocuqueers." The voices of those discussed—contemporary undocuqueer artists and activists—reflect one of the most significant interventions into the Latina/o public sphere and ideas about the public sphere more broadly. These artists and activists explicitly challenge the role of "citizens" within this space, demonstrating that noncitizen Latina/os have been and will continue to be important voices within the US public. In so doing, they continue to break down the boundaries of the nation-state that often demarcate discussions of the public sphere and suggest that Latina/os are and have been integral to new iterations of publics.

In the days following the Trump administration's September 2017 decision to repeal Deferred Action for Childhood Arrivals (DACA) and to allow no further renewals past March 2018, the poet and arts activist Yosimar Reyes used his already substantial following on YouTube and Facebook to discuss his own experiences and perspectives as a queer undocumented, or undocuqueer, person.[1] The coining of

---

1. As of the writing of this section, the future of DACA and DACA recipients remains unclear. Trump has articulated his desire to tie any future benefits to DACA

the term and the fact that it has been taken up as an identity points to the overlap between queer and undocumented peoples and to the sharing of political tactics and cultural interventions undertaken by both groups. Most recently, undocumented people have drawn very explicitly on the tactics of the post-Stonewall gay and lesbian rights movement by encouraging people to "come out" as undocumented and committing to lives "out of the closets" and "out of the shadows." For those who are both queer and undocumented, this dual coming-out did not always occur at the same time. In a 2013 interview, Salgado remarked that as an undocuqueer artivist (a term combining *activist* and *artist*), his coming out as queer was more difficult than coming out as undocumented. He attributes this to being from California, where legal status was "talked about" and "[he] always knew someone who was undocumented" (Seif, "'Layers'" 306). Being queer, on the other hand, "felt more solitary," and it was not until he was in college that he came out to his parents (306). Salgado's narrative highlights the fact that issues of racial/ethnic identity, including one's relationship to the state in terms of legal status, are often shared among family members, whereas sexual identity may not be a commonality shared by members of a family unit. It's also worth noting that queer immigrants have been at the forefront of the immigrant rights movement for at least a decade now, ensuring that questions of sexuality are placed alongside questions about the right to live free from fear, deportation, and detention. Nevertheless, unfortunately, the mainstream gay and lesbian rights movement has not responded similarly to the immigrant rights movement. While some progress and coalitions have been made, gay rights organizations continue to be overwhelmingly white and middle-class in terms of leadership, and thus it is not surprising that undocumented queer immigrants often find greater community in either Latinx or queer Latinx organizations. Drawing on tactics of earlier, related social movements like the LGBT movement of the late twentieth century, these activists implicitly point out which peoples and identities have been excluded from queer US publics while asserting that queer people are already formative members of Latinx publics.

---

recipients to the construction of a border wall, whereas a federal judge in San Francisco ruled in early January 2018 that protections for DACA recipients must remain in place while litigation concerned with ending the program plays out.

Salgado, who studied journalism at California State, Long Beach, channeled his talents and passions into what he terms *artivism* following the 2010 defeat of a national DREAM Act. He works frequently with Reyes and other organizations such as United We Dream's Queer Undocumented Immigrant Project (QUIP). Salgado became well known for his series of posters, "I Exist," which highlight the voices and experiences of undocumented people, including undocumented folks who are students and/or queer. Both Salgado and Reyes have sought to offer visibility to segments of the population that are overlooked, ignored, or even assumed to not exist. What is most fascinating about the work of both artists is that they do not demand inclusion in the US public sphere; rather, they assert that they and others like them are already an important part of it. They may do this through stark visual images as well as narratives that challenge common tropes about immigration. In a YouTube video of a public talk, Reyes creates humor around what are often thought of as "tragic" experiences, such as immigration. "I'm gonna spare you the migration story," he tells a laughing audience, "cuz I only say that when I need to apply to scholarships. . . . if it comes with a check, I'll cry" (Aran). Similarly, in a video made by the arts collective Culture Strike and released just days after the Trump administration announced the end of DACA, Reyes narrates—promising to sell stories of undocumented youth for the price of $495.00—the cost of the renewal fee for DACA applications. Throughout the five-minute video, called "*1 (800) SAVE - DACA*," Reyes offers several variations on typical immigrant stories, charging potential buyers for more-elaborate narratives. Playing on the stereotype that all undocumented migrants work in agriculture, he says: "Need someone to hold or pick a fruit during an interview? For an additional 100 dollars, that can be yours." He also uses ideas that viewers may have about the trauma of crossing the border without documentation as comedic fodder: "Need a DREAMer to recount a traumatic border-crossing story, even though they don't remember because they came when they were three? For an additional 500 dollars we can make something up," he says, as the text "'Reliving' the Trauma: $995.00!!" flashes across the bottom of the screen. The video turns ideas about the disempowered, pathetic immigrant on their head, showing his own agency and pointing out the limitations of such tropes. But the piece also critiques those of us who may be drawn to these narratives for our own reasons, who find in such tearjerker stories a way to access our own feelings about migration. The piece pokes fun at overly narrow and simplistic narratives about undocumented migration and undocumented people as well as viewers' emotional investments in such stories, pointing out that we shouldn't need the pathetic stories of immigrants to convince us that our immigration system is inhumane and flawed. As Reyes emphasizes, "undocumented people are not puppies that need to be saved. We are people with agency, with dignity and with power" (Aran). The video asserts that common ideas about undocumented migrants—as agricultural workers and traumatized children—represent at best only a small fraction of this larger population. At the same time, Reyes's comedic take on the trope of the tragic immigrant gestures to a much larger, more diverse, and complex community of undocumented peoples living in the US.

"*1 (800) SAVE - DACA*" pushes back against the supposedly empathic feelings that viewers may express toward undocumented people by recognizing that these are likely expressions of pity. The piece explores the affective dimensions of the public sphere, critiquing the role that emotions such as pity and sympathy may play in expanding notions of the public and asking that we reject those emotions while nonetheless investing in this larger iteration of a US public. In rejecting emotions such as sympathy and pity while nevertheless asserting his place and belonging, Reyes points out the affective dimensions of who is considered part of a public while simultaneously affirming his place *in* this public—without requiring permission or an invitation to enter. At the same time, the video asks us to question which stories and which people elicit emotional responses. What about those immigrants for whom empathy may come less easily, those migrants who were not brought as "innocent children," those who might have a criminal record? Since 2010 there has been a push on the part of immigrant activists to advocate with and for a more diverse population of undocumented migrants. Speaking of one activist organization, Tania A. Unzueta Carrasco and Hinda Seif explain that the Immigrant Youth Justice League of Chicago (IYJL) explicitly challenges both the conflation of "immigrant" and "criminal" and the tendency to distinguish between "good" and "bad" immigrants, even when young DREAMers may rhetorically benefit from being labeled the former. In work that emerged after 2010, young activists have explicitly challenged rhetoric that sought to divide them from their parents; as one activist said: "We publicly expressed discontent with these framings [that children shouldn't be punished for the illegal acts of their parents], refused to be divided from our parents and broadened our challenge of who was being defined as worthy, culpable or deportable" (289). These activists are very conscious of how images of DREAMers as "deserving" migrants who are college students or graduates, English-dominant, and so forth conform to hegemonic ideas of "model citizens" that are rooted in race, class, and gender hierarchies and unattainable for many migrants (281). Furthermore, while DREAMers might be the most public face of the undocumented immigrant community, they are a small minority of this larger group. The program "67 Sueños" (67 Dreams), sponsored by the American Friends Service Committee, is meant to draw attention to the fact that as it currently stands, 67 percent of migrants would be excluded from the DREAM Act. These challenges to normative ideas of "good immigrants" have permeated youth activism and cultural production, reshaping how immigrant youth think of themselves in relation to others. A poster by Salgado (see figure 2) similarly resists the impulse to separate DREAMers or youth from their parents, explicitly refuting the idea that young undocumented immigrants are being unfairly punished for their parents' "crimes." Rather, with text stating that "my parents are courageous and responsible," the poster seeks to remove the stigma associated with adults who migrate without documentation and to reframe them as conscientious and honorable. The poster doesn't seek to justify or ask permission for considering undocumented migrants as part of the US Latina/o and US public; rather, with a phrase such as "I am here!" they emphasize that these individuals are vibrant and valuable constituents of these publics.

While Salgado's poster presents a heteronormative biological family, it forms part of his larger collection of work that explicitly questions norms of gender and sexuality while giving voice to undocumented people who are queer and/or trans. This attention to issues of gender and sexuality is also a hallmark of post-2010 youth activism; illustrating their harnessing of ideas and iterations of subaltern publics as they exist in relation to larger publics, activists continually confront uncomfortable issues. For example, a young activist interviewed by Carrasco and Seif notes that he has made choices about which deportation cases

**FIGURE 2.** "Courageous and Responsible" by Julio Salgado

to oppose publicly based on personal and societal norms. Francisco states that he recently "drew the line on a sexual assault case" because he "felt personally and strategically it was not wise" (293). Whether or not he felt that a perpetrator of sexual assault merited deportation, and it appears that he was unsure, Francisco recognized that he was still operating within a context that would view such a person as worthy of deportation. The questioning of the use of state institutions—in this case, Immigration and Customs Enforcement—to "solve" the problem of sexual assault, however, is indicative of an intersectional feminist stance that questions a reliance on state institutions that engender violence to adequately respond to interpersonal violence. Young activists such as Francisco acknowledge how immigrants and their allies are viewed by mainstream publics and negotiate their work and rhetoric accordingly as they seek to bring immigrant issues to the public sphere.

This intersectional framework and commitment to examine immigrant publics as they exist within and alongside other publics and within the context of race, class, gender, and sexuality is an important aspect of Reyes's and Salgado's artivism. Reyes often does this in a humorous manner. In a video uploaded to Facebook and featured in an online article entitled "Meet the Immigrant Comedians Making Deportation Funny," Reyes speaks about how all the TV exposure he is getting is going to help him find a partner and get married (Aran). He also, however, calls out the mainstream LGBTQ movement: "as queer people and as someone that's part of a community it's time for other LGBT mainstream groups to step up and acknowledge undocumented people as integral parts [of the larger LGBT community]" (Aran). Salgado references intersectional feminism explicitly, speaking about how his own approach to undocuqueer organizing was influenced by women of color who responded to and refuted white women's leadership in feminism. Thus, he builds on and departs from aspects of the subaltern white feminist public. As a result, he is careful to think about whose voices are represented and amplified and to pay attention to issues of difference, for example how his experience as an undocumented man from California is different from that of an undocumented woman from the Midwest (Seif 2014, 305). Not only is this commitment to speaking openly about gender and sexuality and the place of difference reflective of intersectional feminism, the artivists, like the IYJL activists discussed earlier, also bring a suspicion of state institutions to solve social problems in a way that draws on radical feminist and feminist of color theory and activism.

Salgado and Reyes both emphasize that undocuqueer people are not victims and that they are not waiting for state institutions or white-led movements to "save" them. Reyes is explicit, saying that undocumented people are not "puppies that need to be saved." He also affirms this stance when talking about domestic violence. In a poem titled "U-Visa," he tells the story of a woman abused by her husband who nevertheless does not / cannot rely on protection from the state. The title of the poem references a visa program through the US that offers migrants protection if they have been victims of a crime and cooperate with law enforcement to prosecute perpetrators. While the program commonly assists survivors of domestic violence, it can also tear families and communities apart, as a survivor may assist the state in deporting an abuser who is also the economic provider for their family. Reyes's poem explains:

> Tio beats tia
> purple and blue
> one day is an eye
> another is an arm
> no cops are called
> because here on this block
> cops are bad
> here
> cops separate families
> here on this block cops
> are the last resort
> (Reyes)

The speaker of the poem goes on explain that Tía has acquired a U visa, which the aunt describes as "the only good thing he left me." The speaker, however, sees a larger metaphor connecting the visa and US treatment of immigrants, saying that it is "A metaphor for what this country will do to you / beat you purple and blue until you prove / you can still stand." The poem suggests that only "victims" receive sympathy and that one must suffer and conform to / articulate a particular narrative of suffering to receive relief. As a result, the work exposes the problems of viewing immigrants, like survivors of domestic violence, as in need of saving by state institutions. If the only way we can help survivors of state violence is to force them to prove themselves victims, and if the only way we can accept immigrants is to view them as defenseless and agentless, then we are not accounting for their full humanity. In speaking of a social community located outside (in fact excluded from) state institutions such as citizenship that might grant them protection, the poem recognizes the subordinate place of particular people while enacting and illustrating the necessity of a public sphere similarly unbound by ideas of citizenship and state policies and boundaries.

While "U-Visa" is a poem, in the work Reyes blurs the line between news and cultural production. The poet is in fact informing his audience about the realities of undocumented immigration and the sensibilities of such migrants. In this sense he reflects a new era of mass communication, an era that *Univisión* correspondent Jorge Ramos similarly describes. Speaking of the difference between the past and present of mass communication and the blurring of boundaries between news, entertainment, and business, Ramos writes: "There used to be a clear differentiation between national and international news. Not anymore. Journalists used to work for one form of media. Not anymore. Journalism used to be clearly separated from entertainment and from mass media's concerns with profit. Not anymore. One language was enough to report [the news]. Not anymore" (149).[2] Reyes moves beyond the common debate concerning advocacy versus objectivity to show that the person telling his own story is the greatest authority on the topic. At the same time, he doesn't purport to speak for all undocumented immigrants, encouraging us to see this story as singular. Culture Strike's *1 (800) SAVE - DACA* video similarly skirts this line between entertainment, information, and cultural production. Collec-

---

2. My translation. Original: "Antes había una clara diferenciación entre noticias nacionales e internacionales. Ya no. Antes los periodistas trabajaban para un sólo media de comunicación. Ya no. Antes el periodismo estaba claramente separado del enteretenimiento y de las preocupaciones por las ganancias en los medios de comunicación. Ya no. Antes bataba un idoma para informar. Ya no."

tively, these pieces serve as necessary information that counters overly simplistic views on immigration and immigrants, pointing out the lack of attention to the emotional state of migrants and the way that gender and sexuality are intertwined with questions of immigration, race, class, and citizenship.

These artivists and their work actively contribute to questioning and furthering a public sphere because they speak to and from a population commonly excluded from normative notions of the public sphere. In fact, undocumented people, or noncitizens, have been excluded from ideas concerning the public sphere. As Hector Amaya reminds us, "the 'who' of publicity is typically the citizen" and therefore "noncitizens are not the typical concern of public sphere theories" which in turn equate citizenship with political agency (46). These state-centric notions of citizenship and agency risk obscuring how publics operate beyond and in between nation-states, not to mention the work of individuals who may not be citizens. For Raymond Rocco, this focus on the nation overlooks both how some individuals (in this case, Latina/os) create their own networks and associations and the extent of membership in communities not bounded by nation-states. Rocco asserts that "there is a disjunction between the forms of governance still based exclusively on territorially defined notions of sovereignty and the actual social space created by the organic sets of relationships that define the real boundaries of a particular community," and he suggests looking closer at regional circuits of belonging (for example, the Southern California region that includes Northern Mexico) to define people, culture, and territory (17). The artivists discussed here respond to these contradictions by vociferously asserting their relationship to the public sphere, whether we define that as a US public sphere, a Latina/o public sphere, or something else, and by redrawing lines of community and kinship. One of the activists interviewed by Carrasco and Seif discusses how his status and activism have caused him to think about family and community differently, explaining that if someone is arrested and put in deportation, he "[sends] a message to someone that knows them asking how to help. I say, this is basically my brother, this is part of my community" (290). This kind of alternative understanding of kinship, one based not on biological ties but on shared social standing, is familiar to LGBTQ peoples who similarly have redrawn and rearticulated ideas of family and evidences how undocumented youth are rewriting norms of belonging as articulated by both the nation-state and the family.

The work produced by Salgado, Reyes, and their contemporaries reflects a new kind of Latina/o engagement with the public sphere that draws on their status as undocumented people in the US but also on their age. In this sense, the artivists join others of their generation and, in particular, DREAMers who rely heavily on telling their individual stories via social media to advocate for immigration reform (Báez 419). While undocumented youth, like youth more generally, have a specific level of comfort and access to social media, they are also influenced by their relationship to state institutions. In fact, the rights of undocumented youth to access state institutions such as public education are protected by federal law (Seif, "'Wise up!'" 267). This means that, unlike their parents, undocumented youth "have a direct, daily relationship with a government entity that is not constructed as illegal" (257). While DREAMers and other undocumented youth have used personal stories to articulate their lived experiences and to connect with each other, the artivists discussed here connect with a larger public that includes US citizens and people who are not undocumented. The work of Salgado and Reyes is well known and well circulated within Latina/o youth communities, which include people from a variety of immigrant and non-immigrant backgrounds. Moreover, both artivists focus not on just telling their own personal stories but on amplifying the voices and experiences of others, whether that be family members or unknown strangers. As a result, their work intervenes on a larger scale within the public sphere to question hegemonic notions of citizenship and to foreground how those commonly thought of as outside of or irrelevant to the public sphere (noncitizens) are in fact already an active part of several publics. This work is done in a way that builds upon existing forms of mass communication and upon existing social movements and approaches to social justice, namely intersectional and women of color feminism. This suggests a powerful outgrowth that shows their connection to earlier iterations of mass media activism as well as their knowledge and skill in using a variety of mediums—public speaking, YouTube, and internet-based platforms—to publish literature. Their access to digital media platforms expands the boundaries of the Latina/o public sphere while showcasing its already existing internal contradictions, contradictions that can nevertheless be a source of power. In this continued moment of uncertainty, when the fate of millions of undocumented people in the US and migrants and refugees around the world remains unknown, these artists remind us of the power and ability of marginalized peoples to speak and reflect their own realities and offer more emancipatory visions of the future.

# WORKS CITED

Acosta, Oscar Zeta. "Jailed Attorney Complains," undated newspaper article. Box 1, Folder 1. Oscar Zeta Acosta Papers, 1936–1990. Chicano and Latino Collections, Special Research Collections, University of California, Santa Barbara Libraries, Santa Barbara, CA.

———. Letter to the Editor of *Playboy.* 15 October 1973. Box 2, Folder 36. Oscar Zeta Acosta Papers, 1936–1990. Chicano and Latino Collections, Special Research Collections, University of California, Santa Barbara Libraries, Santa Barbara, CA.

———. Letter to Helen. Undated. Box 2, Folder 38. Oscar Zeta Acosta Papers, 1936–1990. Chicano and Latino Collections, Special Research Collections, University of California, Santa Barbara Libraries, Santa Barbara, CA.

———. Letter to Alan. 12 November 1972. Box 2, Folder 36. Oscar Zeta Acosta Papers, 1936–1990. Chicano and Latino Collections, Special Research Collections, University of California, Santa Barbara Libraries, Santa Barbara, CA.

———. Personal papers, Box 2, Folder 32. Oscar Zeta Acosta Papers, 1936–1990. Chicano and Latino Collections, Special Research Collections, University of California, Santa Barbara Libraries, Santa Barbara, CA.

———. *The Revolt of the Cockroach People.* New York: Vintage Books, 1989.

———. Undated paper, Box 7, Folder 29. Oscar Zeta Acosta Papers, 1936–1990. Chicano and Latino Collections, Special Research Collections, University of California, Santa Barbara Libraries, Santa Barbara, CA.

———. "Zeta expone racismo en las cortes," undated newspaper article. Box 1, Folder 1. Oscar Zeta Acosta Papers, 1936–1990. Chicano and Latino Collections, Special

Research Collections, University of California, Santa Barbara Libraries, Santa Barbara, CA.

Alarcón, Norma. "Traddutora, Traditora: A Paradigmatic Figure of Chicana Feminism." *Cultural Critique,* no. 13, Autumn 1998, pp. 57–87.

Aldama, Frederick Luis. *Postethnic Narrative Criticism: Magicorealism in Oscar "Zeta" Acosta, Ana Castillo, Julie Dash, Hanif Kureishi, and Salman Rushdie.* Austin: U of Texas P, 2003.

Alurista. "Acosta's *The Revolt of the Cockroach People*: The Case, the Novel, and History." *Contemporary Chicano Fiction: A Critical Survey,* edited by Vernon E. Lattin. New York: Bilingual Press / Editorial Bilingüe, 1986, pp. 94–104.

Amaya, Hector. *Citizenship Excess: Latina/os, Media and the Nation.* New York: NYUP, 2013.

Apel, Dora. *War Culture and the Contest of Images.* New Brunswick: Rutgers UP, 2012.

Aran, Isha. "Meet the Comedians Making Deportation Funny." *Splinternews,* 4 Oct. 2017, https://splinternews.com/meet-the-immigrant-comedians-making-deportation-funny-1819144808?utm_medium=sharefromsite&utm_source=Splinter_facebook

Arau, Sergio, director. *A Day Without a Mexican.* Eye On The Ball Films, 2004.

Arias, Arturo. "What Are Central American Studies?" *Latino Studies,* vol. 15, 2017, pp. 99–103.

Báez, Jillian. "Spreadable Citizenship: Undocumented Youth Activists and Social Media." *The Routledge Companion to Latina/o Media,* edited by María Elena Cepeda and Dolores Inés Casillas. New York: Routledge, 2017, pp. 419–32.

Bahadur, Gaiutra. "Sleeping with the Enemy." *The New York Times,* 24 June 2009, p. BR14.

Bahramitash, Roksana. "The War on Terror, Feminist Orientalism and Orientalism Feminism: Case Studies of Two North American Bestsellers." *Critique: Critical Middle Eastern Studies,* vol. 14, no. 2, 2005, pp. 221–35.

Barrera Ortíz, Byron. *Desinformación: el lado oscuro de la democracia.* Guatemala City, Guatemala: Colleción Fundamentales, 1999.

Bartrop, Paul R., and Steven Leonard Jacobs. *Modern Genocide: The Definitive Resource and Document Collection.* Santa Barbara, CA: ABC-CLIO, 2015.

Baxter, Katherine Isobel. "Memory and Photography: Rethinking Postcolonial Trauma Studies." *Journal of Postcolonial Writing,* vol. 47, no. 1, 2011, pp. 18–29.

Bebout, Lee. *Whiteness on the Border: Mapping the U.S. Racial Imagination in Brown and White.* New York: NYUP, 2016.

Berlant, Lauren. *The Female Complaint: The Unfinished Business of Sentimentality in American Culture.* Durham: Duke UP, 2008.

Berlant, Lauren, and Michael Warner. "Sex in Public." *Critical Inquiry,* vol. 24, no. 2, Winter 1998, pp. 547–66.

Bickford, Donna. "A Praxis of Parataxis: Epistemology and Dissonance in Lucha Corpi's Detective Fiction." *meridians: feminism, race, transnationalism*, vol. 5, no. 2, 2005, pp. 89–103.

Bishop, Sara. "'Cockroach Aztlán': Oscar Zeta Acosta's Queer Take on the Indexical Trace and Chicano Nationalism." *LIT: Literature, Interpretation, Theory*, vol. 25, no. 3, 2014, pp. 201–19.

Blackwell, Maylei. *¡Chicana Power! Contested Histories of Feminism in the Chicano Movement*. Austin: U of Texas P, 2011.

———. "Contested Histories: *Las Hijas de Cuauhtémoc,* Chicana Feminisms, and Print Culture in the Chicano Movement, 1968–1973." *Chicana Feminisms: A Critical Reader,* edited by Patricia Zavella, Gabriela F. Arredondo, Aida Hurtado, Norma Klahn, and Olga Najera-Ramirez. Durham: Duke UP, 2003, pp. 59–96.

Brady, Mary Pat. *Extinct Lands, Temporal Geographies: Chicana Literature and the Urgency of Space*. Durham: Duke UP, 2002.

Bruce-Novoa. "Fear and Loathing on the Buffalo Trail." *MELUS*, vol. 6, no. 4, Winter 1979, pp. 39–50.

———. "Homosexuality and the Chicano Novel." *Confluencia,* vol. 2, no. 1, Fall 1986, pp. 69–77.

Butler, Judith. *Frames of War: When Is Life Grievable?* London: Verso Books, 2010.

———. "Performative Acts and Gender Constitution: An Essay in Phenomenology and Feminist Theory." *Theatre Journal*, vol. 40, no. 4, Dec. 1988, pp. 519–31.

———. "Performativity, Precarity and Sexual Politics." *AIBR. Revista de Antropología Iberoamericana*, vol. 4, no. 3, Sept–Dec. 2009, pp. i–xiii.

Calderón, Héctor. *Narratives of Greater Mexico: Essays on Chicano Literary History, Genre, and Borders*. Austin: U of Texas P.

Caminero-Santangelo, Marta. *Documenting the Undocumented: Latino/a Narratives and Social Justice in the Era of Operation Gatekeeper*. Gainesville: UP of Florida, 2016.

Carrasco, Tania A. Unzueta, and Hinda Seif. "Disrupting the Dream: Undocumented Youth Reframe Citizenship and Deportability through Anti-deportation Activism." *Latino Studies*, vol. 12, no. 2, June 2014, pp. 279–99.

Casillas, Dolores Inés. *Sounds of Belonging: U.S. Spanish-Language Radio and Advocacy*. New York: NYUP, 2014.

Castañeda, Mari. "The Importance of Spanish Language and Latino Media." *Latina/o Communication Studies Today,* edited by Angaharad N. Valdivia. New York: Peter Lang, 2008, pp. 51–66.

Castillo, Debra. "Impossible Indian." *Chasquí: Revista de Literatura Latinoamericana*, vol. 35, no. 2, 2006, pp. 42–57.

Cepeda, María Elena. "Beyond 'Filling In the Gap': The State and States of Latina/o Feminist Media Studies." *Feminist Media Studies*, vol. 16, no. 2, 2016, pp. 344–60.

Coppedge, Whit. "Interview with Francisco Goldman." *Pif Magazine*, 1 May 2000, http://www.pifmagazine.com/2000/05/interview-with-francisco-goldman/. Last accessed 1 Feb. 2018.

Coronado, Raúl. *A World Not to Come: A History of Latino Writing and Print Culture*. Cambridge, MA: Harvard UP, 2013.

Corpi, Lucha. *Eulogy for a Brown Angel*. Houston, TX: Arte Público Press, 1992.

Craft, Linda J. "International Adoption as a Fictional Construct: Francisco Goldman's *The Long Night of White Chickens*." *Romance Languages Annual*, edited by Jeanette Beer, Patricia Hart, and Ben Lawton. West Lafayette, IN: Purdue Research Foundation, 1996, pp. 430–35.

Croteau, David, and William Hoynes. *The Business of Media: Corporate Media and the Public Interest*. Thousand Oaks, CA: Pine Forge Press, 2006.

Culture Strike (C/S). "1 (800) SAVE - DACA," https://www.youtube.com/watch?v=fowAKzAPTjY. 12 Sept. 2017.

Cutler, John Alba. "Chicano Narrative's Hidden Print Cultures and the Chicano/a Literary Counterpublic." *Bridges, Borders and Breaks: History, Narrative, and Nation in Twenty-First-Century Chicana/o Literary Criticism*, edited by William Orchard and Yolanda Padilla. Pittsburgh: U of Pittsburgh P, 2016, pp. 139–58.

Cutter, Martha J. "Malinche's Legacy: Translation, Betrayal, and Interlingualism in Chicano/a Literature." *Arizona Quarterly*, vol. 66, no. 1, 2010, pp. 1–33.

Damjanova, Ludmila. "Lenguage de prensa y realidad social en Guatemala." *Mesoamérica*, vol. 18, no. 34, Dec. 1997, pp. 585–94.

Darby, Brandon. "Leaked Images Reveal Children Warehoused in Crowded U.S. Cells, Border Patrol Overwhelmed." *Breitbart News*, 5 June 2014, http://www.breitbart.com/texas/2014/06/05/leaked-images-reveal-children-warehoused-in-crowded-us-cells-border-patrol-overwhelmed/.

Dávila, Arlene. "El Barrio's 'We Are Watching You' Campaign: On the Politics of Inclusion in a Latinized Museum." *Aztlán*, vol. 30, no. 1, Spring 2005, pp. 153–78.

———. *Latinos, Inc.: The Marketing and Making of a People*. Updated edition with a new preface; foreword by Junot Díaz. Berkeley: U of California P, 2012.

Dávila, Arlene, and Yeidy M. Romero. *Contemporary Latina/o Media: Production, Circulation, Politics*. New York: NYUP, 2014.

Davison, Phil. "Zedillo Halts Offensive against Zapatistas." *The Independent*, 14 Feb. 1995, http://www.independent.co.uk/news/world/zedillo-halts-offensive-against-zapatistas-1573127.html.

Del Castillo, Adelaida. "Malintzin Tenépal: A Preliminary Look into a New Perspective." *Essays on La Mujer* (Part 1), edited by Rosaura Sánchez. Los Angeles: Chicano Studies Center Publications, University of California, Los Angeles, 1997, pp. 124–49.

Enloe, Cynthia. *Maneuvers: The International Politics of Militarizing Women's Lives*. Berkeley: U of California P, 2000.

Fanon, Frantz. *Black Skin, White Masks*. New York: Grove Press, 1967.

Filkins, Dexter. *The Forever War*. New York: Vintage, 2009.

Fineman, Mark. "Mexican Government, Indian Rebels Agree to New Talks in Peace Effort: Concessions: Meeting Is Arranged after Zapatistas Extend a Temporary Cease-Fire and Oppositions Party Declares a Truce." *Los Angeles Times*, 14 Jan. 1995, http://articles.latimes.com/1995-01-14/news/mn-20009_1_opposition-party.

Fisk, Robert. "Baghdad: The Day After; Arson, Anarchy, Fear, Hatred, Hysteria, Looting; Revenge, Savagery, Suspicion and a Suicide Bombing." *The Independent*, 11 Apr. 2003, p. 1.

Fraser, Nancy. "Rethinking the Public Sphere: A Contribution to the Critique of Actually Existing Democracy." *Social Text*, no. 25/26, 1990, pp. 56–80.

Gallego, Carlos. *Chicana/o Subjectivity and the Politics of Identity: Between Recognition and Revolution*. New York: Palgrave Macmillan, 2011.

García, Mario T. *Border Correspondent: Selected Writings, 1955–1970*. Berkeley: U of California P, 1995.

Garza Ramos, Javier. "Being a Journalist in Mexico Is Getting Even More Dangerous: Drug Cartels and Others Know They Can Attack the Media with Little Fear of Consequences." *The Washington Post*, 18 Feb. 2016, https://www.washingtonpost.com/posteverything/wp/2016/02/18/being-a-journalist-in-mexico-is-getting-even-more-dangerous/?utm_term=.6f25eb00fb23.

Goldman, Francisco. *The Long Night of White Chickens*. New York: Grove, 1992.

———. "Sad Tales of Libertad de Prensa." *Harper's*, 1 Aug. 1988, pp. 56–62.

González, Juan. "'A Voice from Another Part of New York': Hear Juan González's NY Journalism Hall of Fame Speech." *Democracy Now!*, 4 May 2016, https://www.democracynow.org/2016/5/4/a_voice_from_another_part_of

Gräbner, Cornelia. "'But how to speak of such things?' Decolonial Love, the Coloniality of Gender, and Political Struggle in Francisco Goldman's *The Long Night of White Chickens* (1992) and Jennifer Harbury's *Bridge of Courage* (1994) and *Searching for Everardo* (1997)." *Journal of Iberian and Latin-American Studies*, vol. 20, no. 1, 2014, pp. 51–74.

Greenberg, Linda Margarita. "Learning from the Dead: Wounds, Women, and Activism in Cherríe Moraga's *Heroes and Saints*." *MELUS: Multi-Ethnic Literature of the United States*, vol. 34, no. 1, Spring 2009, pp. 163–84.

"'Growing Concern'—Did Chemicals Cause Children's Deaths?" *48 Hours*. CBS News. Airdate: 18 Apr. 1990.

Gutiérrez, Félix. "Spanish-Language Media in America: Background, Resources, History." *Journalism History*, vol. 4, no. 2, Summer 1977, pp. 34–67.

Habermas, Jürgen. *The Structural Transformation of the Public Sphere: An Inquiry into a Category of Bourgeois Society*. Translated by Thomas Burger. Cambridge, MA: MIT P, 1991.

Hames-García, Michael. "Dr. Gonzo's Carnival: The Testimonial Satires of Oscar Zeta Acosta." *American Literature*, vol. 72, no. 4, Sept. 2000, pp. 463–93.

Haney-López, Ian. *Racism on Trial: The Chicano Fight for Social Justice.* Cambridge, MA: Belknap Press of Harvard UP, 2003.

Hariman, Robert, and John Louis Lucaites. *No Caption Needed: Iconic Photographs, Public Culture and Liberal Democracy.* Chicago: U of Chicago P, 2007.

Hondagneu-Sotelo, Pierrette. *God's Heart Has No Borders: How Religious Activists Are Working for Immigrant Rights.* Berkeley: U of California P, 2008.

"How This Happened." *LatinoUSA,* 12 Sept. 2014, https://latinousa.org/2014/09/12/happened/. Last accessed 27 Oct. 2018.

Kollin, Susan. "On the 'Ragged Margins' of History: Burdens of Truth and National Identity in Ana Menéndez's *The Last War.*" *Studies in American Fiction,* vol. 40, no. 1, Spring 2013, pp. 131–53.

Kozol, Wendy. *Distant Wars Visible: The Ambivalence of Witnessing.* Minneapolis: U of Minnesota P, 2014.

Libretti, Tim. "The Zapatista Unconscious: Chicana and Latin American Connections in Graciela Limón's *Erased Faces.*" *Latin American Indian Literatures Journal,* vol. 24, no. 1, Spring 2008, pp. 92–122.

Lima, Lázaro. *The Latino Body: Crisis Identities in American Literary and Cultural Memory.* New York: NYUP, 2007.

Limón, Graciela. *Erased Faces.* Houston, TX: Arte Público Press, 2001.

Lingis, Alphonso. "One's Own Voice." *Mosaic: A Journal for the Interdisciplinary Study of Literature,* vol. 45, no. 4, 2012, pp. 21–35.

López, Marissa. "¿Soy Emo, Y Qué? Sad Kids, Punkera Dykes and the Latin@ Public Sphere." *Journal of American Studies,* vol. 46, no. 4, 2012, pp. 895–918.

López, Tiffany Ana. "Emotional Contraband: Prison as Metaphor and Meaning in U.S. Latina Drama." *Captive Audience: Prison and Captivity in Contemporary Theater,* edited by Thomas Fahy and Kimball King. New York: Routledge, 2003, pp. 25–40.

López-Calvo, Ignacio. "Chicanismo Meets Zapatismo: U.S. Third World Feminism and Transnational Activism in Graciela Limón's *Erased Faces.*" *Chasquí: Revista de Literatura Latinoamericana,* vol. 2, no. 33, Nov. 2004, pp. 64–74.

Majid, Anouar. *We Are all Moors: Ending Centuries of Crusades Against Muslims and Other Minorities.* Minneapolis, MN: U of Minnesota P, 2009.

Maloof, Judy. "The Chicana Detective as Clairvoyant in Lucha Corpi's *Eulogy for a Brown Angel* (1992), *Cactus Blood* (1996), and *Black Widow's Wardrobe* (1999)." *Ciberletras: Revista de crítica literaria y de cultura,* no. 15, 2006.

Mayorga, Irma. "Invisibility's Contusions: Violence in Cherríe Moraga's *Heroes and Saints* and *The Hungry Woman* and Luis Valdez's *Zoot Suit.*" *Violence in American Drama: Essays on Its Staging, Meaning, and Effects,* edited by Alfonso Ceballos Muñoz, Ramón Espejo Romero, and Bernardo Muñoz Martínez. Jefferson, NC: McFarland, 2011, pp. 151–71.

"McFarland Farm Workers Struggle to Discover Why Their Children Are Contracting and Dying of Cancer." *CBS This Morning.* CBS News. Airdate: 30 Dec. 1997.

Méndez-García. Carmen M. "Private (Brown) Eyes: Ethnicity, Genre and Gender in Crime Fiction in the Gloria Damasco Novels and the *Chicanos* Comic Series." *Altre Modernita,* no. 15, May 2016, pp. 70–82.

Mendoza, Louis. "On Buffaloes, Body Snatching, and Bandidismo: Ilan Stavans's Appropriation of Oscar Acosta and the Chicano Experience." *The Bilingual Review,* vol. 26, no. 1, Jan. 2001–Apr. 2002, pp. 79–86.

Menéndez, Ana. *The Last War.* New York: HarperCollins, 2009.

Mercado, Antonieta. "*El Tequio*: Social Capital, Civic Advocacy Journalism and the Construction of a Transnational Public Sphere by Mexican Indigenous Migrants in the US." *Journalism,* vol. 16, no. 2, 2015, pp. 238–56.

"Mexico's Zapatista Rebel Leader Subcomandante Marcos Steps Down." *BBC,* 26 May 2014, http://www.bbc.com/news/world-latin-america-27569695

Mohanty, Chandra. *Feminism Without Borders: Decolonizing Theory: Practicing Solidarity.* Durham: Duke UP, 2005.

Moraga, Cherríe. *Heroes and Saints and Other Plays.* Alexandria, VA: Alexandria Street Press. E-book, 2005.

———. "A Long Line of Vendidas." *Loving in the War Years: Lo Que Nunca Pasó Por Sus Labios.* Cambridge, MA: South End Press, 2000, pp. 173–90.

———. *A Xicana Codex of Changing Consciousness: Writings, 2000–2010.* Durham: Duke UP, 2011.

Mulvey, Laura. "Visual Pleasure and Narrative Cinema." *Screen,* vol. 16, no. 3, Autumn 1975, pp. 6–18.

Nance, Kimberly A. *Can Literature Promote Justice? Trauma Narrative and Social Action in Latin American* Testimonio. Nashville: Vanderbilt UP, 2006a.

———. "Only Connect? Empathy and Exotopy in Teaching Social Justice Literature," *Notes on Teaching English,* vol. 30, May 2006b, pp. 10–14.

Nishikawa, Katsuo A., Terri L. Towner, Rosalee A. Clawson, and Eric N. Waltenburg. "Interviewing the Interviewers: Journalistic Norms and Racial Diversity in the Newsroom." *Howard Journal of Communications,* vol. 20, no. 3, 2009, pp. 242–59.

Noel, Urayoán. "Counter/Public Address: Nuyorican Poetries in the Slam Era." *Latino Studies,* vol. 9, no. 1, 2011, pp. 38–61.

Noriega, Chon, editor. *The Future of Latino Independent Media: A NALIP Sourcebook.* Los Angeles: UCLA Chicano Studies Research Center, 2000.

Olguín, Ben. "Of Truth, Secrets, and Ski Masks: Counterrevolutionary Appropriations and Zapatista Revisions of *Testimonio*." *Nepantla: Views from the South,* vol. 3, no. 1, 2002, pp. 145–78.

Ontiveros, Randy. "No Golden Age: Television News and the Chicano Civil Rights Movement." *American Quarterly,* vol. 62, no. 4, Dec. 2010, pp. 897–923.

Paredes, Raymund. "Los Angeles from the Barrio: Oscar Zeta Acosta's *The Revolt of the Cockroach People.*" *Los Angeles in Fiction: A Collection of Essays: From James M. Cain to Walter Mosley.* Albuquerque: U of New Mexico P, 1995, pp. 239–52.

Perla, Hector Jr. "Explaining Public Support for the Use of Military Force: The Impact of Reference Point Framing and Prospective Decision Making." *International Organization*, vol. 65, Winter 2011, pp. 139–67.

Poole, Deborah. "Ethnography, Race, and Visual Technologies." *Annual Review of Anthropology*, vol. 34, 2005, pp. 159–79.

Pratt, Mary Louise. "'Yo Soy La Malinche': Chicana Writers and the Poetics of Ethnonationalism." *Callaloo*, vol. 16, no. 4, Autumn 1993, pp. 859–73.

Ramos, Jorge. *Atravesando Fronteras: La Autobiografía de un Periodista en Busca de su Lugar en el Mundo*. Waterville, MA: Thorndike Press, 2004.

Reyes, Yosimar. "U-Visa." 4 Oct. 2017. https://giftsinopenhands.wordpress.com/2017/10/04/u-visa-by-yosimar-reyes/.

Rivera, Christopher. "The Brown Threat: Post-9/11 Conflations of Latinas/os and Middle Eastern Muslims in the US American Imagination." *Latino Studies*, vol. 12, no. 1, 2012, pp. 44–64.

Robinson, M. Michelle. *Dreams for Dead Bodies: Blackness, Labor, and the Corpus of American Detective Fiction*. Ann Arbor: U of Michigan P.

Rocco, Raymond. "Transforming Citizenship: Membership, Strategies of Containment, and the Public Sphere in Latino Communities." *Latino Studies*, vol. 2, 2004, pp. 4–25.

Rockwell, Rick. *Media Power in Central America*. Urbana: U of Illinois P, 2003.

Rodríguez, America. *Making Latino News: Race, Language, Class*. London: Sage, 1999.

Rodríguez, Ana Patricia. "Toward a Transisthmian Central American Studies." *Latino Studies*, vol. 15, 2017, pp. 104–8.

Rodríguez, Ralph. *Brown Gumshoes: Detective Fiction and the Search for Chicana/o Identity*. Austin: U of Texas P, 2005.

Romano, Angela, ed. *International Journalism and Democracy: Civic Engagement Models from Around the World*. London: Routledge, 2010.

Rosell, Sara. "La detectivesca de Latinas en los Estados Unidos: Lucha Corpi, Alicia Gaspar de Alba, Michele Martínez y Carolina García-Aguilera." *Ciberletras*, vol. 21. http://www.lehman.edu/ciberletras/v21/rosell.htm.

Rothenberg, Daniel, editor. *Memory of Silence: The Guatemalan Truth Commission Report*. New York: Palgrave Macmillan, 2012.

*Rubén Salazar: Man in the Middle*. Directed by Phillip Rodriguez. City Projects, LLC. 2014.

Said, Edward. *Orientalism*. New York: Vintage Books, 1979.

Sánchez, Marta Ester. *"Shakin' Up" Race and Gender: Intercultural Connections in Puerto Rican, African American, and Chicano Narratives and Culture (1965–1995)*. Austin: U of Texas P, 2005.

Sandoval, Chela. *Methodology of the Oppressed*. Minneapolis: U of Minnesota P, 2000.

Santa Ana, Otto. *Juan in a Hundred: The Representation of Latinos on Network News*. Austin: U of Texas P, 2013.

Schleifer, Theodore. "Univision Anchor Ejected from Trump News Conference." *CNN*, 26 Aug. 2015, http://www.cnn.com/2015/08/25/politics/donald-trump-megyn-kelly-iowa-rally/.

Seif, Hinda. "'Layers of humanity': Interview with Undocuqueer Artivist Julio Salgado." *Latino Studies*, vol. 12, no. 2, 2014, pp. 300–309.

———. "'Wise up!' Undocumented Latino Youth, Mexican-American Legislators, and the Struggle for Higher Education Access." *Latinos and Citizenship: The Dilemma of Belonging*, edited by Suzanne Oboler. New York: Palgrave Macmillan, 2006, pp. 247–72.

Siddiqui, Sabrina. "Trump Press Ban: BBC, CNN and Guardian Denied Access to Briefing." *The Guardian*, 25 Feb. 2017, https://www.theguardian.com/us-news/2017/feb/24/media-blocked-white-house-briefing-sean-spicer.

Sontag, Susan. *On Photography*. New York: Farrar, Strauss and Giroux, 1973.

Stiehm, Judith Hicks. "The Protected, the Protector, the Defender." *Women's Studies International Forum*, vol. 5, no. 3–4, 1982, pp. 367–76.

Thompson, Hunter S. *Fear and Loathing at Rolling Stone: The Essential Writing of Hunter S. Thompson*. Edited and with an introduction by Jann S. Wenner. New York: Simon and Schuster, 2011.

———. *The Great Shark Hunt: Gonzo Papers*. Vol. 1, *Strange Tales from a Strange Time*. New York: Simon and Schuster, 1979.

Torres, M. Gabriela. "Art and Labor in the Framing of Guatemala's Dead." *Anthropology of Work Review*, vol. 35, no. 1, 2014, pp. 14–24.

———. *The Paper Trails of Counterinsurgency Violence: The Documented Design and Implementation of Political Violence in Guatemala, 1976–1984*. Doctoral dissertation, York University, Ontario, Canada, 2004.

Versényi, Adam. "Translation as an Epistemological Paradigm for Theatre in the Americas." *Theatre Journal*, vol. 59, no. 3, Oct. 2007, pp. 431–47.

Vigil, Ariana. "Photography, Self-Knowledge and Solidarity in Graciela Limón's *Erased Faces*." *Revista de literatura mexicana contemporánea*, no. 53, Apr.–June 2012, pp. viii–xiii.

———. *Understanding Franciso Goldman*. Columbia, SC; U of South Carolina P, 2018.

———. *War Echoes: Gender and Militarization in Latina/o Cultural Production*. New Brunswick, NJ: Rutgers UP, 2014.

Warner, Michael. *Publics and Counterpublics*. New York: Zone Books, 2005.

———. "Publics and Counterpublics." *Public Culture*, vol. 14, no. 1, 2002, pp. 49–90.

Weld, Kirsten. 2014. *Paper Cadavers: The Archives of Dictatorship in Guatemala*. Durham: Duke UP.

"World News Tonight." *ABC News*. Airdate: 3 Dec. 1987.

Yarbro-Bejarano, Yvonne. *The Wounded Heart: Writings on Cherríe Moraga*. Austin: U of Texas P, 2001.

Ybarra, Patricia. "The Revolution Fails Here: Cherríe Moraga's *The Hungry Woman* as a Mexican Medea." *Aztlán: A Journal of Chicano Studies,* vol. 33, no. 1, Spring 2008, pp. 63–88.

*Zapatista!* Directed by Benjamin Eichert, Rick Rowley, and Staale Sandberg. Santa Barbara, CA: Big Noise Films, 1998.

Zimmerman, Marc. "'Woody Allen visita Guatemala' o una reivindicación frustrada. Consideraciones sobre la novela de Francisco Goldman." *Mesoamérica,* vol. 18, no. 34, Dec. 1997, pp. 651–66.

# INDEX

*ABC World News Tonight*, 72, 75
Acosta, Marco Federico, 36, 38
Acosta, Oscar Zeta, 19, 27, 27n1; FBI surveillance of, 37–38, 47; as gonzo journalist, 36, 39; heterosexuality in, 40; homophobia in, 39–40, 42; journalism, relationship to, 29, 35–37, 39, 40; masculinity in, 40–41; misogyny in, 39–40, 42; political engagement of, 40. See also *Autobiography of a Brown Buffalo* (Acosta); *Revolt of the Cockroach People, The* (Acosta)
activism: "artivism," 158–67; in *Heroes and Saints*, 68, 69, 73–74, 75, 77–78, 84–85, 88, 91; and media representation, 69
agency: and citizenship, 165; and performativity, 91–92; and spectatorship, 120
Alarcon, Arthur, 37n6
Alarcón, Daniel, 106
Aldama, Frederick Luis, 39

Alurista (Urista Heredia, Alberto Baltazar), 42
Amaya, Hector, 20, 165; on Latina/o public sphere, 69; on public sphere paradox, 89–92
American Friends Service Committee, 160
Árbenz Guzmán, Jacobo, 102
Arendt, Hannah, 91, 92
Arias, Arturo, 115
artivism, 158–67
*Autobiography of a Brown Buffalo* (Acosta), 35, 63; authenticity in, 39; scholarship on, 38–39
Azcárraga Vidaurreta, Emilio, 7, 9, 42

Bahramitash, Roksana, 140
Bakhtin, Mikhail, 132
Barrera Ortíz, Byron, 104
Baxter, Katherine, 132
Bebout, Lee, 141–42

belonging: and citizenship, 16; in *Erased Faces*, 147–48; in *Heroes and Saints*, 145; in *Last War*, 144, 145–48
Berlant, Lauren, 14; on intimate publics, 16
Bickford, Donna, 51, 53
Biltmore 6, 37n6
Blackwell, Maylei, 10, 15–16
Blaya, Joaquín, 33
Brady, Mary Pat, 70
*Breitbart News*, 122
Breslin, Jimmy, 18
Brown Berets, 10n3, 33
Brown Threat, 147n4, 151–52
Bruce-Novoa, Juan, 39
Bush, George W., 140, 151n6
Bush, Laura, 140
Butler, Judith, 91–92; on framing, 119; on photography, 122, 123

*Californian, The* (newspaper), 6
Caminero-Santangelo, Marta, 16, 18; on undocumented narrators, 22
cancer clusters: in *Heroes and Saints*, 68, 71, 77; in McFarland, CA, 69, 72, 76; and race, 75. See also pesticide poisoning
*Caracol*, 9
Carrasco, Tania A., 159, 160, 165
Casillas, Dolores Inés, 7, 11
Castañeda, Mari, 11, 83
Castillo, Debra, 150
Castro, Sal, 10n3, 33
*CBS This Morning*, 76
Central America: migration from, 97–98, 115; US intervention in, 20–21, 98, 114
Central American studies, 115
Central American-Americans: gendering of, 100; transmigration of, 100
Central American-American studies, 115
Central Americans: gendering of, 100; indigenous, 115; migrants, 115–16

Cepeda, María Elena, 11, 12, 20
Chávez, César, 67–68, 73–74; in *Heroes and Saints*, 67
Chicana/o movement: Chicana/o newspapers, role of, 9; and Chicano nationalism, 63–64; and cultural identity, 51; in *Eulogy*, 28, 50; and gender, 56; and masculinity, 63–64; media coverage of, 68; and misogyny, 58; radical politics of, 32; in *Revolt*, 28, 41, 46; and Salazar, 28, 33; visibility of, 67–70
Chicana/os: "Chicana/o" as term, 31, 43–44, 150–51; and gender, 56, 65; as identity, 150–51; media coverage of, 68; Zapatista uprising, response to, 149–50, 150n5
Chicano Moratorium, 26; in *Revolt*, 35, 47. See also Chicana/o movement
Chicano Youth Liberation Conference, 34
citizenship: and agency, 165; and belonging, 16; and critical witnessing, 77–78; hegemonic notions of, 166; and Latina/o public sphere, 156; and political agency, 165; and public sphere, 22, 164–65
Clinton, Bill, 126
CLUE (Clergy and Laity United for Economic Justice), 74n4
colonization, 125; and *Erased Faces*, 126–27
*Con Safos*, 9
Coronado, Raúl, 14–15, 16
Corpi, Lucha, 19, 28; scholarship on, 50. See also *Eulogy for a Brown Angel* (Corpi)
Cortez, Raúl, 8
counterpublics, 14, 60, 62; feminist, 62; Latina/o, 15–17, 50, 60–62, 65–66; and print culture, 15
counterpublics, Chicana/o, 15, 16; Chicana feminist journals as, 16; and Chicana/o literature, 15; in *Eulogy*, 60–62, 65–66; and gender, 50; lexi-

con of, 62; and media, 62; in *Revolt*, 65–66
cultural studies, 18
Culture Strike, 158, 164
Cutler, John Alba, 15, 16

DACA (Deferred Action for Childhood Arrivals), 156, 156n1; Trump policy on, 156, 158
Damajanova, Ludmila, 104
Daves, Betty, 36
Dávila, Arlene, 11, 75
Davis, Ed, 34–35
*Day Without a Mexican, A* (film), 3–4, 17, 93; journalism in, 4
*De Colores* (periodical), 9
de la Rocha, Zack, 150n5
del Toro, Guillermo, 8, 26
del Valle, Mayda, 15
detective fiction, 29; ethnic, 51
Diaz, José (Angel Gilberto Diaz), 26, 54
digital media: democratization of, 155–56; and journalism, 164; and social movements, 155; and undocumented youth, 166–67
*Dirty Girls Social Club, The* (Valdés-Rodríguez), 150
DREAM Act, 158, 160
DREAMers, 159, 166; as "deserving" migrants, 160

East LA blowouts, 33, 37
East LA Thirteen. 13, 9–10, 37; in *Revolt*, 41
East LA Welfare Rights Organization, 34
*El Grito*, 9
*El Heraldo de México* (newspaper), 6
*El Misisipi* (newspaper), 5
*El Paso Herald-Post* (newspaper), 31
*El Pocho-Che*, 9
ELZN (Zapatista Army of National Liberation). *See* Zapatistas
emo culture, 16

*Encuentro Femenil* (newspaper), 15
*Erased Faces* (Limón), 21, 124–34, 136; belonging in, 147–48; and colonization, 126–27; ethical spectatorship in, 120, 123, 129, 147; gender in, 132–33; and Latina/o public sphere, 124, 149, 151, 153; loss in, 129; mirrors in, 127–28, 129, 130; photography in, 127, 128–34, 137, 147, 148, 149; photojournalism in, 21, 119–20, 151, 152–53; and transnationalism, 148; and transnational Latina/o publics, 121; trauma in, 120, 126, 127, 146, 153; truth in, 130–32; war, framing of, 120; Zapatistas in, 21, 125, 138
Escalante, Alicia, 34
*Eulogy for a Brown Angel* (Corpi), 52–61; and Chicana feminism, 52; Chicana/o counterpublic in, 60–62, 65–66; Chicana/o movement in, 28, 50; Chicana/o public of, 19, 29, 60; as feminist text, 60–61; gender in, 29–30, 51–52, 56–58; intersectionality in, 51, 58; journalism in, 50, 56, 58; LAPD in, 53, 54; masculinity in, 56–58; misogyny in, 60–61, 63; Salazar in, 49–50, 52–64; scholarship on, 50–51; sexuality in, 29–30

*fafa* system, 108n6; in *Chickens*, 107–8
Fanon, Frantz, 140
Faulkner, William, 39
*Fear and Loathing in Las Vegas* (Thompson), 25–26, 36
feminism: intersectional, 17–18, 22, 162; Western, 140–42; white, 140
feminism, Chicana: and *Eulogy*, 52, 60–61; and *Heroes and Saints*, 69; organizations and publications, 10, 15–16
feminisms, Latina: interdisciplinarity of, 17–18; intersectionality of, 17–18, 22
feminists of color, 163
Filkins, Dexter, 137–38
Fisk, Robert, 121

*Forever War, The* (Filkins), 137–38
*48 Hours,* 72–73, 75
Foucault, Michel, 140
Fraser, Nancy, 14, 15, 16; on public sphere, 89n8

Gallego, Carlos, 46
Gallegus, Manuel, 76
García, Mario T., 30, 34, 82n7
Garciá, Rupert, 27–28
García Márquez, Gabriel, 106
gender: and Central American migration, 115–16; and Chicana/o community, 56; and Chicana/o movement, 56; and Chicana/o public, 65–66; in *Chickens,* 100, 109–11, 113; in *Erased Faces,* 132–33; in *Eulogy,* 29–30, 51–52, 56–58; in *Heroes and Saints,* 68, 69, 79–80, 82; and Latina/o public sphere, 5; media coverage of, 76; and performativity, 91–92; and power, 98; in *Revolt,* 29–30; in Reyes, 162–63; in Salgado, 160; and visual technology, 133; in war photography, 122
Goldman, Francisco, 20, 98; journalism of, 99, 105n5, 105–6. See also *Long Night of White Chickens, The* (Goldman)
Gonzales, Rudolfo "Corky," 34, 37; in *Revolt,* 46
González, Juan, 18
gonzo journalism, 27, 36, 39
Gräbner, Cornelia, 111n7
Greenberg, Linda Margarita, 70
Guatemala: genocide in, 103; US intervention in, 20–21, 101, 102
Guatemalan Civil War, 20; in *Chickens,* 98–100, 101–2, 114; human rights violations during, 102–3; repression of mass media during, 23, 103–5, 105n4, 107
Gutiérrez, Félix, 6
Gutiérrez, José Ángel, 65

Habermas, Jürgen, 13–14, 15
Hames-García, Michael, 39, 40
Hariman, Robert, 121, 122
*Heroes and Saints* (Moraga), 20, 67–71, 77–93; activism in, 68, 69, 73–74, 75, 77–78, 84–85, 88, 91; belonging in, 145; cancer cluster in, 71, 72, 77; and Chicana/o feminism, 69; gender in, 68, 69, 79–80, 82; in-betweenness in, 82–83; journalism in, 68, 71, 73–74, 75, 85, 92; and Latina/o media studies, 69; pesticide poisoning in, 20; political power in, 76; race in, 69, 75–76; scholarship on, 70–71; sexuality in, 81, 83; translation in, 20, 69–70, 79–84, 85, 90; violence in, 71; visibility in, 69–71, 78–79, 87–88; voice in, 69–70, 79–80, 85–87, 88, 93; witnessing in, 77–78, 87
Hinojosa, María, 98
Hinojosa, Rolando, 50
*Hispanic,* as term, 75
Hussein, Saddam, 121

Immigrant Youth Justice League of Chicago (IYJL), 159, 163
immigration reform, 91, 166; and Spanish-language radio, 8
Iñárritu, Alejandro González, 8
intersectionality, 162; in *Eulogy,* 51, 58; and immigration, 162; of Latina feminisms, 17–18, 22
Iraq: 2003 invasion of, 119, 121

journalism: in Acosta, 9, 35–37, 39, 40; and Chicana/o public sphere, 30, 62–63; in *Chickens,* 99–100, 106–10, 112, 113; in *A Day Without a Mexican,* 4; and digital media, 164; in *Eulogy,* 50, 56, 58; of Goldman, 99, 105n5, 105–6; gonzo journalism, 27, 36, 39; in *Heroes and Saints,* 68, 71, 73–74, 75, 85, 92; as literature, 18–19, 106; and objectivity, 65; public, 86; transnational, 100. *See also* photojournalism

journalists: threats to, 22–23; Latin American, 105–6

journalists, Latina/o: as translators, 80, 82–83

Kennedy, Robert F., 67

King, Martin Luther, Jr., 74n5

KMEX: in *Revolt*, 42; Salazar tenure at, 33–35

Kollin, Susan, 135, 136–37, 141n3

Kozol, Wendy, 118, 122; on ethical spectatorship, 123–24, 129; on neoliberal spectatorship, 137; on war photography, 123

*La Prensa* (newspaper), 6

*La Raza* (newspaper), 9

LaCapra, Dominic, 132

LAPD (Los Angeles Police Department): in *Eulogy*, 53, 54; in *Revolt*, 48; and Salazar, 27, 34

*Las Hijas de Cuauhtémoc* (newspaper), 10, 15

*Last War, The* (Menéndez), 21, 134–45; belonging in, 144, 145–46, 147–48; engagement, lack of, 120, 136, 138–39, 143, 145, 153; and Latina/o public sphere, 124, 149, 151, 153; misrecognition in, 146; neoliberal spectatorship in, 137; and Orientalism, 139–42; photography in, 135–37, 139–40, 143, 145, 147; photojournalism in, 21, 119–20, 152–53; spectatorship in, 120, 147, 148–49; and transnational Latina/o publics, 121; trauma in, 120, 142; war, framing of, 120

Latin media boom, 12

Latina/o feminist media studies, 11–13, 17; transnational orientation of, 20

Latina/o studies, 120; and transnationalism, 116

Latina/os: counterpublics of, 15–17, 50, 60–62, 65–66; heterogeneity of, 9;

mass media, relationship to, 5–11, 61–62; media coverage of, 76; radio listenership of, 8

*Latino USA* (radio program), 97; US Latina/o public, relationship to, 98

LGBT rights: and undocumented people, 157

Libretti, Tim, 126–27, 133

Lichtenberg, Judith, 86

Lima, Lázaro, 15, 16

Limón, Graciela, 21. See also *Erased Faces* (Limón)

literary studies: Latina/o, 17; and mass media studies, 18–19

literature: and journalism, 18–19, 106; media studies approaches to, 17

*Long Night of White Chickens, The* (Goldman), 13, 20–21, 23, 98; *fafa* system in, 107–8; gender in, 100, 110–11, 113; gendered relationships in, 109–11; Guatemalan Civil War in, 98–100, 101–2, 114; humor in, 101, 104, 109; in-betweenness in, 101, 113; journalism in, 99–100, 106–10, 112, 113; masculinity in, 110–11; race in, 100; sexuality in, 100; threat to journalists in, 23; transnationalism in, 113, 115; violence in, 104–5

López, Marissa, 16

López, Tiffany Ana, 77–78

Lucaites, John Louis, 121, 122

Majid, Anoua, 147

Malinche, 79, 80–81; and *Heroes and Saints*, 20, 80–82, 83–84, 86; and sexuality, 81–82

Marcos (Subcomandante Marcos), 117–18, 150

Martínez, David, 33

masculinity: in Acosta, 40–41, 61, 64; and Chicana/o public, 49; and Chicano nationalism, 63–64; in *Chickens*, 110–11; in *Eulogy*, 56–58; and militancy, 5 mass media: as fourth estate, 89n9; and Latina/o cultural production, 156; Latina/o relationship to, 88; and political power, 89; repression of during Guatemalan Civil War, 23, 103–5, 105n4, 107; and social justice, 114

mass media, Latina/o: history of, 5–11; and representation, 61–62

mass media studies: and literary studies, 18–19

MAYO (Mexican American Youth Organization), 65

McFarland, CA, 71–73; cancer cluster in, 69, 72, 76; media coverage of, 76. See also *Heroes and Saints* (Moraga)

media, Chicana/o, 62

media, English-language: segregation of, 31

media, Latina/o: defined, 11–12; heterogeneity of, 6; Latina/o publics, relation to, 4–5, 83; marketing of, 12; and public sphere, 92–93; as transnational, 5, 10, 12, 13

media, Spanish-language: and public sphere paradox, 89–90

media studies: and literature, 17; feminist, 120

media studies, Latina/o, 11–13, 17; and *Heroes and Saints*, 69

Mendoza, Louis, 36n4, 38n7

Menéndez, Ana, 134, 137–38. See also *Last War, The* (Menéndez)

Mercado, Antonieta, 114

Mexican-American War: and Spanish-language newspapers, 6

*Mexican Music* (radio program), 7

Mexican Revolution: and Spanish-language newspapers, 6

Mexicans: racialization of, 8

migrants, Central American, 97; indigenous, 115; and sexuality, 115–16

migrants, undocumented, 158–67

migration, Central American: and gender, 115–16

military-entertainment complex, 118n1

misogyny: in Acosta, 39–40, 42; in Chicana/o movement, 58; in *Eulogy*, 60–61, 63

Mohanty, Chandra, 140

Montag, Gustav, 26

Moraga, Cherríe, 20; "A Long Line of Vendidas," 80–81; Malinche in, 80–81. See also *Heroes and Saints* (Moraga)

Moriarty, Erin, 72

Muller, Marcia, 51

Nance, Kimberly A., 132

Nava, Gregory, 50

Nava, Michael, 50

Navarro, Bob, 45

neoliberalism, 125; and spectatorship, 137

newspapers, Chicana/o and Latina/o, 6; and Chicana/o movement, 9. *See also individual titles*

newspapers, Spanish-language, 9; and Mexican American War, 6; and Mexican Revolution, 6; ownership of, 7; as transnational, 10

Nicaragua, 103–4, 114; US intervention in, 114n8

*Nine Parts of Desire* (Brooks), 141

Noel, Urayoán, 15, 16–17

Nuyorican poetry, 15

Obama, Barack, 122

Obejas, Achy, 106

"1 800-SAVE-DACA" (video), 158–59, 164

Ontiveros, Randy, 67–68, 73n3, 74, 74n5

Orientalism, 139–40; and *Last War*, 139–42; and the Middle East, 140; and Western feminism, 140–42, 141n3; and white supremacy, 142

INDEX · 185

*Pan American Nights*, 7
Paredes, Raymund, 39
performativity, 91–92
pesticide poisoning, 68; in *Heroes and Saints*, 20; media coverage of, 12–13, 72
photographers: as colonizers, 123; as tourists, 123
photography, 122, 123; in *Erased Faces*, 127, 128–34; in *Last War*, 135–37, 139–40, 143, 145, 147; and Latina/o public sphere, 149; war photography, 120, 121–24, 128, 152
photojournalism: in *Erased Faces*, 21, 119–20, 151, 152–53; and ethnocentrism, 123; and human rights, 118–19; in *Last War*, 21, 119–20, 152–53; and social justice, 123; and spectatorship, 119
Poniatowska, Elena, 106
Poole, Deborah, 123
precarity, 91–92
*Prensa Libre* (periodical), 105n4, 108
Proposition 187 (CA), 43n10
publics, Chicana/o: of *Eulogy*, 19, 29, 60; and gender, 65–66; and individualism, 49; and masculinity, 49; and sexuality, 65
publics, Latina/o: and Latina/o media, 4–5, 83; and *Latino USA*, 97; and transnationalism, 121; and queer people, 157
public sphere, 89n8; affective dimensions of, 159; and citizenship, 22, 164–65; development of, 13; Latina/o engagement with, 166; and Latina/o media, 92–93; and sexuality, 13; and undocumented people, 165; and visibility, 92
public sphere, Latina/o, 14–15; and citizenship, 156; and *Erased Faces*, 124, 149, 151, 153; and gender, 5; and *Last War*, 124, 149, 151, 153; and the Middle East, 21; paradox of, 69, 70, 88–92; and photography, 149; and print culture, 14–15; as transnational, 21, 100, 116, 121, 148; and transnational journalism, 100; and undocuqueers, 156; and war photography, 152; and Zapatistas, 21

Queer Undocumented Project (QUIP), 158

race: and cancer clusters, 75; in *Chickens*, 100; and essentialism, 4; in *Heroes and Saints*, 69, 75–76; media coverage of, 76
radio, Spanish-language: early history of, 7–8; and immigration reform, 8; Latin American programming, 8; ownership of, 7; as transnational, 10
Rage Against the Machine, 150n5
Ramos, Jorge, 22, 23, 164
Razo, Joe, 9–10, 10n3
*Reading Lolita in Tehran* (Nafisi), 141
Reagan, Ronald, 37, 114
*Regeneración* (newspaper), 6
REMHI (Recuperación de la Memoria Histórica), 103, 104
representation: linguistic, 71; and mass media, 61–62; and speech, 79; and voice, 4
representation, media: and activism, 69; and power, 69, 76; and social justice, 71
Restrepo, Guillermo, 27, 34, 35
*Revista Chicano-Riqueña*, 9
*Revolt of the Cockroach People, The* (Acosta), 38, 41–49, 63; and Chicana/o counterpublics, 65–66; Chicana/o movement in, 41, 46; Chicana/o public of, 19, 29; gender in, 29–30; homophobia in, 42; LAPD in, 48; masculinity in, 61, 64; media workers in, 47–48; misogyny in, 42; racism in, 48; Salazar ("Zanzibar") in, 35, 39–40, 42–49, 53, 59–64, 66; Salazar ("Zanzibar")

murder in, 45–49; sexuality in, 29–30
Reyes, Yosimar, 22, 156, 158–59, 162, 166; gender and sexuality in, 162–63; poetry of, 163–64; videos of, 158–59
Ríos Montt, Efraín, 104, 105n4
Risco, Eliezer, 9–10, 10n3
Rivera, Christopher, 146, 147n4, 151–52
Rivero, Yeidy M., 11
Robinson, M. Michelle, 51
Rocco, Raymond, 165
Rodríguez, América, 7, 9, 10; on KMEX, 43; on Latina/o journalists, 82–83; on Latina/o media consumption, 43n11
Rodríguez, Ana Patricia, 115
Rodríguez, Ralph, 59, 60
Rose, Donna, 72, 73
*Rubén Salazar: Man in the Middle* (documentary film), 27, 44

Said, Edward, 139–40
Salazar, Rubén, 12, 18, 19; biography of, 30–33; Chicana/o community, relationship with, 29–30, 31–32, 33; Chicana/o movement, relationship to, 28, 33; in *Eulogy*, 49–50, 52–64; and LAPD, 27, 34; legacy of, 64–65; move to KMEX, 33–35, 44–45, 64; murder of, 25–27, 29, 48, 49, 53–55, 59–60; political philosophy of, 32; postage stamp of, 27 fig. 1; in *Revolt* (as "Zanzibar"), 35, 39–40, 42–49, 53, 59–64, 66; as translator, 82n7
Salazar Cook, Rachel, 35
Salgado, Julio, 22, 156–58, 160–62, 166; gender and sexuality in, 160; posters of, 160, 160 fig. 2
Salinas, Marta, 76
Sánchez, George I., 31
Sánchez, Marta E., 39n9
Santa Ana, Otto, 11, 76, 88
Schell, Tom, 72
segregation: of Mexican Americans, 32

Seif, Hinda, 159, 160, 165
sexuality: and Central American migrants, 115–16; and Chicana/o publics, 65; in *Chickens*, 100; in *Eulogy*, 29–30; in *Heroes*, 81, 83; and Malinche, 81–82; in *Revolt*, 29–30; in Reyes, 162–63. *See also* undocuqueers
*Shrunken Head of Pancho Villa, The* (Valdez), 70
"67 Sueños," 160
Smith, Andrea, 141
social justice: and Latina/o media, 18, 20; and mass media, 114; and photojournalism, 123; and representation, 71; visibility, 67, 78–79
social media, 155; and undocumented youth, 166
Sontag, Susan, 123
Spanish International Network (SIN), 9
spectatorship: and agency, 120; ethical, 120, 123–24, 129, 147; in *Last War*, 120, 137, 147, 148–49; neoliberal, 137; and photojournalism, 119
Stavans, Ilan, 36, 36n4, 38n7

Televisa, 9
television, Spanish-language: early history of, 8–9; Latin American programming, 8; ownership of, 7; as transnational, 10
Thomas, Bill, 34, 35, 55
Thompson, Hunter S., 25–26, 36; forward to *Revolt*, 38; gonzo journalism of, 39
Tijerina, Reies López, 34
Tobar, Héctor, 106
Torres, M. Gabriela, 105n4, 108n6
translation: and accommodation, 80; in *Heroes and Saints*, 20, 69–70, 79–84, 85, 90; and Latina/o journalists, 80, 82–83; and theater, 84
transnationalism: in *Chickens*, 113, 115; and *Erased Faces*, 121, 148; and jour-

nalism, 100; of Latina/o feminist media studies, 20; and Latina/o media, 5, 10, 12, 13; and Latina/o public sphere, 21, 100, 116, 121, 148; and Latina/o studies, 116; and Spanish-language media, 10

trauma: in *Erased Faces,* 120, 126, 127, 146, 153; in journalism, 132; in *Last War,* 120, 142; in literature, 132; in war photography, 119, 121, 122

Trump, Donald, 22; DACA policy of, 156, 158

Turkey, 137, 138; and Brown Threat, 152

UMAS (United Mexican American Students), 10n3, 33, 34

undocumented people, 158–67; and gay rights, 157; and public sphere, 165

undocuqueers: coining of term, 156–57; and immigrant rights movement, 157; and Latina/o public sphere, 156

United Farm Workers (UFW), 37, 73–74

United We Dream, 158

Univisión, 9; Ramos incident, 22–23

US foreign policy: in Guatemala, 20–21, 101, 102; and interventionism, 20–21, 32, 101–2, 114n8, 138, 151n6, 152; in Latin America, 151n6; in Mexico, 120, 125–26; in Middle East, 138, 151n6; in Nicaragua, 114n8; in Turkey, 120

Ut, Nick, 121

Valdés-Rodríguez, Alisa, 150

Valdez, Luis, 70, 70n1

Valdivia, Angharad, 11

Vargas Llosa, Mario, 106

Versényi, Adam, 84

Villanueva, Danny, 32, 35

violence: in *Chickens,* 104–5; in *Heroes and Saints,* 71; state, 164; and video games, 118; and war, 118

visibility: of Chicano movement, 67–70; in *Heroes and Saints,* 69–71, 78–79, 87–88; and public sphere, 92; of queer undocumented people, 158; and social justice, 67, 78–79

war, media coverage of, 118; in *Erased Faces,* 120; in *Last War,* 120

Ward, Lyn, 26, 54

Warner, Michael, 14, 15; on counterpublics, 60, 62; on new media, 155; on publics, 62

war photography, 120, 121–24; gendered suffering in, 122; and Iraq invasion, 121; and Latina/o public sphere, 152; of nursing babies, 128; trauma in, 119, 121, 122

Wenner, Jann, 38

white supremacy, 141–42; and Orientalism, 142

Yarbro-Bejarano, Yvonne, 70, 82, 83

Ybarra, Patricia, 81

Young, Iris Marion, 110

Young Lords, 18

Zapatistas, 117–18, 120–21; in *Erased Faces,* 21, 125, 138; and Latina/o public sphere, 21; media strategies of, 118

Zapatista uprising (1994), 119; Chicana/o community response to, 149–50; US involvement in, 125–26; and US Latina/o public sphere, 149–50

Zimmerman, Marc, 103

*Zoot Suit* (Valdez play), 5n2, 70n1

## GLOBAL LATIN/O AMERICAS
FREDERICK LUIS ALDAMA AND LOURDES TORRES, SERIES EDITORS

This series focuses on the Latino experience in its totality as set within a global dimension. The series showcases the variety and vitality of the presence and significant influence of Latinos in the shaping of the culture, history, politics and policies, and language of the Americas—and beyond. It welcomes scholarship regarding the arts, literature, philosophy, popular culture, history, politics, law, history, and language studies, among others.

*Public Negotiations: Gender and Journalism in Contemporary US Latina/o Literature*
ARIANA E. VIGIL

*Democracy on the Wall: Street Art of the Post-Dictatorship Era in Chile*
GUISELA LATORRE

*Gothic Geoculture: Nineteenth-Century Representations of Cuba in the Transamerican Imaginary*
IVONNE M. GARCÍA

*Affective Intellectuals and the Space of Catastrophe in the Americas*
JUDITH SIERRA-RIVERA

*Spanish Perspectives on Chicano Literature: Literary and Cultural Essays*
EDITED BY JESÚS ROSALES AND VANESSA FONSECA

*Sponsored Migration: The State and Puerto Rican Postwar Migration to the United States*
EDGARDO MELÉNDEZ

*La Verdad: An International Dialogue on Hip Hop Latinidades*
EDITED BY MELISSA CASTILLO-GARSOW AND JASON NICHOLS